BACK TO LIFE

BACK TO LIFE

Getting Past Your Past with
Resilience, Strength, and Optimism

Alicia Salzer, M.D.

WILLIAM MORROW
An Imprint of HarperCollinsPublishers

This book is written as a source of information only. The information contained in this book should by no means be considered a substitute for the advice, decisions, or judgment of the reader's medical advisor.

All efforts have been made to ensure the accuracy of the information contained in this book as of the date published. The author and the publisher expressly disclaim responsibility for any adverse effects arising from the use or application of the information contained herein.

Some names and identifying characteristics, situations, and symptoms of patients have been changed in this book in order to preserve their privacy and anonymity. The goal in all cases was to protect the individual without damaging the integrity of the work and advice provided.

HarperCollins books may be purchased for educational, business, or sales promotional use. For information please write: Special Markets Department, HarperCollins Publishers, 10 East 53rd Street, New York, NY 10022.

FIRST EDITION

Designed by Lisa Stokes

Library of Congress Cataloging-in-Publication Data has been applied for.

ISBN 978-0-06-177106-4

11 12 13 14 15   OV/RRD   10 9 8 7 6 5 4 3 2 1

For Piper, my starfish

*And for Leslie, who keeps a roof over our
heads and the ground beneath our feet*

In a world blinded by the pursuit of pleasure, I am here to say that people are in pain. In a world rushing to get ahead, I am here to say that people are being left behind. In a world obsessed with the value of the market, I am here to speak for the value of life . . . and I am alive. This will be no quiet fight, for I am the voice of audacity in the face of apathy. I am the spirit of bravery in a world of caution. I am a commitment to action in the face of neutrality. I am alive.

—Dan Pallotta, *activist/survivor*

| CONTENTS |

| INTRODUCTION |

AS CHILDREN WE SEE THE WORLD with a sense of wonder. We imagine that we are princesses or superheroes, and we inhabit those roles with conviction. As adolescents we fall wildly and romantically in love. We plan our lives and plot our dreams, and we bask in the assurance that we will become who we are meant to be. What happened to that passion and vibrancy? Well, life happened—disappointments, setbacks, tragedies. We don't often stop to consider these collective losses and what causes them, but accumulate too many of them and life starts to feel dull and hard.

Most of us have had experiences in our past that we feel have changed us forever and changed us for the worse. Many of us look in the mirror and see a person who has become bitter and angry or fearful and uncertain. We have trouble getting past our pasts. We continue to feel thin-skinned, damaged, powerless, ashamed. Life certainly takes its toll.

Yet in our midst are people who do overcome life's tragedies and challenges and do so with apparent grace. We read their biographies. We go to hear them speak. We watch them on TV and we ask ourselves: *How did they do it?*

How does a person live through a life-altering challenge yet emerge still self-possessed, still hopeful, still empowered? How did they retain—or regain—a sense of safety and trust?

For us, the people on those TV shows are a real mystery. We scan their faces and stories for clues, longing to know what they have that we don't have and whether it's possible to get there from here. What gave them the courage to move forward? How did they lay the anger to rest? How did they find purpose from something so senseless? What did they think and do in their darkest hour to get them back to the positive place they seem to be in now? *How did they overcome?*

Unfortunately, the "how" doesn't make for good television, so we tend to see the wretched "before" and the glorious "after" punctuated by an epiphany that miraculously turned their life around. This makes it seem like some kind of healing magic appeared in their lives and helped them get past their past.

In fact, they are working hard to earn the ease with which they seem to move through life. They are practicing the art of survivorship. They know what and who makes them feel good, safe, and vibrantly alive and they pursue those things and people with discipline and vigor. They know how to soothe themselves, how to reassure themselves, how to restore their own sense of self, their faith, and their ability to cope. When we look at these people, these resilient overcomers, we tend to notice their impressive *actions*. But what I find most significant and compelling is the way these survivors take charge of the *thoughts* that they allow to inhabit their minds, the *emotions* that they cultivate in their hearts.

Resilient survivors have a special way of *thinking about* what they have been through that enables them to thrive.

And everything they know, you can learn. In the course of my work, I have met a lot of heroes, some famous, most not, who have taken the challenges of being human and woven from them a life in the aftermath that is a magnificent tribute to the resilience of the human spirit. I am always looking—just as you are—for the "how." And I have found some concrete answers that really help.

As a psychiatrist I have focused on trauma for the past ten years. At times I have found myself in the trenches with my patients in the immediate aftermath of major psychological trauma. I have worked as an attending psychiatrist in the psychiatric emergency room of a New York City hospital where people turn when their life is at its very worst. I have worked with disabled New York City mass transit workers who sustained psychological trauma on the job. After my hometown was attacked on September 11, I worked with an organization called Disaster Psychiatry Outreach and treated hundreds of New Yorkers. At first I volunteered at Ground Zero, talking with firefighters and paramedics, ironworkers and neighbors, all of whom had found themselves unexpectedly in a war zone. Later I volunteered at the heartbreaking family assistance center that was set up to help the families of those missing, injured, or killed.

While it is valuable to help support and advise people in the midst of their crisis, it is in the months and years afterward that real progress is made, as they struggle to get back to a life that a psychological trauma derailed. It is in the long term that certain individuals emerge who seem blessed with an ability to move forward with grace. For three years after 9/11, I worked at the Mount Sinai World Trade Center Clinic, which provided free treatment for Ground Zero rescue workers and volunteers. I also worked, for five years, as the trauma expert and aftercare director for *The Montel Williams Show,* where I had the opportunity to meet and to help hundreds of remarkable survivors. In my years as a trauma psychiatrist, I have had the opportunity to see people at their very worst and their very best. What moves me most is when a person finds a way to be simultaneously both. But make no mistake, the people we call heroes face doubts, just like the rest of us; they have lost hope, and floundered, and fallen on their faces, too. But they have specific skills and strategies that they implement in moments of doubt and crisis and they utilize these skills in a way that is part life raft and part religion.

A rare few heroic overcomers seem to have been born with an intuitive sense of how to surmount life's psychological traumas; maybe they were taught some of these skills in childhood. But most of them made an active decision that enough was enough. At which point they took control over the thoughts they allowed to inhabit their heads. It's an impressive discipline that they have cultivated, but there is no bar to admission. Everyone can learn the habits they practice and the outlooks they take. Everyone can try on the skills that these resilient survivors use in the face of life's inevitable challenges. And everyone can use them to feel better.

I use the word *trauma* a lot in this book. As in "life's traumas came along and robbed you of your sense of hope." For many the word may sound alarming.

What exactly qualifies as a psychological trauma?

> **For the purposes of this book, a trauma is *any* event or situation that fundamentally shakes our understanding of the world and of our place in it.**

Certainly this includes all the horrors that one typically thinks of when the word "trauma" is used. But in my opinion it also includes a host of other experiences that leave us reeling because the "rules" of life seem to have suddenly changed. In this view, a trauma might be a health issue, a betrayal, the loss of an apartment or job. When a life event robs you of your sense of well-being and self-esteem and leaves you feeling unsafe or out of control—that's a trauma, too.

But it's important to acknowledge that when we speak of trauma there are really two different things we are referring to. There's the traumatic event itself, and then there's "take-home trauma," the way that the trauma changes our views, the rules we live by, and the way we see ourselves. The long-lasting casualties after trauma are the spiritual, emotional, and cognitive hits you've taken—and how those changes affect how you subsequently move through the world.

Traumatic events pose a challenge to our sense of justice and order; a world that once seemed fair no longer does. You thought that if you were loyal and caring that your marriage would work, but it didn't—and now you feel less able to love and trust. You thought you were making smart investments, but losing the bulk of your savings has made you feel unsure that your intelligence is a sound guide. Somehow, the rules have changed: because of your experiences, you can no longer believe that being careful will keep you safe, or that a healthy lifestyle will keep you well.

> **It's important to distinguish between the trauma itself and the "take-home trauma."**

This rule-changing that underlies the take-home trauma is devastating. Sometimes it feels as if there's a ghost life running right next to yours on a parallel track. You can see very clearly the person you should have been, the person you *would have been* if it hadn't been for the trauma, and you can see, very clearly, everything you lost.

When we try to live by these new rules it feels like the ground has become shaky under our feet. This state consists of a blend of grief, anxiety, and distrust that I call living in **permatrauma.** In an attempt to protect ourselves from a recurrence of the trauma, we adopt maladaptive behaviors, bringing the lessons we learned on the worst day of our lives—distrust, a lack of self-confidence and self-efficacy, a feeling of victimhood—to every day afterward. We stop doing things; we stop trusting people. And we cling to these maladaptive behaviors long after the storm has passed, not realizing how this perpetuates our sense of disempowerment and danger.

As these maladaptive strategies become habits, our lives get really, really small. Suddenly, there's a lot of stuff you don't *do* anymore. But more importantly, there's a lot of stuff you don't *feel* anymore, as your repertoire of emotions shrinks to be more congruent with this new permatrauma worldview.

The rules we make for ourselves after trauma feel like they protect us, but they really narrow our emotional range. Essential emotions like safety, trust, love, tenderness, intimacy, and empowerment often fall by the wayside. Yet these emotions are precisely the things we need to feel in order to lead a full and fulfilling life. That's why the real wages of trauma occur in the aftermath.

Trauma narrows our emotional bandwidth.
That's why the spiritual and emotional costs are the focus of this book.

It's not easy to be a loving and supportive parent or partner from a state of fight-or-flight. It is impossible to experience intimacy while keeping someone "safely" at arm's length. If you're white-knuckling your way through life, it's going to be very hard to feel grateful, or creative, or to laugh until you cry. If you have embraced the notion that you are a victim, you cannot feel empowered, emboldened, or fierce. Over the course of this book, you will come to see that these "lost emotions"—and the activities they allow us to enjoy, the relationships they allow us to have—are what make life worth living. Permatrauma takes them away, but you can take them back.

Why This Book Is Different

This probably isn't the first book you've picked up on the topic of getting past your past. Perhaps you've even tried therapy in an effort to feel better. Chances are, things didn't work out quite as well as you'd hoped. Rest assured: this approach will feel very different from what you've done before.

First of all, I aim to show you that you are not alone and what you are going through is not unusual. One of the great myths about trauma in our culture is that it's rare, which is one reason so many survivors feel so alone.

I was once at a seminar on a topic completely unrelated to trauma. In order to make a point about our inherent ability to overcome challenges, the speaker asked people in the audience—and there were close to a thousand—to stand if they'd ever experienced a particular kind of trauma. Tons of people stood. He asked about another type of hardship, and more people got to their feet. After he'd named a handful of traumas, most of the room was standing.

Interestingly though, the people remaining in their seats had experienced difficult, profound, emotionally challenging, life-altering traumas as well. "My husband of ten years left me and the kids for someone else." "When I didn't turn out to be the kind of athlete my dad wanted me to be, it seemed like I became invisible to him." "I invested everything I had in a dream and my business partner stole it out from under me." "I worked hard to provide a cozy home and a stable life for my wife and kids, and then we lost our house." There was no one—and I mean no one—in that room who hadn't experienced the lasting effects of a profound psychological blow.

Rape, assault, war—those are what I call "Big-T Traumas." But for every combat veteran, 9/11 widow, or woman who has survived a brutal attack, there are scores of people who got sideswiped by some other life-altering, rule-changing situation. I call these "little-t traumas" but there's nothing little about them; they certainly don't feel inconsequential or trivial when you're going through them.

> **Life's "little-t traumas" can be as profoundly affecting as what we think of as the "Big-T Traumas."**

My goal is not to label, or even to diagnose, but rather to remove the shame that comes from feeling that we are alone and that what we are going through is unusual.

We survivors are a strange tribe, deeply in need of solidarity and kinship, yet largely invisible to each other. And strangely, while we think we are alone in our struggle, we really aren't. I am on the speakers' bureau of an organization called RAINN, the Rape, Abuse and Incest National Network. To raise money and awareness, RAINN sells a number of pendant necklaces, each engraved with a single word: "Hope." "Courage." "Strength." "Survivor."

When I wear the necklace that reads "Hope," people often ask me where they can get one for themselves. Who doesn't love hope? When I wear one inscribed "Courage" or "Strength," people often ask where they can get one to give to a friend going through a hard time. (No one ever says they want one for themselves; after all, you wouldn't be wearing a pendant that said "Strength" or "Courage" unless you felt you needed some, and that's hard to admit.)

It took me a long time to put on the one that says "Survivor." What would I say if people asked me, "A survivor of what?" Was I prepared to share? Would people wind up hearing more than they bargained for?

I was completely unprepared for what happened when I finally found the courage to wear that necklace. That afternoon, I noticed a young woman who kept hovering near and looking my way. Finally she approached me, choking back tears, and simply said, "It's cool that you wear that necklace." She clearly wanted to say more, but I could tell that it had taken her considerable strength just to say what she did.

Subsequently, others came up to me, touched and emboldened by my survivor necklace. It's not because I'm a psychiatrist that these people felt safe making their disclosures to me—they didn't know anything about me, except that I was bold enough to wear my survivor status as a badge of honor.

To this day, every time I wear it, that necklace reminds me how many of us there are living in pain and trying to pass ourselves off as "normal." I see signs of the walking wounded all around me—in the boy who jumps when a car backfires, in the posture of a woman as she passes a group of men on the sidewalk, in a friend's sarcastic aside about the fecklessness of the opposite sex. Shame keeps us hidden from one another.

> **The reality is that by the time we reach adulthood most of us are carrying around some unhealed trauma.**

This affects our ability to love and feel lovable, to stick up for ourselves and get our needs met, to take risks and be hopeful. Living in this permatrauma mode affects our ability to get and accept the emotional soul food we need in life. In that sense, even those supposedly inconsequential little-t traumas can really do a number on us.

So, no matter what happened to you, I'd like you to take your past challenges seriously and to acknowledge the ways they may have changed you into a person you don't want to be. At the same time, it is my hope that over the course of this book you will find that there is a way back.

If Traditional Therapy Failed You, You're Not Alone

Recognizing that our lives have shifted off course, many of us have reached for the life ring of therapy. Some people do find relief in therapy. But trauma therapy as it is traditionally practiced doesn't work for everyone. There are no published statistics on trauma therapy dropout, but the dirty little secret that anyone in clinical practice will tell you is that the numbers are astronomically high.

In my years at *The Montel Williams Show* our guests from the show often related their trauma treatment nightmares and I was pained to see the excruciating downward spiral that therapy can set into motion when it's done badly. Truly, it is my belief that my profession is in collective denial about the type of damage this sort of therapy can leave in its wake, and that we will look back at our current techniques with the same shame and regret with which we now regard lobotomies or the Victorian bedlam wards. Our profession is in dire need of better trauma treatments.

In our psychiatric training, we were taught that encouraging patients to retell their trauma stories helps them bring unconscious feelings to the surface, where they could be released. We were taught not to backpedal when our patients cried, but to create a safe place for them to express and explore these feelings. "Telling" and "talking" was cathartic, we learned, and would help our patients become desensitized to the disturbing content: watch a horror movie enough times, and there's nothing left to jump out and scare you. We were trained to tolerate and encourage this opening of Pandora's box—no matter what flew out.

Once I was a therapist, I noticed that clients tended to dive right into the thick of what they went through, reexposing themselves very aggressively and often leaving themselves utterly overwhelmed: they, like their therapists, had been schooled to think that they were there to retell and that doing so would help.

It's widely accepted that the patient will go through a period of feeling worse before she or he gets better. But in reality, many, many people find that they quickly become so symptomatic they can't function. In our field there is much written about the things that we therapists must do to prevent *ourselves* from becoming overwhelmed by what our patients are describing and going through. It seems incredible to me that we're willing to acknowledge that the experience of retelling and reliving may be too much for a trained professional to handle while remaining committed to the idea that it's somehow helping the survivor.

When you read the "bibles" of trauma therapy you find lines like "trauma survivors never really heal" and "you can't undo what's been done." Indeed, I have seen very little—in my training, in my personal experience, or in my practice—to show that this approach actually helps the majority of trauma survivors.

I do not find that there is convincing research or scientific evidence to support the "retelling" approach or to justify that it is worth its potential hazards. As psychiatry moves toward more evidence-based models, it's becoming pretty apparent that our methods of doing trauma therapy are flawed and that the poor outcomes do not justify the considerably painful means.

One study acknowledging that half of all patients fail to respond to cognitive behavioral therapy as a treatment for PTSD looked to our neuronal responses for a reason that might help us understand why. The researchers found that some people respond to trauma with an excessive fear response in the amygdala, the part of the brain that controls how we process and remember emotions. Because traditional therapy rekindles the trauma, therapy for these patients acts in a very similar way to the trauma itself. It overwhelms them. Clearly there are some people who are not good candidates for therapy that invites the reopening of this Pandora's box. At the very least, we need to have a better way to figure out who will benefit from therapy like this, so we can spare the ones who won't.

Another study looked at critical incident stress debriefing (CISD, or *debriefing*), a technique favored by what Jerome Groopman called "the Grief Industry" in his article on the subject in the *New Yorker*. Debriefing consists of structured, one-session group interventions, in which survivors discuss their emotions about and reactions to the event. (Education and follow-up opportunities are also provided.) The argument for this type of therapy, which was developed in the late seventies and early eighties, is that it allows survivors to begin processing immediately; it takes them out of fight-or-flight mode and prevents them from getting numb or going into denial. In theory, this concept seems like a great way to avert permatrauma. It was widely used at Ground Zero; indeed, we were proud to have been trained in this technique because we really felt we were practicing good preventative medicine. But follow-up studies showed that debriefing doesn't prevent PTSD or alleviate symptoms. And in some, it may make them worse.

So for a long time, we've been under the spell of this idea that it's good to talk about your trauma, to share, to get it "off your chest." But it's a very painful process to ask someone to go through, especially if you're not 100 percent sure that they're going to end up better. In other areas of medicine, when we are offering a potentially harmful treatment, we offer a cost-benefit analysis. Aggressive chemo might make sense in a healthy, hearty, middle-aged patient, but not in a frail, elderly person who can't be assured that the potential good will outweigh the sizable risks. In either case, a physician is obligated to explain the potential side effects and the likelihood of failure. It's called "informed consent," and if trauma therapists were obligated to obtain it, I think that most people would not embark on therapy as it is currently done.

And the self-help books that address life after trauma—of which there are hundreds—are not much better than conventional therapy. They, too, encourage you to lay your emotions bare without giving you adequate tools to cope with them. Like you, I bought them all with the best intentions and plunged in, highlighter in hand. But after a few chapters, I'd find myself overwhelmed by the emotions the exercises stirred up in me. My mind would drift from the page into the past, and it would get stuck there. And as my fears increased, my function suffered. I have a complete library of trauma self-help books—each one of them abandoned halfway through. I never doubted that there was a wealth of information in there, but I couldn't tolerate what I had to go through to get that information; it was a prescription with side effects too painful to tolerate.

Do people recover from trauma? Sure they do. But often they do so in spite of, not because of, established trauma therapies.

> Established techniques encourage us to return, over and over, to the "scene of the crime." But in constantly revisiting the event, we also retraumatize ourselves.

And we never gain what we really need: the tools we need to feel better and move forward. So while other books focus on symptoms, with an eye toward reducing them by revisiting "the incident," I want to begin in a different place—with the radical idea that you don't need to hurt yourself to get better.

Can this be promising a "feel-good" book about getting past your past? It is. You won't have to retell what happened to you. You won't be asked to journal or scrapbook your trauma story. You won't be writing letters to your attacker or to your ex. Traditional therapy, and the books spawned from it, would ask you to return to the trauma in search of insight. But that's a place you've already visited—and revisited. If that had worked you wouldn't be here reading this book. My goal is to help you get *out* of that pattern.

> **You don't have to relive every terrible moment of what you went through in order to get better.**

If you're reading this book, you undoubtedly acknowledge that your past has left its mark on you. We will take stock not of your symptoms, but of the ways you lack balance in your daily diet of emotions and experiences. There is much to be learned from the people we think of as resilient survivors, the people we call heroes or who are moving forward in their lives in a way we admire. So we'll study some of these people to see what *they* do when their past starts to creep into their present and they find themselves feeling lousy. We'll try on their techniques and coping skills.

We're not sweeping what happened under the rug but figuring out what emotions and beliefs it robbed you of and finding shortcuts to taking them back. Efficacy, safety, power, well-being, trust, optimistic hopefulness: this book is about getting those things back into your emotional repertoire and back into your life.

Responsibility, Not Blame

I have developed my approach to working with trauma patients over a number of years. My goal in my private practice, as well as in this book, is to synthesize helpful ideas from many disparate fields of research, as well as some of the newer schools of thought in the world of psychiatry.

This eclectic approach to trauma has its roots in positive psychology, resilience theory, cognitive therapy, and learned optimism. I draw on the relatively new field of happiness psychology to provide insight into the techniques of people who want to feel more than just better; they want to feel good. I have incorporated concepts from the fields of mindfulness, gratitude, and savoring and apply them to people who are trying to get past their past.

There is fascinating research going on in all of the above fields, and yet often the outcomes being studied are not specific to trauma survivors. I hope that researchers in these fields take an interest in trauma and design studies that apply these techniques in the treatment of PTSD and other trauma related ailments. I myself am not a researcher. I am a clinician. But in my experiences, both personal and professional, I have found that this eclectic approach to trauma links stepping-stones from many fields into a footbridge and is an exciting, effective alternative to traditional trauma therapy.

> **Just as you can't live on junk food alone, you can't live on a steady diet of the bad feelings that brought you to this book.**

Using the techniques of this book, you can begin to widen your emotional bandwidth. You'll learn what emotions and actions have value and meaning to you and find ways to get those things back into your life. And you'll strengthen a sense of yourself as a survivor, not a victim. All of this will mean getting reacquainted with who you *used* to be (or perhaps who you were *meant* to be) while acknowledging something you may not have ever considered—that you may even be better, wiser, and stronger because of the challenges you have overcome.

You will take away a set of highly individualized, personal coping strategies—a chart for these new waters you find yourself in. These strategies not only can be used to quiet the traumas of your past but will give you the confidence to know that you can handle what happens in the future. This is the protective nature of resilience.

The fields of positive psychology and resilience have so much to offer people drowning in the feelings so common after trauma: depression and anxiety coupled with a loss of self-esteem and personal power. But they have never before been applied specifically to trauma as a treatment.

And I think I know why. These psychological schools put a tremendous amount of personal responsibility on *us*. They presume that we can and should take charge of our emotions instead of letting them control us. They operate on the principle that whether or not we thrive despite hardships depends on what we do with the struggles life deals us. In the wrong hands, that can feel like we're being told that it's our fault, to snap out of it, to pull ourselves up by our bootstraps and move on.

But in my experience, my patients are more than capable of incorporating these pearls in a constructive way. They've been watching survivor stories on daytime TV and reading trauma texts for years, trying to answer the elusive question "How do I get there from here?" They have been demoralized by seeing others recover while they themselves cannot. If they're getting in their own way, they're eager to hear what they can do differently. When offered with support and compassion, these techniques can be a real lifeline, one that they grab with both hands.

> **You may not have had any control over or responsibility for what happened in your past, but you are in control of what happens now.**

One of the things that you will be asked to do in the pages that follow is to abandon a mind-set in which you live the remainder of your life as if you are still experiencing your trauma. You may argue that given what you went through you are permanently damaged or scarred, that your baggage will be with you forever. I'm not here to tell you to get over it. I'm here to help you get past it. I will make the argument that you're richer now—stronger, more empathic, and more in touch with your core values—than you were before you were challenged by what you went through. I don't just believe that trauma survivors can go on to live rich, happy lives; I believe that they're uniquely suited to do so.

> **It is possible that what you experienced left you with an enhanced appreciation of what is wonderful, rare, and special about life.**

I will use a three-pronged approach by asking you to look first at the way you think, then at what you do, and finally at how you feel. First, we will look at some of the ways you think about yourself and the world around you, and we'll see if there isn't a more positive, empowering approach to take. Next, I'll encourage you to do something different, by trying on the habits of resilient survivors. The third section of the book is about how to take control of the emotions that fill your mind and dominate your day. You'll create a toolbox, unique to you, stocked with tricks that you can deploy when permatrauma feelings threaten to overwhelm you.

What I'd like to offer you is the rare chance to remove the dark glasses you have been wearing and give you a peek at the world through the eyes of the resilient heroes you most admire.

It will probably feel unnatural in the beginning; standing up straight after a lifetime of bad posture is bound to feel awkward. But if you are reading this book, you've likely tried other approaches and still find yourself battling the same old demons. I hope that you will find the courage and the optimism to take a leap of faith for the duration of this book. In the end, it will be up to you to choose whether you want to try to wear these rose-colored glasses full-time or not.

This book is for everyone who feels their life has left them dented. It is for those of us who define ourselves by the checklist of symptoms that hold us back from the life we feel we lost. Every one of us deserves to have what we have survived be acknowledged and honored. We deserve to be reminded to show compassion for ourselves, and we deserve to hold someone's hand as we walk a path of healing. It is my hope that you will think of this book as a companion on your journey, a source of support and encouragement. There's no reason to spend the rest of your life with your nose pressed up against the glass. You deserve a life that is rich in love and laughter and happiness, and you can have it. You may not believe me right now. But I promise: we will get there together.

PART I | Changing How You Think

The Car Behind the Dent
Getting Reacquainted with Yourself

VIOLET SURVIVED TERRIBLE DOMESTIC VIOLENCE but was eventually able to leave her relationship and has spent the last five years becoming a powerful and passionate advocate for women like herself.

During an event held by the National Domestic Violence Hotline, I watched while she brought a hotel ballroom full of supporters to tears with her story. As she came down from the podium, the audience surged forward, desperate to engage with her and to tell her how they'd been affected by her words. I felt so glad that she had given herself the gift of that moment: too many people who have gone through what she has never get to have one like it.

I found myself wishing that I could bottle the empowerment and confidence and support she was feeling in that ballroom, and travel back in time to when she had needed it most—while she was contemplating leaving her husband, when she was afraid she couldn't make it on her own, when she looked to the criminal justice system for closure but had to endure her statement being ripped apart for inconsistencies. What effect would it have had on her if I could have told her *then* that she would one day be surrounded by hundreds of adoring, grateful, respectful people rushing up to tell her how much they admired her courage and resilience?

That's what I hope to do for you. *That's* the way I want you to think of yourself after reading this chapter—like a hero. Because it is only once you experience that level of compassion and admiration for yourself that you will allow yourself to imagine a world in which you live the vibrant and courageous life you've earned. Once you can see past the scars, you can start to feel good about one of the greatest accomplishments of your life: having survived your past.

TRY THIS: CELEBRATING THE UNDERDOG

Why is it that we watch heroes and survivors on TV or read about them in books? What does it do for us?

At a very basic level, these stories show us that overcoming is possible— and they give us a little shot of what it feels like to overcome. In preparation for the work in this chapter, I'd like you to take a few minutes to make a short list of books, songs, movies, or news stories in which an underdog triumphs. Consider both classic hero stories and those of quirky unexpected overcomers who may not have gotten what they thought they wanted but found meaning and satisfaction somewhere else.

Which underdogs do you root for? Gandhi? Wilbur from *Charlotte's Web*? The senior citizen on the news who beat the would-be burglar with her cane? A breast cancer survivor who ran a 5K? Little Miss Sunshine? Rocky? Which are the stories that stick with you? How do these underdog overcomers make you feel?

As we will explore later in this chapter and throughout this book, these stories give us the opportunity for great insight. Our heroes are not arbitrary. The stories that resonate most for us—the ones that speak to us and inspire us specifically—are often the ones in which the survivor is doing what we ourselves need to do.

A Dent, with a Car Attached

Mere minutes into Pauline's session she was already berating herself. "I'm such a wreck. I used to be really well put together, but now I'm jumpy and anxious all the time. I can't sleep, I smoke too much, I can't concentrate; I'm amazed I still have a job. I tell my boyfriend I wouldn't blame him if he found someone less screwed up. I don't have the energy to do anything fun."

Pauline seems to think she's a disaster! A violent incident that happened at work left her badly shaken and has completely clouded how she perceives herself. But, from my perspective, her description of herself leaves out quite a bit. Pauline's pretty, smart, and capable; she's sensitive and loyal, and a generous friend despite her heavy heart. Where are *those* qualities in Pauline's own description of herself? Pauline has many gifts, as you do, but she can't see past her trauma.

If Pauline were a used car on the lot, she would price herself low and her sticker would tell everyone up front that she had been totaled in a wreck. She'd show potential buyers the big rusty dent in her front end, while neglecting to mention that her motor runs just fine and gets great gas mileage to boot. She wouldn't brag about her snazzy, comfortable interior, and you'd never know from her low price that during the crash—which was not her fault, incidentally—all the seat belts functioned, and all the air bags deployed, which is why everyone walked away alive.

To hear Pauline tell it, she's just a dent with a car attached. That's how we see ourselves after trauma. And it's one of the reasons that life after trauma is so painful; we're grieving for not just what happened to us, but for the parts of ourselves—aspects that we used to take pride and comfort in—that feel like they're permanently lost.

When I began to list some of Pauline's wonderful traits she began to cry. She wept because all her wonderful characteristics felt inaccessible to her after what she'd been through. Her calm competence, her sense of humor, her genius for steady friendship—all these things felt lost, buried under scar tissue, superseded by feeling crazy, broken, and out of control. Pauline was mourning the loss of those pieces of herself.

> **Part of the pain we feel after a trauma comes from mourning the loss of a former self.**

My job was to help Pauline see that her past self wasn't gone; she'd just gone into hiding and needed to be coaxed out. In fact, the metaphor I use with patients is that of a battered suitcase: although you've traveled far and show some wear, dinged from countless taxi rides and ungentle baggage handlers, the precious contents inside remain intact. All the qualities that made up your past self are in that suitcase. It's time to crack it open and dust them off. And that's precisely what we'll do in the next exercise.

TRY THIS: WHO YOU ARE AND WHAT YOU LIKE

If I asked you to make a list of everything you don't like about yourself, I'm guessing you'd dive right in starting with all your perceived physical flaws and moving swiftly through character traits you feel you are lacking. Like Pauline, you could probably readily fill pages with the ways in which you've "fallen apart" since what you went through. Traditional therapy focuses on the dent and how to smooth it out. But that's not what we're doing here. Remember? I promised you a feel-good book!

So, quickly make a list of ten things you like about yourself: your warped sense of humor or the way your feet look when they're tan. Just as quickly, make a list of ten things you like to *do.* List your talents and interests, the things you want to do before you die, the things you dream of doing, if only you could get a week off.

Read your list back to yourself, starting with phrases like, "I am good at _____. I am interested in _____. I have a talent for _____."

We'll delve into this in a more meaningful way in a minute, but with this simple, easy exercise, you've just taken a first step toward recognizing that you're more than your dent. Most of us, regardless of the personal war we may be in with ourselves, *like* the person we are deep inside, even if we don't spend much time hanging out with her anymore. So notice how it feels to focus on what makes you *you* and the effect it has on your spirits.

Connecting with the Car Behind the Dent: Identifying Your Signature Strengths

You are much more than what happened to you. Connecting with the values that inspire you and the activities that energize you is a very useful coping mechanism. And yet when asked, "What values are you most passionate about?" many people find they have to pause and reflect. So let's take a deeper look at what you stand for, what you like, what you are good at.

In positive psychology, these are called your "signature strengths" and knowing them and incorporating them into your life is highly correlated with life satisfaction. We are going to use them to get back in touch with the car behind your dent. (The list in this chapter comes from *Character Strengths and Virtues,* a handbook published by the researchers Christopher Peterson and Martin Seligman of the VIA Institute on Character.)

Your signature strengths are more than just talents—they're the things that make you come alive. We each have between two and five of these that particularly resonate.

Before you read the list, I'd like to make it very clear that there's no hierarchy here. These are universally observed traits that are valued, fostered, and praised across a wide variety of cultures. You may have exhibited aspects of all of these strengths at different times in your life. But you will undoubtedly find that some items on the list *feel* superior or more important; that's a good indication that you've hit on one that "lights up" for you.

Circle the signature strengths below (up to five of them) that resonate for you:

Appreciation of beauty and excellence: Some of your most powerful emotional moments have been when you have been struck by something beautiful—music, art, something in nature. You're awestruck and grateful in the presence of a great talent or something that has been done really well. The profundity of the emotions that can be evoked in you when you are experiencing something beautiful borders on the spiritual, and these experiences are deeply nourishing to you.

Authenticity: What matters most to you is the truth. It is very important to you that you're genuine, not phony or a liar. People know you to be "real," never pretending to be someone you are not. If a misunderstanding occurs, it is important for you to set it straight. A sense of being comfortable in your own skin, knowing yourself, and owning and celebrating that definition feels like a life path to you.

Bravery: You speak your mind, even if your idea is unpopular or controversial. You stick up for those who are wronged. You don't let fear rule your decisions regarding how to act if you're sure that action is the right thing to do. The universe makes more sense to you if you know that you are an agent of justice, even if only in some small way.

Creativity: You get fired up when you can solve a problem in an unorthodox way or find a novel use for something. You dive headlong into tangled challenges and tend to think of solutions that no one else has considered. Although you like to see the fruits of your labor, you equally enjoy the "process" that got you there. You are always eager to sign up for something that allows you to express your ingenuity, flexibility, resourcefulness, and originality.

Curiosity: You love to try new things, learn new skills, and experience adventures you haven't yet had. You feel most alive when navigating uncharted waters. Many people love the familiar and feel uncomfortable in new or different surroundings; that is definitely not you. Instead, you feel comforted by—and excited by—the knowledge that there will always be new things out there for you to experience.

Fairness: You feel that everyone, regardless of their rank or status, deserves to have a say and to be treated equally. You are the one in a group setting who makes sure everyone gets a chance. If you are wrong, you admit it. You would never want to take credit for someone else's achievement but instead delight in making sure that praise and accolades accrue to the person who truly deserves it. You are frustrated and pained when you see others treated unfairly, and to the extent you can prevent this, you are always glad to make a difference.

Forgiveness: You are not one to hold a grudge. Revenge doesn't interest you. You do not seek to wrong or hurt someone because they injured you in the past. While you observe others carrying the enormous burden of hurt, blame, and anger, you have a gift for letting go, and you feel the world might be a better place if more people had access to this gift that comes easily to you.

Gratitude: Regardless of what has happened to you in your life, you feel that you've been blessed. People in your life know you appreciate them because you make a point of letting them know; in fact, some of the most meaningful times of your life have been when you have been able to find expression for the appreciation you feel. Even in the midst of hard times, you maintain perspective based on all the good things in your life, and you feel lucky that small gifts can give you great joy.

Hope: You feel fairly certain that your future will be bright and that your goals are within reach. Even if an outcome is not what you had hoped it would be, you can still see the good that came of the situation. It is easy for you to access the reassuring sense that everything will ultimately be okay.

Humor: Your friends can count on you to lighten the mood with your ability to have fun, to tease and to laugh. You have a gift for making people feel better through humor. And when times get tough, you can still see what's funny about your own situation. Doing so has been a touchstone for you, keeping you sane and grounded.

Kindness: You love to help. You often lend a hand to friends, sometimes by anticipating their needs and doing something for them that they didn't even ask for. When you help a stranger, it puts a spring in your step. In fact, in your view, small acts of kindness have the enormous power to balance out the bad in life. It is important for you to see for yourself—and to show to others—that no matter what, there are good people out there.

Leadership: You have a knack for organizing people and for appreciating what gifts each individual will bring to a task. You love to plan and see things through. Your friends know you to be a diplomat—facilitating dialogue, smoothing out differences, and motivating everyone to get on the same page. Helping to mobilize others to achieve a goal gives you enormous satisfaction. Faced with a chaotic or challenging situation, it feels great to know that you can step in and make sense of it all.

Love: You feel that what matters most are the connections between people. You enjoy the feeling that you are important to someone else, and you cherish the people in your life. You measure wealth in terms of the quality of your relationships. The ability to give love is a nourishing feeling, one that you will always have in abundance.

Love of Learning: You are constantly seeking to learn more about new things you encounter. It's not enough to hear a new fact; you want to look it up online and read more about it. You love nonfiction books. Just as someone who exercises derives joy from feeling fit, you feel great about yourself when your knowledge base grows.

Modesty: While others may love to be the center of attention, you enjoy the feeling that you are no different than anyone else. Rather than talking about yourself, you would prefer to focus on and listen to others, and let your achievements speak for themselves. This sense of yourself is the source of a great deal of dignity for you.

Open-mindedness: You feel that the world would be a better place if we all weren't so sure that we were right. You don't consider yourself knowledgeable on a topic until you've considered it from all sides and often can see that even people on opposite sides of an argument have valid points. Your lack of rigidity in this regard is a source of great pride.

Perseverance: If a task calls for someone who can get the job done despite all kinds of obstacles, then you are the person for the job. You are good at focusing, prioritizing, and executing. In your life, you know that your stick-to-itiveness has helped you accomplish things that others could not have, and there is a special satisfaction you derive from executing this discipline. The fruits of hard-earned labors are much more satisfying to you than those that are easily won.

Perspective: People turn to you for your wisdom and advice, in part because you are truly considered. They often describe you as wise or "an old soul." When others are confused, you have a gift for offering clarity. Your ability to see the big picture is a source of great comfort to you.

Prudence: Being reckless and hasty has never appealed to you. You're not a risk taker—in fact, you feel that taking time to consider your actions first has been a major contributing factor in your success. You know you can count on yourself not to succumb to impulsivity, leaving you to deal with a world of regret later. Your motto is: anything worth doing is worth the moment it takes to think it through first.

Self-regulation: Moderation and discipline are your formula for success. You have a remarkable ability to balance your urges and desires with a sense of realism about the outcome of overindulgence.

Whether this means sticking to a diet or exercise plan, adhering to a budget, or simply reassuring yourself that the reward is worth the work and the wait, you know your impulses aren't going to get the best of you and undermine the big picture. It is great to know you can count on yourself not to get in your own way.

Social intelligence: People are complex, but you have always had insight into the reasons they do what they do and the feelings they are experiencing. This not only makes you gifted at fitting in and connecting with others, it also gives you the gifts of empathy, insight, and perspective into the motivations of others. You feel alive when experiencing others in 3D and are drawn to experiences that bring you into their inner worlds.

Spirituality: Many people live entirely in the earthly realm, but you are a person with ready access to something more transcendent. Your internal dialogue about the meaning of life and your purpose in it helps you make decisions in life and provides insight and comfort during hard times. At ease with abstract thought and in touch with universal forces that may or may not have evidence in the scientific/ physical world, your insight and understanding provide a context for your life.

Teamwork: You're the kind of point guard who makes sure that everyone gets the chance to shoot and score. You are happiest when you feel like you are part of a group. Helping others, doing your part, and sharing in the collective identity and shared accomplishments of your group make you feel alive.

Zest: You're the dictionary definition of "joie de vivre." You make stuff happen, and you make it fun. You love your life, are excited about your plans, and are blessed with the energy and enthusiasm to seize the day. Life is full of possibilities for you.

The items that you circled above are your signature strengths. They represent your core values. *This* is who you are—not what happened to you. You've been focused on the dents, but these strengths are what make up the car. (Quickly, look back at the underdog exercise earlier in this chapter; you may notice that these underdogs share many of your signature strengths.) When you look back on your life from your old age, these traits and the accomplishments that stemmed from them will be your crowning achievements.

Cultivating your signature strengths is important because *using them makes you feel good.*

Doing things that give our signature strengths a chance to shine makes us feel vibrantly alive; recognizing and using them helps us inhabit our skin in a way that gives shape and meaning to our lives. You learn quickly when what you're learning draws on one of these strengths, and exercising them makes you feel invigorated rather than exhausted. Your signature strengths can help you understand what you need more of in your life—and why you find some things enjoyable and restorative while others drain you.

The psychologist Mihaly Csikszentmihalyi began studying famous Hungarian painters in the 1950s. He noted that when they were "in the zone," it was as if they were oblivious to hunger, pain, fatigue, and cold. In his book of the same title, he called this state *flow:* "Flow is an invigorating sense of presence in the absence of time. Accompanying it is a loss of sense of self. One is not preoccupied with whether one is competent or what the outcome will be. It is a state of complete absorption in one's activity. Flow is incredibly beneficial in making us feel refreshed and alive. It requires a balance of skill and challenge . . . too much challenge and it is frustrating, too much skill and you are bored. But fortunately the concept is open to anyone at any skill level."

That feeling of total concentration and absorption, of being "in the zone"—both completely in the moment and lost to it—is most often found when we're exercising a signature strength. The outcome isn't at all important; it's not what you create but how you feel while you're creating it. Csikszentmihalyi speaks of shared flow (derived from a conversation with someone else, a team sport, or playing ensemble music) and micro-flow (short-duration flow-producing activities that help restore concentration, such as doodling). Any activity with the proper balance of challenge and mastery can give you a dose of flow: jogging, painting, knitting, debating, conversing.

In fact, there may be an evolutionary advantage to pursuing flow. Since this wonderful feeling fades as we achieve mastery, we keep pushing the envelope and increasing our challenge-to-mastery ratio. In so doing, we strive and improve. Flow is the reward feeling that keeps us chasing our best.

It's easy to devalue the importance of flow or to blow off the things that give us this feeling, thinking that they are merely hobbies or luxurious diversions for people with more time and money than we ourselves have. But you actually don't need money, or talent, or a lot of time to get a dose of flow. And, unlike self-soothing acts that are hedonistic or all about pleasure and therefore short-lived (a donut, say, or a bath), flow is both productive and has a lasting effect.

Flow is great for us—it may be correlated to greater longevity and is certainly correlated to success and life satisfaction. For someone who has come to identify himself exclusively with the trauma, a dent with a car attached, taking a closer look at the activities that give you flow (or used to) can be a great way to reconnect with the car behind the dent.

TRY THIS: WHAT GIVES YOU FLOW?

When I described flow, what was the activity that popped into your head? When was the last time you felt flow? What were you doing? Were you alone or with someone else? Is there something you do in your life—crossword puzzles, sex, swimming, work—that can be depended on to deliver you to this state?

We all have mindless but nonetheless good-feeling activities that help us check out and relax. Those are not the ones I'm talking about here. Which feel-good actions and thoughts do you pursue that are deeply rooted in your values? List five activities that give you a feeling of flow.

But wait, why are we discussing values and signature strengths and flow in a book about getting over trauma? Here's why. Being in victim mode is a passive state, in which our thoughts and feelings sweep over us like the weather, leading us to actions that seem inevitable and beyond our control. Getting past your past will necessitate exercising conscious control over what you think and the activities you pursue in your life. And one of your goals will be to seek out the things that allow you to exercise your signature strengths, activities that give you a dose of flow. "Why do we skim trashy novels instead of poring over great literature? Why do we chatter casually with friends rather than talk about things that really matter? Why do we take the easy path rather than the ones filled with challenge?" Csikszentmihalyi asks. To choose flow when *Seinfeld* reruns and a pint of ice cream beckon may turn out to be a real tool of healing for you.

One of the things I have learned from resilient people is that they take responsibility for the thoughts they allow to inhabit their heads. We make active choices about what fills our closet, balancing work wardrobe with workout garb; we make sure the fridge is stocked with stuff for breakfast and for dinner; but we are quite passive about what thoughts fill our heads and what emotions fill our hearts.

> If it is true that we are what we eat, it is even more true that we are what we *think*.

So if the emotional diet of a resilient survivor has become too heavy on emotions that make them sluggish, they see to it that they get a few portions of the good stuff into their day. People who have been through trauma tend not to eat their veggies, in terms of the colorful, crunchy, feel-good emotions. That's not to say that experiencing a measure of anxiety, depression, grief, poor self-esteem, doubt, and hurt isn't perfectly natural after a trauma—in fact, they're part of a balanced repertoire of emotions. But while this is absolutely normal, it is also not a place anyone should get stuck.

As the saying goes, you can't pursue peace while preparing for war. And you can't pursue feeling good if you constantly devalue and neglect good feelings. We need a well-rounded, multicolored diet of emotions. Positive emotions aren't a luxury, something you'll make time for when your schedule lightens. They're essential, and you must have them every day.

So we're going to make it a point to get back in touch with things that make you feel good, the things that give you flow, things that resonate with your values and signature strengths. You will be asked to commit to keeping these feelings in your daily life with the same conviction you would have in promising to eat more salad if you were working on making your diet healthier. And if you're going to go looking for positive emotions (and we are), they might as well be ones that pack a lot of juice for you.

TRY THIS: WHO ARE YOUR HEROES—AND WHY?

Each year *Time* magazine lists the most influential people of our times. As I read down the list this year, I noted which of the stories "spoke" to me and which ones I merely scanned. I noted which ones I wanted to cut out for my own bulletin board and which ones I wanted to mention to a friend, or to my mom, or to my spouse. Our heroes, famous or not, offer evidence of something in human nature that we either wish *we* had more of or wish humanity in general had more of.

Our heroes are not arbitrary.

At first glance, the reasons why we grant someone hero status may seem obvious. Your sports hero has broken world records and redefined the game;

who wouldn't admire him? But, in fact, if we pause to look at who our heroes are in order to try to understand the role they play in our lives, it becomes apparent that what draws you to Mr. Basketball Icon is more than just his athletic ability. Our heroes are our heroes for a reason.

> **Our heroes can tell us something about ourselves that will ultimately help us tap into what we need to heal.**

So it's worth it to take a moment to look not at their titles and accomplishments, their awards or achievements, but at what their story and their presence does for us emotionally. Who are *your* heroes—and *why*?

As I look at *Time*'s list, I see Richard Phillips, captain of the *Maersk Alabama,* which was captured by pirates off of Somalia. Captain Phillips offered himself up as a hostage in order to save his crew. He is undoubtedly a hero to many, but for different reasons: his courage, his selflessness, the clarity of his decision making, his dedication to his job. If someone like Captain Phillips is your kind of hero, ask yourself what he represents that makes him so. Is it that you wish someone had stepped in during your trauma to rescue you? Do you hope that you would be able to dig deep and find the courage to do something similar? Does it make you feel safe to know there are people like him in the world? Does it make you feel that there is some measure of good in humanity to balance out the evil?

Sometimes our heroes are people who were courageous enough to try to change the world. Maybe they're advocates for the underdog or do something we wish we ourselves could do. If so then Somaly Mam, also on *Time*'s list, might appeal to you as a hero. Sold into sexual slavery by her own grandfather in Cambodia at age twelve, Somaly escaped but later returned to that country to fight against the trafficking of women and girls. Despite death threats Mam persists in her struggle. Is it her staggering and persistent hope in the face of all odds that inspires you? Does the fact that Mam got a second chance at life inspire you not to waste yours? Or does her beauty and courage help you see past a damaged, ugly image of yourself?

Don't limit yourself to what I call the obligatory "Martin Luther King answer." Perhaps one of your heroes is a real-estate mogul or a rock star. I suspect that you don't admire them just for their wealth and fame, but rather for something about their journey that has significance to you. Does their success give you the courage to think big? Does your favorite singer's voice make your emotions soar unbridled? Do they make you feel understood? Part of a greater community?

One of my heroes is Dan Pallotta. When his partner committed suicide Dan turned his grief into action and founded a twenty-six-mile overnight walkathon called Out of the Darkness that has raised 1.3 million dollars for suicide prevention. Dan has made a career out of finding ways to harness grief and indignation to mandate change in the world. His company, Pallotta TeamWorks, has netted $305 million for charitable causes ranging from breast cancer to AIDS to world hunger. He sounds like a businessman, and he is . . . but he is also a poet and a songwriter, deeply affected by loss and pain, yet powerfully motivated to move mountains. He is my hero because in the face of what might have made him numb or bitter, angry or helpless, he has emerged full of feelings, fierce as hell and vibrantly alive.

Your heroes have made choices in life that you respect and admire; crystallizing what those choices are will be helpful to you. Sometimes our heroes represent rescuers, or role models, or aspirations. But they always carry something that we see the seeds of in ourselves. So, emotionally speaking, what do your heroes do for you? What values are demonstrated in their lives? When you review your own list of signature strengths, do you notice that your heroes embody traits that you can identify in yourself?

I admire my heroes because:
they evoke beautiful and transcendent emotions in me
their spirituality has remained intact despite the challenges they faced
they have the courage to be vulnerable
they are beloved despite their flaws
they make it okay to be different
they have made the world a safer place for me and others
their courage reassures me that there are good people in the world

their ingenuity opens a world of possibility

they make me feel proud of who I am

they make me feel heard/speak on my behalf

they achieved what they did against all odds, which helps me believe
    my dreams are possible

they have been able to move on constructively

they give back/give thanks/demonstrate appreciation

they have made a place in their lives for so much love

they are able to inspire others

their humor gives me perspective/relief

they are fierce, and no one messes with them

they know how to take on the system and get something done

they are amazing at connecting with others

they are able to solve other people's problems

they mobilized the masses and made a difference

they are tirelessly persistent

Can you see the way what you admire about your heroes resonates with your signature strength? Captain Phillips might speak to your core value of bravery while Billie Jean King speaks to your core value of perseverance.

List three activities that would enable you to capitalize on your signature strengths while emulating the actions of your heroes. This is a fantasy exercise, so these activities don't have to be realistic: for the purposes of this exercise, it's less important that you be in a position to build an orphanage than it is to get in touch with the feelings you'd have if you could. The items on your list can also be the smallest of acts, like buying a cup of coffee for a homeless person or starting to learn a new language.

Don't worry if your activities are ones that are completely out of reach to you. You may not be able to go to Cambodia to fight the trafficking of women, but there's nothing stopping you from volunteering with an organization that helps women. While you may not have the opportunity to ride into battle to defend the weak and the meek, there are probably kids being bullied at your neighborhood school who need an adult spokesperson. And if what you admire most about your sports hero is his or her perseverance, then there's no reason you can't make yourself a push-up chart and increase the number by five every week.

If you can create a small local version of what your heroes do that embody your values and your signature strengths, you will get yourself a dose of what it feels like to experience their triumphs.

You've taken an important first step. Even if you don't yet have ways to celebrate your signature strengths on a daily basis, take comfort in knowing that what you went through cannot rob you of these fundamental qualities. Hold these clues close. No matter how you feel right now, these are a well that you will always be able to draw upon when you need to. Throughout this book we will elaborate on these insights about yourself, and you will find realistic ways not only to incorporate them into your life, but to turn to them when you feel blue, like a nonpharmaceutical medication. This is the very beginning: you're learning to reach for an emotional carrot instead of a cupcake.

Before you leave this section, write down your signature strengths someplace that you will see them every day, so that ultimately you can commit them to memory.

Reconceptualizing Your Symptoms

Another way that trauma survivors focus on the dent, as opposed to the car attached to it, is to reduce themselves to a list of post-traumatic or depressive symptoms. Patients often come into my office and tell me about the cold sweats, the panic attacks, the flashbacks, the nightmares, the low energy, and the tearfulness, as if these things are their pedigrees.

There's a precedent for this. In psychiatry we have worked hard to turn ill-defined problems into a constellation of symptoms that facilitate diagnosis and treatment. In many ways this approach is very helpful: to recognize that someone has schizophrenia or bipolar disorder is far preferable to merely thinking them "mad," as was the case a century ago.

And these lists of symptoms do provide an objective way of tracking improvement. That's why a weekly visit is not considered complete without a rundown of these "target symptoms" and whether or not they're improving. But this also schools the survivor to start thinking about him- or herself in terms of this list.

These symptom lists, and the diagnoses that go with them, can pathologize and stigmatize the person attached to them. While it can be a great relief to see your inner life laid out in textbook form— "Yes! That's me!!"—a lot of my patients tell me that they had no idea what a mess they were until they encountered a list of PTSD symptoms in a self-help book.

Symptoms are a tempting way to track progress because they're measurable. You either had a nightmare last night or you didn't, and if you didn't, you must be getting better—right? But such a narrow focus on symptomatology can also make you feel like you're nothing more than a laundry list of the crazy stuff you do and feel. It's yet another way of focusing on the dent at the expense of the car.

Again, I'd like to get away from this conventional line of thinking. While you may suffer from some post-traumatic symptoms, your symptoms don't define you. Just because you had a nightmare last night doesn't mean you can't have a wonderful, life-affirming day today. Nor is my ultimate goal simply to get you back to zero, or an asymptomatic life; I have much bigger plans for you than that.

If you have a tendency to define yourself by your pathology, I would encourage you to think about this in a different way. Instead of seeing your symptoms as a sign of how irrevocably screwed up you are, evidence of illness and pathology, see them for what they are: your mind and body's attempt to protect you from a recurrence of your trauma.

Your symptoms are evidence of your innate survival instinct. They're a conserved response, left over from a time when there were benefits to all the physiological stuff that goes along with the fight-

or-flight response—like being able to run away a little faster from the saber-toothed tiger on your heels. So you're jumpy and can't sleep because you're still looking over your shoulder; your brain is trying to stay alert so that you "win" the next time. Your nightmares are your brain's attempt to work all the angles, to figure out how you can be better prepared next time. That sense of impending doom in which you feel certain that something terrible is about to happen is your mind screaming "I want to live!"—and employing every one of your senses to locate and preempt the threat.

This physiologic effort at self-protection is misguided, and the results can be very disruptive and upsetting. But, given what you've been through, it's also completely normal, and, I think, a pretty brave thing for your brain to be trying to do on your behalf.

You may find that the methods in this book result in considerable improvement in your symptoms, but you may also find, as most survivors do, that some remain. What will be different is that when you have the occasional nightmare or find yourself ruminating about a dark period in your past, you will have tools to take charge of the way you are feeling.

Connecting with Your Survivor Pride

"Isn't it *depressing*?" people always ask me when I tell them what I do.

The honest answer is no. Yes, I have heard about some astonishing atrocities, things that might have shaken my faith in humankind. But I am inspired, every single day, by the courage, dignity, humor, and clarity of survivors. There is no question in my mind that tremendous character and fortitude are forged in the fire of trauma. My first challenge is always to help my patients see those extraordinary qualities in themselves.

Survivors are quick to consider themselves damaged goods,

irrevocably broken and considerably less valuable than they were "before." But navigating a path through traumaville, while still trying to accomplish all the things our lives demand of us, is like carrying an enormous, invisible weight—all the time. So although it can feel like a burden to face life post-trauma, it's important to know that this kind of resistance training builds serious muscle mass—not just "coping" muscle mass, but real character definition.

This is why I love trauma survivors so much. Persisting in the face of something that has threatened to rob you of your sense of safety and your very sense of self is a heroic and noble accomplishment.

> **Something bad happened to you, and it has changed you. But you are not inexorably damaged.**

It's now time to change the way you think about yourself, to embrace and celebrate your survivor status. You are a veteran, not a victim, and here is your monument, your Purple Heart ceremony, your ticker-tape parade. My goal is to help you think like a person who believes in herself, her potential, and her future, as someone who celebrates life instead of living in fear of death. In other words, to help you see yourself as a survivor, not a victim.

You might be asking, "What's so wrong with identifying as a victim?" After all, you *were* one once—nobody can deny that. But the simple truth is that continuing to see yourself that way is an unrealistically passive and ultimately disempowering way to live.

When you feel like a victim, you believe that your emotional diet is dictated by your circumstances; like a prisoner, you eat what's on the tray that's shoved through the bars. Your ability to take control of the thoughts and emotions that inhabit your head becomes atrophied. When you're trapped in "victim thinking," instead of seeing yourself as someone who moves through the world with purpose and direction, you see yourself as someone who is acted upon, someone from whom anything and everything can be taken at any minute.

> **Victim thinking keeps you in permatrauma.**
> **You may have been helpless and powerless while your**
> **trauma was ongoing, but you are not powerless now.**

So our goal must be to help you move through this state, eventually arriving at a more positive, empowered sense of yourself. And you've just taken the first step toward doing that: getting back in touch with *you*—the person you were and the person you hoped to be before trauma got in your way.

Finding Meaning in What Happened to You

WHEN CHARLIZE THERON WAS FIFTEEN, she saw her mother shoot and kill her alcoholic and abusive father in self-defense. In an interview she said, "I don't know how to say this without sounding strange. But I feel like having this tragedy at such a young age has given me a leg up from other people. Because, man, from sixteen, I knew the value of life and I knew how quickly it could be taken away."

In many cultures, a person is not considered a man or a woman until they have endured certain rites of passage that challenge them much in the way that what you went through challenged you. In these cultures, survivorship is a badge of honor, to be worn with pride. It may be a journey to see yourself as someone who has endured a rite of passage and grown because of it, but you deserve to wear that badge of honor, too.

The ability to reframe trauma as a rite of passage, one that inoculates you and from which you emerge stronger and better, is a common theme among resilient survivors. What happened to you may be completely senseless, but that doesn't mean that we can't find meaning in the ways we have grown because of what we lived through.

You are changed, yes. But it is time now to appreciate and celebrate the person you've become *since* the trauma.

Looking for a Positive Meaning

In the last chapter you met Violet, a domestic violence survivor turned activist. Violet genuinely believes that she was put on this earth to empower other women in the same position she was once in. To hear her tell it, her own destructive relationship was just an incubation period for her activism. Every act of violence and humiliation that she suffered at the hands of her ex now motivates her to fight for legislation and resources on behalf of battered women. No one can know what might have happened if her own marriage had been different, but Violet believes with an unshakable conviction that the trauma she suffered while she was in it awakened something in her that might have stayed dormant otherwise. She is proud of who she is now.

> **Developing an appreciation for what you have gained confers meaning on what you have endured and is a valuable part of moving forward.**

But there's an elephant in the room, and, for most survivors, it's the "how." How can you possibly be expected to turn these horrible and destabilizing events into an empowering part of your personal story?

I told you we'd be popping into the heads of resilient people, looking at the world—and your own past—the way they do. So let's go ahead and do it. We'll start with one of my own heroes, the South African antiapartheid activist Nelson Mandela, who spent twenty-seven years in prison for his civil rights activism before his release in 1990. He went on to be elected president of South Africa in that country's first fully representative democratic election—and eventually to win a Nobel Prize for Peace.

Mandela is one of my heroes, not just because of his world-changing political and human rights achievements, but because he emerged from his challenges with his spirit intact when most of us would have become bitter and defeated. He is candid about his inner emotional life in his autobiography, *Long Walk to Freedom,* and there is much to learn from how he coped.

In his book, he describes his circumcision, the rite of passage that marks a Xhosa boy's transition into a man. In the very moment when the cut is made, it is traditional for the boy to transform his pain into a scream of victory as he yells *"Ndiyindoda!"* or "I am a man!"

Adult circumcision without anesthesia sounds absolutely horrible. One could easily understand if an experience like this one became the source of a lifelong trauma. Yet to hear Mandela describe it is to understand that the event made him feel special, powerful, part of his tribe, and ready to embark on his life. "It was a sacred time; I felt happy and fulfilled taking part in my people's customs and ready to make the transition from boyhood to manhood. I felt stronger and prouder that day."

Here we can clearly see the importance of *meaning* in helping a survivor integrate what might have been the worst thing that ever happened to him. Imagine how different that story would be if a marauding gang had jumped Mandela in an alley, inflicting an identical wound. Would the pain have been greater? No. But the suffering would have been unhitched from a sense of purpose and community. And that would have been enough to transform it into a trauma. Instead, the physical pain has a positive, affirming meaning for Mandela and other Xhosa boys because it is attached to a coming-of-age ritual. It isn't random or even violent in Mandela's view; it *means* something. It doesn't humiliate or diminish him; in fact, it confers a sense of power to have endured it.

Now, many things differentiate Mandela's circumcision experience from the kind of traumas we are speaking about in this book. First of all, he never felt that his life was in danger, because every man he knew had lived through a circumcision. Unlike most of us, he had the benefit of knowing he was not alone and that such things could be endured and overcome and mastered. And in his view, the rite, although frightening, was not against his will. Rites of passage have a context, a meaning.

That's not true for most traumas. Indeed, for most survivors, the horror of what happened to us is amplified by its senselessness. But some trauma survivors succeed in finding a way to make sense of what they have endured. They do so by *assigning* a sense of meaning to their ordeal.

The best example I can think of is the psychiatrist Viktor Frankl, who spent several years in a Nazi concentration camp during World War II. His experiences there helped him forge a number of theories about how we endure terrible events, and the resulting book, *Man's Search for Meaning*, is an account by a resilient survivor that shows how it is possible for people to come out on the other side, even after some of the worst atrocities in recorded history.

According to Frankl, there are three ways people find meaning in their lives:

1. through their accomplishments and acts, their work, and their work legacy,
2. through their connections with people and the quality of their intimate connections,
3. *through the way they have endured, and made sense of, the inevitable suffering that life offers.*

I'm sure the first two ring true: they are the stuff of our values and our signature strengths—and besides, these are the things our society tells us give life meaning. Number three, however, may give you pause. In some cultures, such as Nelson Mandela's, where ordeals of coping are part of what defines you as an adult, number three might seem more intuitively correct. I offer that one reason Frankl's book is one of the bestselling books of all time is that it holds a lesson about the value of overcoming hardship that our society has failed to adequately teach us.

Clearly, Frankl is not saying that he's glad the Holocaust happened; he's not grateful for the chance he was given to spend time starving and demoralized in a work camp while his loved ones and millions of other people were slaughtered. But the experience taught him valuable lessons about the choices we have, even when life deals us something horrible. Even as we walk to our death, he has said, we have the choice to do so with head held high and a prayer on our lips. Of the people with him in the camps, Frankl writes that "the way they bore their suffering was a genuine inner achievement. It is this spiritual freedom—which can not be taken away—that makes life meaningful and purposeful."

This is a gruesome example chosen on purpose to illustrate an important lesson to all survivors. I would have thought that there were things in life so horrible that one could never again return to any sense of happiness, peace, or meaning. But then I met people who defied this assumption. Frankl's quest for the silver lining is a hallmark of people who move past their past and are able to return to a life that feels meaningful.

There's no question that sometimes finding meaning in trauma feels like a stretch. But what we learn from resilient survivors is that—stretch or no—this step is an essential part of processing your past.

Someone in the camps actually asked Victor Frankl for help in doing this, in creating meaning out of what appeared to be senseless suffering. What meaning, he asked, should he derive from the fact that his entire family had been massacred? Frankl noted that if the man's wife had been the family's sole survivor instead of him, she'd be the

one doing the suffering. Would he have wanted that? Maybe, he suggests to the man, you endured all you did so she could be spared what
you are feeling now. In this reinterpretation of events, the man's suffering and loss takes on a purpose: he would surely have chosen the
suffering if he knew that doing so would have spared his beloved wife
the same grief. In this fragile space, Frankl invites the mourning widower to see himself as a man of honor rather than as a victim.

We learn from Frankl that we can choose to ascribe meaning to
what happened to us, even after the fact. We do that by taking pride
in the people we have become. You have gained new skills out of
your hardship. You know things about yourself now that you would
never have known if you had not been put to the test. And it is not
unusual, in my experience, for the skills and confidence forged in the
fire of trauma to become the things about ourselves that give us the
most pride.

How Are You Better Now?

You would not have chosen to get better and smarter and stronger in this way. But this thing happened to you—and you are better
and smarter and stronger for it.

The evidence for this is not merely anecdotal. Psychologist
Christopher Peterson, who is one of the founding fathers of positive psychology (and one of the authors of the signature strength
list in the previous chapter), has done a number of studies on people
who have had a brush with death. He found that people who had
lived through a life-threatening illness showed elevated levels of the
following:

- appreciation of beauty
- curiosity
- fairness

- forgiveness
- gratitude
- humor
- kindness
- love of learning
- spirituality

This jibes completely with my own experience working with survivors. I believe that survivors are special people; in my work with them, I have found that they have a unique depth, thoughtfulness, and sense of purpose. Survivors often have a touching ability to separate the things that are important in life from the superficialities. One of my patients spent a year recuperating after a car accident. She'd previously been frustrated by the fact that her husband's idea of romance was to grab a cheap chocolate heart at the drugstore on Valentine's Day after she'd dropped him several hints. But he spent the year of her recovery going with her to every doctor's appointment. He rose to the occasion and changed bedpans and surgical dressings without a word of complaint.

Needless to say, her definition of "Prince Charming" has radically changed. At the end of the day, a loyal friend, a true supporter, someone who loves you at your absolute worst, trumps just about anything else on earth; this is something you don't have to tell someone who has lived through a trauma.

Trauma survivors know what really counts.

If there is a pretty little flowering weed sticking up out of the concrete on the ugliest block in Manhattan, in my experience, it's the trauma survivor who stops and points out that single green shoot. And this isn't in spite of his trauma—it's *because of it*.

Researchers Lawrence Calhoun and Richard Tedeschi coined the phrase "post-traumatic growth." They found that many people experience some kind of positive change—stronger relationships, increased compassion and sympathy, and an increase in their own perceived strength—after a traumatic experience. In general, the growth is experienced in three domains: relationships with others, a change in sense of self, and a change in philosophy of life. Ben Sherwood, author of *Notes from the Survivor's Club,* quotes the work of Jeff Moore, a neuropsychologist at the Robert E. Mitchell Center for RPOW Studies. Most POWs felt stronger because of the experience, he reports, and 61 percent reported favorable psychological changes after captivity, including clearer priorities and a deeper understanding of self.

Met with financial devastation, people find they have a drastically altered perception of value and worth, especially of the things that money cannot buy. When you know how common it is for people to cheat, to lie, to hurt, or to leave, you develop a heightened appreciation for the preciousness of trust. When you have been struck by illness or accident, you rediscover with awe the magic of your body's ability to repair itself.

You may not have been oblivious to these things in the past, but would you not agree that you have an enhanced awareness of them now?

And I have always found that what they have been through allows survivors to uncover astonishing depths of compassion and empathy in themselves. Scratch beneath the surface and you will find that survivors are the driving force behind every movement to make the world a better place, to fight for civil rights, to protect the underdog, to rescue those in danger, and to provide for those in need. It is no secret that domestic violence shelters are staffed largely by survivors of domestic violence like Violet, and that the healing professions are filled with people who have themselves overcome emotional challenges. Every human rights movement we have ever had was born of the pain, the injustice—the trauma—of those who led it.

Counterintuitively perhaps, these qualities are part of the equipment that will help you enjoy your life. Caitlin, who survived sexual assault, entered therapy with lots of ideas about reclaiming her sexuality: "I'll know I'm better when I can do a raunchy striptease or have a quickie in the backseat of a car again." Reclaiming her sexuality was, of course, a worthy goal, but was there more she could do with the hard-won, vital information about trust and intimacy that she'd gained as a result of what had happened to her?

What Caitlin had endured had given her some very precious and rare insight into what it means to agree to consensual sex. The involuntary nature of her experience helped her appreciate the potential for intimacy that can happen when vulnerability is mutual. Many people spend a lifetime without learning this. I offer that the intimacy she experiences next may be of a higher quality than what some other people call intimacy. Although she would never have chosen to learn what she did the way she learned it, when the smoke cleared, Caitlin found herself ideally positioned to get something wonderful out of her relationships.

Survivors identify themselves by what they've lost. But what you have endured has given you an enhanced capacity for precisely those things.

This is one of the reasons that I am so insistent on this theme of survivor pride—because understanding the ways in which your trauma has given you insight and compassion is instrumental in your recovery.

Trauma as Inoculation

There's one last reason to embrace what has happened to you, and that is this: overcoming past obstacles helps you overcome future obstacles.

Trauma survivors often describe themselves as weakened by what has happened to them; their experiences, they feel, have left them helpless to navigate life in general, let alone the rough patches. But in fact, trauma (and our ability to survive it) inoculates us.

There is strength to be taken from simply knowing that we can endure. As Eleanor Roosevelt, another hero of mine, once wrote: "You gain strength, courage and confidence by every experience in which you stopped to look fear in the face. You are able to say to yourself, 'I have lived through this horror. I can take the next thing that comes along.'"

But if we can also learn from what helped (and what didn't help) us cope, then the experience can help prepare us for the future challenges that life will inevitably throw our way.

Let us return to Nelson Mandela. Although his circumcision was not psychologically traumatic it was undoubtedly challenging. Later in life, he repeatedly applied the coping strategies from that experience.

Shortly after circumcision the newly initiated young men gathered to hear the chief of their tribe speak about racism. "We are a conquered people, tenants on our own soil. We as a people have no strength, no power." For the first time, Mandela, who had enjoyed a peaceful childhood free from knowledge of discrimination, recognized himself as a victim of a crime of power.

The rest, as they say, is history; Mandela began a lifelong (and ultimately successful) quest to end apartheid in his country. But what's interesting to me is how he took the lessons of the horrible, painful moment of his circumcision and used them every day in the years of struggle that followed, including twenty-seven years of wrongful imprisonment. Always, his reflexive response was to cry out, "I am a man!"

In a highly ritualized way, the ceremony of his circumcision taught him to cope with hardship by asserting his own power and dignity. Even in the face of a sadistic system that was designed to make him feel helpless, Mandela got himself through the hard times by finding opportunities to combat humiliation with the expression of his own pride, dignity, and power. When his jailers attempted to demoralize black prisoners, not only by failing to provide them with adequate or nourishing food, but by making them wear short pants, as only a South African child would wear, Mandela demanded that prisoners be treated with dignity, like men. For twenty-seven long years of imprisonment, he continued to cry out, "I am a man!"

Mandela's and Frankl's ordeals taught them that despite what happened they could conduct themselves with dignity and not allow themselves to feel like a victim. Their life lessons taught them that they had what it takes to get through it. And if you so choose, this can be the lesson of your trauma as well. If you've never been tested, then you don't know what it's like to have to dig deep just to get through the day. If you haven't had to rely on yourself, then you don't know the depth of your powers of resilience and recovery. Everyone will experience injustice, pain, heartbreak, discrimination, disease, or defeat at some point in their lives. The difference is that when these things happen to you, as they surely will, you will know that you have what it takes to get through.

If you survived this, what can't you do?

**TRY THIS: CULTIVATING YOUR SURVIVOR PRIDE—
WHAT HAVE YOU GAINED?**

Complete the following:

I am stronger, wiser, and better since my trauma in the following ways:

_____, _____, _____. (name three)

Since my trauma, I have an increased appreciation for _____,

_____, _____, _____, _____. (name

five)

Before my trauma, I never had to _____ (name three skills that

you have acquired); now I know that I can.

Maybe the previous exercise was easy for you; if so, you're ahead of the game. But I know that if I asked most of you now to look in the mirror and to read the statements above out loud, they'd probably ring hollow. Even if they felt authentic when you were writing them, they might feel fraudulent once you were looking yourself in the eye and saying them aloud. It's interesting, isn't it? It doesn't feel false to hear Nelson Mandela or Viktor Frankl describe how they grew from their traumas, but this may be a new and strange way to see yourself. Indeed, for many of us, this is what we feel separates us from our heroes: they not only survived but seem to be thriving in spite of it all.

Let me let you in on a little secret: heroes rarely identify themselves as heroic. One of the most amazing things about working at *The Montel Williams Show* for five years was the opportunity to meet and to get to know a lot of people who are hailed as heroes, and most were the first to confess that they had no idea how they got on top of the pedestal.

And when I worked at Ground Zero the same guys on the covers of the magazines spoke openly about how the thank-yous and flowers and baked goods felt undeserved. "A hero is the guy who emerges from a burning building with a rescued baby in his arms," they told me, again and again. But there was no one at Ground Zero to be rescued. What those guys were doing was struggling to keep their hearts and souls together as they worked on a smoking pile of rubble and body parts.

But they were heroes, and I'll tell you why: because every day that they stepped out on the job, they rescued themselves. They were engaged in active combat in a war zone of emotions where everything conspired to defeat them, to rob them of their power and efficacy, to rob them of their love of life, and they emerged out of that hailstorm of emotions with themselves intact. They bore witness to things that others could not. They were able to go on in spite of their grief, able to face another day of work in spite of exhaustion, able to muster belief in themselves long enough to keep the faith—all this, in spite of a reality that threatened to crush them.

This is what a hero does. Sometimes he rescues someone else; sometimes he rescues himself.

The same thing that makes those rescue workers heroes is what makes Victor Frankl and Nelson Mandela heroes, too: the ability to rescue one's own soul from defeat. And it's what makes you a hero, too.

> **Sometimes, your ability to rescue *yourself* is what makes you a hero.**

Your challenge is simply to recognize that this is what you've been doing all along. If you are reading this book, it's because something came and put a huge weight around your neck. Every day you have been courageously bearing that weight. Despite your heavy heart, you've gone to work. Even though it's impossible to trust, you've tried to love. Every day, you have courageously gone forth into your scary life.

Like the rescue workers at Ground Zero, you have been engaged in active combat in a war zone of emotions where everything conspired to defeat you, to rob you of your power and efficacy, to rob you of your love of life. You have emerged out of that hailstorm of emotions with yourself intact. You bore witness to things that others could not. You have been able to go on in spite of your grief, able to face another day of work in spite of exhaustion, able to muster belief in yourself long enough to keep the faith—and all this in spite of a reality that threatened to crush you.

This is what a hero does.

I hope that, even at this very early stage in the book, you can at least wrap your head around the idea that you may come to feel a real sense of pride in your ability to thrive despite difficult conditions. Can you imagine feeling compassion as you look into your own face? Can you imagine feeling admiration for the person you see there and what he/she has overcome? Can you imagine taking pride and satisfaction in your ability to emerge on the other side?

If you can say yes to any of these, then you're already in good shape, because you've already signed on to a way of thinking that is radically different from the way most people approach healing from trauma. We can't make what happened to you go away. Nothing that either of us can do will strike it from history. But perhaps it doesn't need to cripple you as much as you thought it did; perhaps something that is not unequivocally negative might even emerge from the ashes of your experience.

The version of you that has survived a trauma deserves even more of your love, loyalty, and admiration than the pretrauma version. So what we will focus on next is learning about the obstacles standing between you and that destination—and finding ways to remove them.

In my practice, I usually find that patients feel much better after they've acknowledged the ways in which they were enriched by their trauma. For me, it shows how powerful it can be to change the way you think. That's because your cognitions, or the way you see the world, were damaged when you went through what you did. Those scars linger long after the bodily injuries have healed, and the court case is over, and the rest of the world has moved on. Trauma changes the way you see the world, and not for the better. But it is within your power to alter those perceptions so that you have access to the richest, most wonderful life possible.

You can either allow what has happened to you to mark you as forever damaged, or surviving it can become your most amazing achievement.

A Final Note on Pandora's Box: The Value of Containment

Our societal beliefs have taught us that medicine doesn't work if it doesn't taste bad. So we have a tendency to approach healing work with a rip-off-the-bandage, feel-the-burn, what-doesn't-kill-you-makes-you-stronger attitude.

Why do people tend to delve headlong into the details of their trauma in their very first therapy session? Because they think they are supposed to. But what we'll be doing in the exercises in this book is very different. This approach is supposed to feel good.

Remember that this approach does not ask you to revisit or to enumerate specific details about what you went through. There's nothing to be gained from revisiting the scene of the crime, especially if it's going to mean you spend the rest of the day trying to recover from it.

As you proceed through this book, use your feelings as a guidepost. If you find yourself getting overwhelmed, chances are that you have drifted back into old habits or are reflexively following other techniques. Take a break. Reread the exercise. Catch yourself at the point that your mind drifts and keep yourself in the present. Don't let yourself get in so deep that you're experiencing symptoms (dissociating, flashbacks, panic attacks) or spiraling into ruminations. The intention of this book is to help you to *avoid* being in that state—and to give you the tools to get out, if you should happen to fall in.

Does this sound like I'm suggesting that you don't talk about it or that you sweep it under the rug? If so, there is some evidence that suggests that too much talking, sharing, and communing with others about a trauma may place a person at risk of something called *stress contagion.* Although talking and sharing after a trauma is intended to be helpful, research has shown that increasing doses of this type of support are positively correlated with psychological distress.

I'm not saying that you should enter a permanent state of denial or that you can't look back at what happened. But I do believe that you should do so (and only if you want to) in doses you can handle.

So here's my solution, and it's a pretty simple one: if you feel like an excercise is going to overwhelm you, don't do it. (They're called "Try This" for a reason; if trying one does more harm than good, stop trying.) Limit the amount of time you spend on these exercises; none of them should take you more than five or ten minutes to do. And if you can see that you're going to have a problem with a given exercise, or if you find yourself experiencing symptoms when you're doing it, skip it. Come back to it when you can—or never at all.

There's no single exercise in this book so integral to your recovery that you can't live a perfectly wonderful life without it. The most important thing to me is that you don't hurt yourself in your quest to get better.

Meet Moodith
Conquering the Enemy Within

ASKED TO LIST THE POSITIVES ABOUT HER LIFE, Amy says, "Well, I'm smart." But her voice falters as she says it, because the little voice in her head has chimed in: "Not smart enough to know your husband was cheating."

> **When it comes to permatrauma, our own minds are our very worst enemy.**

Have you ever noticed, as you stand on the cusp of doing something intimidating like asking for a date or a raise, that a little voice in your head pipes up to undermine your confidence? Maybe it tries to talk you out of taking the risk by filling your head with fantasies of negative outcomes, demoralizing failure, and humiliating rejection. Maybe it scoffs at your efforts, gleefully pointing out all the times you've failed in the past. Or it poisons the well by forcing you to doubt people you might otherwise trust or the goodness of the world around you.

What happened to you undoubtedly threw you a real curveball—it's no wonder that this inner voice pops up a lot for trauma survivors. We're invested more intensely than we even know, in our inner voice. We listen to it because we believe in our heart of hearts that it is wise and that its wisdom will keep us safe.

Unfortunately, our inner voice isn't always the calming, prudent source of guidance we think it is; too often, our ability to see all that is joyful and healing in the world is eclipsed by the clouds of paranoia and complaint that it disperses. When we tentatively reach for the soul food we need, our inner voice slaps our hand. We think of our inner voice as our friend, but if we ever had a friend or a shrink or a coach who was this much of a buzzkill, we'd fire her on the spot. What's left in life, after your inner voice has talked you out of all the good stuff, is just all the bad stuff. So it's time to take some control over the thoughts we allow to inhabit our heads.

How We Keep Ourselves in Permatrauma

We talked in a previous chapter about how symptoms like nightmares and flashbacks are misguided but well-intentioned stabs at self-protection. In the same way, much of what keeps us in permatrauma are ways of thinking and coping that were developed in a time of tremendous, overwhelming stress. We bring these coping strategies to our current lives in an attempt to safeguard ourselves from future harm. But the way you learned to cope on the worst day of your life is no way to live the rest of it.

I've named my nasty inner voice Moodith because it's funny and dismissive and reminds me that she's not a good adviser, but Hatelyn, Buzzkill, or Mr. Misery will work just as well. Feel free to come up with your own dismissive moniker.

Now, why in the world would you have this lousy inner voice, if it's such a bad adviser? It's a holdover; in the animal kingdom, there's a distinct evolutionary advantage for those who preferentially attend to danger. From a natural selection perspective, it makes a lot of sense for most animals to make radical negative generalizations—it helps them to avoid the things that have seriously hurt them in the past. If a deer gets sick after eating some red leaves, it will learn to stay away from the red ones. A dog who nabs a burger off the grill and gets a bad burn on his nose isn't likely to try that trick again. Who would blame him for whimpering with his tail between his legs whenever he smells charcoal? In his case, developing a barbecue phobia is a pretty smart survival strategy.

Fortunately, being human confers some advantages over being a deer or a dog: you can tell the difference between poison ivy and radicchio, and you can don an oven mitt before grabbing something hot. Unfortunately, you're still hardwired with the same primitive brain that serves dogs and deer so well. Moodith is the voice of that primitive brain. And if she had her way, you'd stay home every night, locked in your room, taking no risks, shunning love—at least there, you're safe! So just as you think, "Wow, I really like this guy," you hear Moodith whispering, "How do you know you can trust him? He's gonna cheat on you. They always do. Anyway, you're not pretty enough to keep him."

After trauma, our internal voice trends toward the classic profile of depressed thoughts, or what Aaron T. Beck, M.D., the father of cognitive therapy, called the tendency to **personalize, generalize, and catastrophize.**

These three characteristic distortions of thought are known in the field as the "cognitive triad of depression."

For example:

Alan and Steve took an enormous risk when they tried to open their own business. They left their jobs and invested a substantial chunk of their life savings. When a competitor opened two blocks away from their proposed site, Alan said, fuming, "It was a stupid idea, and I was an idiot to think that I could ever do anything more with my life." He saw the failure as *personal* (the business didn't get off the ground due to his stupidity), *general* (his stupidity not only undermined this project but is pervasive and undermines everything he attempts), and *catastrophic* (because this one idea failed, he will spend the rest of his life stuck working a job he hates).

Steve, his partner, had a different take: "Our competitor's success is evidence that it was a good idea and a good location; we just didn't move fast enough. Let's look for another site." Steve understood that there was no conspiracy, no bigger picture, and no reason to criticize himself. He and Alan fell victim to circumstance. So Alan walks away from the experience feeling he got burned and ready to give up, while Steve walks away with his self-esteem unbruised. His dream is still intact and he continues to feel excited about his new career path.

Unfortunately, this PGC triad of personalizing, generalizing, and catastrophizing is a fallback position for survivors—and a failsafe way for us to know when our inner voice is leading us astray. Extreme thoughts like "Now I'll never get married" or "I'm bad luck; stuff like this always happens to me" keep us thinking like victims instead of resilient survivors.

Martin Seligman, Ph.D., is hailed as the father of the field of positive psychology. He and his colleagues took the concept of personalizing, generalizing, and catastrophizing one step farther. They conceptualized optimism, not as a personality trait, but as the tendency to recognize that when bad things happen, they are *not* personal, *not* permanent, and *not* pervasive. Steve, it goes without saying, is an optimist.

What's so great about being Steve? Well, an "optimistic explanatory style," as it's called, is associated with everything from better performance at athletics, college, and work; greater satisfaction in relationships; better coping; better health; and, of course, less vulnerability to depression. It's also interesting to learn that pessimism, as Seligman defines it, is strongly associated with PTSD symptoms.

I call it "spiraling," when we start ruminating, going 'round and 'round with PGC-style thoughts. In this section, you're learning to be aware of the way you think about the world and your place in it, and this pattern of thinking is definitely something to look out for. The next time something doesn't go as you'd planned, and you find yourself spiraling and feeling lousy, stop. Ask yourself instead if there was a reason that it didn't work out that you can learn from or that will help you to do something differently the next time. Remind yourself that the failure was just one incident, and don't allow it to spread like a fungus to every other area of your self-esteem, your current life, and your hopes for the future.

Alternatively, recognizing your habit of spiraling and the futility of the habit, you may just decide to simply stop. Abigail Thomas is the author of a thought-provoking memoir called *A Three Dog Life,* about her life after her husband suffered a traumatic brain injury. Abigail moved out of New York City to be closer to her husband's assisted-living facility and bought a car—but, on one of her first drives to the hardware store to buy garbage pails, she backed into a tree and smashed the back window.

Abigail acknowledges that most of her life she has waited "for a big man to show up and fix things." Her first inclination is to go "belly up." Before her husband's accident, she admits she would have whined and wailed, and then he would have taken care of everything. But instead of spiraling—"Why did this happen to me? Now I'm all alone"—or sinking into PGC thinking, here's what she says: "He wasn't here. There was just the bald fact: I had backed my car into a tree. Nothing else was relevant, the weather, the humble purchases, the small parking lot, nothing. I had backed my car into a tree and accepting this seemed to require less energy." Abigail stopped a spiral dead in its tracks.

Instead of holding a pity party, she calls her daughter, the car dealer, the glass guy, and the insurance company. "To my delight, I discovered myself capable of making phone calls to arrange the repairs and a couple of weeks later I had my car back, almost as good as new. This small accomplishment was thrilling."

Getting Out of the Permatrauma Box

Don't let Moodith's silly name suggest this is a trivial step.

We're making choices every day to see the glass as half-full or half-empty. But what we don't always understand is the tremendous influence our perception of the glass has on the way we feel. The example I use with patients is this one: There are few things in life that I dislike as much as jury duty. Wait. Wait. Wait. Sit. Stand in line. Change rooms. Sit and wait some more. Go home—then return the next day, for more of the same. This, to me, does not warrant canceling patients and hiring a babysitter.

But a friend of mine has an entirely different take. Jury duty fills her with a tremendous sense of civic duty and pride, and she loves every minute of it. It's an honor for her to serve; sitting in that massive room with hundreds of her fellow citizens, she feels like an integral part of the most impressive, sophisticated, democratic justice system on earth.

Neither of us is right—or perhaps both of us are. But I can tell you one thing for sure: for those three days, my cup-half-full friend has a much better time at jury duty. Whereas I go home tired and cranky, she feels energized and enriched. It is an attitude I'm going to do my best to emulate the next time I'm called, but for now, it serves to demonstrate a point, which is this: what you choose to focus on depends on you, and the choice you make drastically impacts the quality of the life you live.

For Moodith, the glass is always half-empty. And the only way for us to truly move on is by identifying and silencing this unsavory voice, to rob her of her authority over us. Otherwise, *she* controls what we think—and how we live.

The person or event that originally *perpetrated* our trauma isn't responsible for *perpetuating* it; Moodith is. But since Moodith originates in your brain, it is your own inner voice that is keeping you in a state of permatrauma.

I recognize that this might sound harsh at first, but it's actually a very empowering message: if we're the ones doing it, we can stop it. There's no denying that something bad happened to you. Now is the time to begin to observe the ways that we allow that inner voice to pick at our scabs, preventing our wounds from healing. It's time to look at what happens when you let Moodith drive you back to old coping strategies, wartime strategies that don't work in the peace-time world—and how you can put her in her place.

Because we are hardwired to think that Moodith has our back, it's hard *not* to hear her siren song. That's why it's a powerful thera-peutic tool to picture Moodith as a nasty little ogre whispering in your ear, not the sage voice of your street smarts. Her advice may be well-intentioned, but it is misguided. Tell her off for trying to impede your efforts to put your past in your past. Curse her out for trying to rob you of the life that awaits you. Do whatever you have to do to deflate and disregard her buzzkill ways.

These techniques, a combination of the cognitive therapy skills of thought-stopping and reframing, offer a way of shutting Moodith up while also exploring the plasticity of our false cog-nitions. In particular, consider ways that the bad outcome you're ruminating about was *not* personal, *not* pervasive, and *not* perma-nent. Look for reasons that might make it the other guy's fault. Check yourself if you find that you are expecting that the circum-stances will last forever, or if you are using the event to predict doom for your entire future.

Once we quantify the damage we carry—our take-home trauma—we can clearly see that our cognitions, our worldview, and our self-esteem have taken the biggest hits. These are all wounds that originate in our thoughts. But when you take responsibility for what you allow in your head, you may be delighted to find that a parallel universe exists all around you, and it's a much nicer place than Moodith would have you believe.

| 4 |

Moodith's Accomplice
The Shame-Blame Game

THE NEGATIVE VOICE IN YOUR HEAD that I call Moodith doesn't operate in a vacuum. Society adds plenty of fuel to the fire.

> *"You were pretty drunk; maybe you just got your signals crossed."*
> *"It's been six months already; don't you think it's time for you to put this behind you?"*
> *"How can you think you were discriminated against because of your race? Look at all the minorities who have achieved great success."*

Our friends, our family, our medical team, the media, and the justice system—all are potential sources of messages that discredit your experience by making you feel like your trauma didn't happen or that you might be lying or exaggerating the event or its effects. Those messages assign a weight to our trauma. They communicate how we should grieve, how it's appropriate to act and feel while healing, and how long that process should take.

As you can clearly see from the quotes above, many of these messages are destructive. They suggest that you shouldn't trust your own perceptions or that you aren't getting over it fast enough. They tell us to want things that run contrary to what we really want, or need, to feel better. Often, they invalidate what happened and devalue our feelings afterward.

In her book *I Can't Get Over It: A Handbook for Trauma Survivors,* Aphrodite Matsakis outlines several categories of this phenomenon, which she calls *secondary wounding,* a term that is now widely used. I call it the shame-blame game, and in my experience, the messages we receive about blame, shame, and damage can be just as or more damaging than the trauma itself.

One of the most insidious things about these societal messages is that they are absolutely impossible to avoid altogether. Like spitballs, they come out of nowhere to whap you in the head. A trigger may even come from a well-intentioned, encouraging comment. For instance, I recently read a newspaper article about a woman who was being hailed as a hero. Badly injured in the midst of a massacre, she had the presence of mind to play dead and was subsequently able to call for help. In the article I read, her brother was quoted as saying, "She's still a little shook up, but I'm sure she's going to move past this."

Still shook up? It had only been *three days* since this poor woman had survived the most terrifying, traumatizing fifteen minutes of her life; her wounds, both physical and emotional, were still fresh. Of course, she was still shaken! Like the rest of the nation, I hope that she will eventually be able to "move past this." But you can see how a comment like the one her brother made might make a person feel like she should be getting on with it sooner rather than later.

Since it's impossible to protect ourselves completely from the shame-blame game, it's essential that we learn to recognize these messages and the way we have integrated them into our perception of ourselves. Because when you internalize these negative messages about yourself, you add fuel to Moodith's fires; her chatter compounds and perpetuates what was done to you. While you can't change what your brother tells a reporter, you can make sure it doesn't affect what you tell yourself.

What follows is by no means a comprehensive discussion of all the ways society fuels the fire, contributing inadvertently to the take-home trauma we carry, but I'll bet that you've picked up at least one of the following societal messages about your trauma and incorporated it into your internal monologue:

#1: "It didn't happen."

They say: Maybe you're not remembering what happened. Maybe you misunderstood. And you hear: Maybe it didn't happen. And if it didn't happen, then you're crazy, lying, or just trying to get attention.

This type of comment is called "discrediting" and it is particularly noxious because it can cause you to question your own perceptions. We all use the people around us as a reality check, so it's fundamentally unsettling when the response we get back from them is one that makes us distrust our own recollections and impressions.

How can you heal, process, share, or find closure about something you've been made to feel might not have even occurred? And since it often takes a tremendous amount of courage to talk about what has happened in the first place, when your story is met with skepticism or disbelief, being discredited can give way to feelings of shame, isolation, and loneliness.

Many survivors incorporate those feelings into the way they think about what happened to them, sometimes to a terrible extreme. Debra, for instance, had grown so accustomed to her mother discrediting her trauma that she eventually stopped trying to talk about it. Years later when she shared her trauma story with me, I responded with shock and compassion—*but Debra thought I was mocking her.*

Being listened to and believed was so far from anything she'd experienced before that she had trouble accepting it when someone finally did. She had adopted the habit of being dismissive of herself. She'd talk for a while, then wave her hand in the air and say, "Oh, it's not that big a deal," "It happened a long time ago," or "You don't really want to be hearing any of this."

Sometimes you can even feel discredited indirectly. We overhear an off-color joke or a snide comment about what someone else went through, or about victims in general, and it cuts deep. More salt in the wound—and the thrower wasn't even aiming at you! One of my patients had a very hard time when a well-known political figure was accused by a female employee of ongoing sexual harassment. Pundits called the woman a publicity seeker, her story was questioned, and old history was excavated as evidence of her loose morals. (Needless to say, no one was talking about the politician's well-known history of womanizing.) The spectacle sent my patient a loud, clear message: "No one will believe you. People will think what happened was your fault."

The physiologic response that accompanies fear, stress, and strong emotions wreaks havoc with our memory, which makes discrediting messages even more confusing. The adrenaline and accompanying cortisol surges that flood our bodies in times of stress can make our own recollections of the incident seem cloudy or confusing. Survivors often describe their traumatic incident as dreamlike or movielike in their memories of it, "as if I'm out of my body watching it all unfold in slow motion." These perceptual alterations prime us to believe that perhaps we *aren't* remembering correctly.

Numbing of the senses is a typical reaction to trauma, and sometimes, due to this numbing, or the fact that it is uncomfortable to talk about, the language we use to describe our traumas may sound vague or childlike to others. This phenomenon is apparent in performer and survivor Rosie O'Donnell's memoir *Celebrity Detox,* in which there is a reference to her childhood abuse. While Rosie normally tells it like it is, her account of the incident becomes so abstract that at first I wasn't sure if she was saying what it seemed she was saying. When others note that you seem to be hedging, that you seem to be leaving things out, or that your language has become childlike or vague, it may cause them to doubt the veracity of your story. And this is exactly what happened to Rosie. After her book came out the Internet was full of skeptics weighing in on what did and didn't happen.

The important thing to remember is that these altered perceptions have everything to do with the chemicals in your brain; they don't mean that your story is fabricated. What happened to you was not a dream, a movie, or a misfire. But can you imagine how this onslaught of doubts and accusations must have felt to Rosie? Talk about secondary wounding adding to the take-home trauma!

#2: "You're making a mountain out of a molehill."

Some people may suggest, in ways subtle and not, that you are overreacting. This is often gender-specific. Our culture is full of messages that teach boys early to toughen up. No wonder, then, that men so often accuse themselves of overreacting or acting soft when they're just going through a normal grieving process.

But accusations of overreaction are certainly not restricted to men. This insulting dismissiveness is also liberally doled out to survivors of little-t traumas. Trudy had made an insightful connection between her intimacy problems and her cold, emotionally unavailable parents and hoped to discuss it with a childhood friend. But her friend flippantly responded by essentially telling her to quit her bitching: "Please, it's not like they beat you. You always had food on your plate and a roof over your head; there are lots of kids in this country who would gladly have traded places with you." The comment made Trudy feel ashamed, as if she was not just a dented car but a big baby, too.

Trudy shouldn't have to justify the strength of her reaction, or apologize for having one, and neither should you. Your goal is to be a person whose compassion is intact, whose outrage is alive, whose indignation and sense of right and wrong are in place. Just because your friend is cynical and hard doesn't mean her attitude has to rub off on you.

#3: "You don't have what it takes to cope."

Sometimes society gives us the message that we are more fragile than we really are. While men are often expected to be tough, women are force-fed the idea that they are fragile. The images that surround us, from fairy tales to romantic comedies, are of damsels in distress, waiting for the knight in shining armor to show up. By the time girls are in their teens, they are already well versed in the so-called romantic notion of an emotionally tortured girl in crisis and the strong, handsome, sensitive guy who shows up and loves her, in spite of it all. We don't see a lot of examples of women rescuing or healing themselves.

If everyone and everything around you is telling you that because you've been through some hard times, you're damaged goods, who are you to say that you aren't? How do you access rage or entitlement—emotions that might help you to feel powerful and in control—when everyone's expecting you to go to pieces?

It's hard to see yourself as something other than a victim when everyone is handling you with kid gloves after a trauma. One of my clients had fantasies about moving to a different city, just so that she wouldn't have to deal with the sober pall that fell over every room when she entered. Sometimes what we need is a break from ourselves, but the reactions of others dictate our behavior and limit us to what is felt to be socially appropriate.

#4 "A person never gets over this kind of thing."

Maybe you're asking if there aren't some things a person can *never* get over. My answer is: no. I would have thought so, too, until I began to meet people who had been through every variation of trauma imaginable: war, the loss of a child, the loss of an entire family. I have met people with permanent, life-changing functional losses from their trauma, like blindness and paralysis. I have met and treated people who have survived brutalities that far surpassed what most of us could even imagine. And although there are many in every category of Trauma or trauma who do *not* move on, there are others who do. And the one thing those survivors don't do is buy into the message that after a trauma like theirs, they can no longer have a rich and fulfilling life.

Certainly, there are widows who wear black forever. Many of us feel it insults the memory of what happened to move on after a trauma. Our suffering is a monument to what we have lost, and we fear that if we stop actively grieving, we will be betraying or abandoning people who did not survive, or somehow denying the event itself. But I don't see what anyone gains when a survivor turns what's left of her life into a living memorial. There are other ways to honor the memory of someone and keep their spirit alive so that you can continue to feel and express your love for them.

If you are committed to living a whole, real, complete life after trauma, it is imperative to develop an awareness of the ways in which we resist feeling happy. Many of us get caught in the lifelong trap of needing acknowledgment and validation surrounding a secret or shameful trauma, hoping someone will finally see how badly we are hurting. There are other ways to make visible what you have kept a secret for so long.

All of these are beliefs that perpetuate a state of chronic suffering; the idea of being happy and whole again presents a serious conflict. Why are these thoughts being mentioned in this section about societal messages of shame, blame, and damage? Because they are beliefs that contribute to the take-home trauma, the emotional aftermath of trauma. And it is in this realm, over the long term, that we have the power to make choices.

I don't for a second mean to rob you of your sorrow or to devalue or dismiss what happened to you. I'm only suggesting that you have a choice in how you go forward. There is grief that becomes action. There is grief that celebrates. There is grief that serves to help us see how precious and poignantly beautiful life is. And then there is grief that is like a cancer, robbing you of all the gifts of life.

#5: "It was your fault."

If there is one thing that is universally true about all traumas it is that they show us a picture of ourselves that none of us wants to see: a picture of helplessness. Is it possible that the universe is so random—and we are so at its mercy—that these horrible things just *happen*?

Humans prefer to imagine that there is a cause-and-effect relationship between our actions and the outcome. This often gets translated into a comment that, directly or indirectly, puts the blame on you.

But not all of these messages come from society. Here's one we are often guilty of slinging at *ourselves*. Almost all trauma survivors share the idea that there was *something they could have done* to prevent their trauma from happening in the first place. "If I hadn't trusted her with my finances . . ." "If I hadn't agreed to go on the trip . . ." "If only I'd been paying closer attention . . ." These are all slightly different versions of the exact same spiral.

We're too quick to enter a guilty verdict on ourselves and to lock ourselves into a life sentence in an attempt to regain a false sense of power over something we couldn't control. It is a paralyzing responsibility to believe that you can prevent bad things from happening. It feels terrible, it misrepresents reality, and it keeps us from moving on.

As difficult as it might be to admit, there are times in life when we are helpless. Sometimes, things go terribly wrong; sometimes the lunatic wins. A lot of people get to be in denial about this. Trauma survivors do not.

But there is a cognitive middle ground between maintaining a guilt-ridden delusional belief that lends you a false sense of control and accepting the fearful belief that random terrible things can happen at any moment. I maintain there is a third option: to acknowledge that there will be brief moments in our life when we are powerless, while knowing that most of the time, we are not.

What about those people who do have something to blame themselves for? One of my patients, Michelle, made the kind of stupid decision that lots of teenagers make: she masterminded something dangerous that she thought would be fun, and three of her friends died. Her shame and guilt cripple her from moving on, and some might say she *should* feel guilty.

I know how bad Michelle feels, but I also know that even someone like her deserves to move on. She caused the accident and she might have prevented it by making a different choice, but she is not the murderer she feels she is.

#6: "There's a 'right' way to cope—and you're doing it wrong."

Judgments about which emotions are appropriate in the immediate aftermath of a trauma are often unintentionally wounding—indeed, this is often a by-product of good intentions. People see you suffering, and they want to help. Unfortunately, they may have only a limited number of moves, which in turn limits the ways they think you should be responding.

For instance, many women crave intimacy after sexual assault, but their partners are frightened to initiate sex. Everyone knows how to offer heartfelt condolences at a funeral but not how to react when the grief-stricken widower uses gallows humor to cope. Given what you went through, people don't expect humor or sex to be helpful.

This "you're doing it wrong" response happens a lot, in my experience, when female victims get angry. In fact, many of my female patients have been coached by their lawyers *not* to show anger on the stand. Apparently it's hard for juries to reconcile the idea that a woman can simultaneously be a victim and be quite pissed off about it.

We are social animals, sensitive to the responses of the people around us. And it may be true that the fragile and vulnerable survivor gets more compassion and support than the angry, entitled one. So there is a real incentive to steer away from feelings that might give us back some of the sense of power and control that we lost.

But just to confuse things, our culture also values people who are able to contain their emotions. Everybody admires the rare mourner at a funeral who delivers the beautifully controlled eulogy—but if you can't lose it at a funeral, then where can you cry?

Who gets to decide when (if ever) it is appropriate to feel okay again? When it comes to mourning, "long enough" seems pretty arbitrary. Jews sit shivah, or formally mourn, for seven days after a death. In Islam, a widow observes *iddah* for four months and ten days. In the courts of nineteenth-century Europe, widows wore black for two years and could not reenter society for twelve months.

Fear of the "you're doing it wrong" response can contribute to the sense of isolation that trauma survivors often feel. One of my patients refused to go to a big annual family reunion because he was afraid people would judge him if they saw him having fun. He didn't want to face endless condolences; he just wanted to have a beer under a tree. Of course, when he didn't show up, then everyone assumed he must *really* be depressed: others' expectations of how "messed up" he was exceeded how "messed up" he really was. It's not that he wasn't grieving. But there is a lot of pressure to grieve a certain way.

If you look to societal messages for clues as to how it's acceptable to act and feel, you may find yourself adrift in contradictory messages. On the one hand we're supposed to keep our feelings covered up, like our bank balances or our underwear. Then again, if you keep your emotions too hidden, people will say, "Let it out—you can't keep it all bottled up inside!" You can't really win.

#7: "It's time to move on."

One of the most common shaming messages that I hear reported is the feeling that a clock is ticking on a survivor's ability to "get back to normal." After political figure Elizabeth Edwards lost her teenage son in a car accident she noted, "If I had lost a leg instead of a boy, no one would ask me if I was 'over it.' They would ask how I was doing learning to walk without a leg."

Our pain makes people uncomfortable. They wish the trauma hadn't happened to us; they wish we didn't still hurt. That's natural. Unfortunately, those sentiments often turn into subtle (and sometimes not-so-subtle) cues, hinting that it's time to pull ourselves together, to man up, to dust ourselves off and get back out there. When your health insurance company will only pay for twenty sessions with a therapist, the implication is clear: you should be able to get better in that amount of time. Your attacker has been prosecuted and will spend the next twenty years as a guest of the state; this was supposed to give you closure, and your friends are jubilant on your behalf. But it just makes you feel like your allotted sad-time is over, and now you have to pretend.

When you feel lousy and let it show, people say, "I'm worried about you." When you fake it, people say, "You look great! Good for you!" And from the difficult emotional state you're in, both the concern and the compliment feel like pressure. It's not enough, apparently, to feel bad—we have to feel bad about feeling bad! The ticking of this trauma stopwatch makes us feel ashamed in the face of our weakness, sorry that we keep boring our friends with our grief, and guilty about what our response is doing to our family.

#8: "Thank God it wasn't worse."

One of the firefighters I treated after 9/11 talked a lot about how supportive everyone had been, but whenever people made comments about how lucky he was to still be alive, he felt angry, guilty, frightened, and alienated. Their remarks were innocently delivered, and he accepted them with the assumption that they were meant to be supportive; it was only afterward that he realized how they'd reopened his wounds.

The repeated message that he should be grateful invalidated the fact that he was in mourning, that he was still in shock from a terrifyingly close brush with death, and that while he had not lost his life, he had lost much and was in fact very changed.

#9: "Trauma is an anomaly."

Bad things happen all the time. No one lives their entire life without losing a loved one, without being betrayed, without suffering a health crisis. When I watch reality TV I always ask myself why they have to go so out of their way to create the artificial drama of a fabricated crisis. Real life has plenty without producers stepping in.

Other cultures seem more realistic than ours about bad things happening; as a result, they are more likely to have rich containment rituals. There is great wisdom in traditions that both allow space to grieve after a trauma and provide guidance on how to do so in a healthy way. When I was working in Zimbabwe, for instance, I was impressed to witness a funeral custom in which relatives provide props from the dead person's life to a funeral actor, who then creates a tribute to the milestones and accomplishments of their life. The result is a festive reenactment that even children attend. This relieves the family of the emotional burden of having to deliver the eulogy themselves. But more importantly, it encourages the family to focus on ways of celebrating and loving the deceased instead of becoming overwhelmed by loss and longing.

The cultural insistence that trauma is rare can fuel "why me" thinking or make us feel we must be cursed or have bad luck. This feeds into that pessimistic thinking we talked about previously. (Remember—optimists don't assume things are personal, permanent, or pervasive). Recognizing the fact that most of us are touched by trauma removes a lot of shame and blame.

We must pull these judgments into the daylight to look at them and at their effect on us. Doing so begins the process of seeing ourselves as something more than damaged goods and allows us to take an important first step out of permatrauma.

In an ideal world, everyone around you would have responded in just the way you needed to make you feel strong, supported, and defended after your trauma. They would have been outraged for you and full of compassion. They would have brought you casseroles and let you cry or punch things when that was what you needed to do. They would have listened to you, and believed you, and sought justice on your behalf.

Did people in your life call the trauma by its name or skirt the topic with euphemisms, creating an atmosphere of shame? Did they let you know they could handle your honesty and grief or did you get the message that you had to protect them from the full force of what you were going through? Did your friends and family acknowledge the anniversary of the event and let you know it was okay to be having a setback or were you left to pretend that it was just an ordinary day? Did anyone in your sphere get angry on your behalf? Rally in your defense? Start a foundation to help?

TAKE NOTE: WHAT MESSAGES DID YOU RECEIVE?

I often encourage my patients to dig into the fantasy of what would have happened if everyone in their lives had done exactly what they'd needed them to do in the aftermath of the trauma. Note that this exercise is not an invitation to ruminate on all the ways your support system fell short. Rather, it is an opportunity to note how you would have felt if everything had gone right.

Fill in the blanks:

"After my trauma, I would have liked it if people had _____ because that would have helped me to feel more _____."

Repeat this simple exercise as many times as you can, noting all the ways your take-home trauma might have been minimized by family and friends, by the police and the courts, by the media and the news, by your church.

> We can't control how others perceive what happened to us, but *we can control how* we *think about it.*

Most of us were not blessed to be surrounded by these ideal healing and empowering experiences. But we can at least make sure that we're not unconsciously reiterating these destructive messages to ourselves.

Hardwired for Hard Times
Seeing the World Through Traumatized Eyes

REMEMBER WHEN WE TALKED ABOUT that primitive animal in us that makes sweeping generalizations about life in order to try to help us learn from our mistakes? In this chapter we will be taking a look at the ways your worldview may have changed after you went through your own ordeal. After something bad happens, it's a natural response to put ourselves on red alert, constantly watchful for a recurrence. From a natural selection standpoint it makes sense for us to be hardwired for hard times. After all, the antelope who is always looking over his shoulder for attack has a better chance of survival than the one who isn't. But let's look at what it means for us as humans when, without even realizing it, we make rules for ourselves in the form of statements of "fact" that predict and anticipate a repeat trauma.

These rules—often unconscious—feel savvy and street-smart. In fact, most people will defend them when they're called on them, claiming that they're better equipped to get through life because of them. But the real truth is that these rules don't really protect us; in fact, they can block the road to healing. These self-imposed strictures make our lives small and dull—and they can lead to feelings of depression and hopelessness.

Ultimately, these perceptions *continue to perpetuate the trauma that you experienced*. That's why I call them **trauma-preserving assumptions,** or TPAs—because they keep the trauma alive and well in your mind instead of helping you to move on. Without realizing it, you are aggressively collecting evidence every day to support your trauma-preserving assumptions; I call this process **harvesting.**

The tricky thing about trauma-preserving assumptions is that people don't realize they have them, aren't aware they have embraced them, and are certainly not aware of the ways they are traveling through life apparently trying to prove that they are correct.

According to my patient Alison, who was betrayed by her spouse, she is wholeheartedly trying to meet someone new. She's gone out on a bunch of dates; she's dressed up and chatted hard. As far as she's concerned she's open to finding a new mate. Alison doesn't realize she's carrying around a trauma-preserving assumption that men are all cheaters, unworthy of her trust. She thinks she's giving her dates a fair shot. But is it a fair shot when every guy you date has to disprove your worst assumptions about him? John was fidgety—he must be hiding something. Bob talked too much about his ex—he's probably still in love with her. Sean, God help him, excused himself to take a call during lunch.

Alison never consciously decided not to trust anyone new. But as she meets new guys she is unconsciously harvesting evidence to prove true her trauma-preserving assumption that all men are cheaters like her ex. And she's finding evidence wherever she looks that serves to give that TPA deeper and deeper roots.

SOME COMMON TRAUMA-PRESERVING ASSUMPTIONS

Someone treats you badly and you go through life thinking—
    I am not good enough to be lovable.
Someone betrays you and you go through life thinking—
    People are always disappointing.
You lose your job and you go through life thinking—
    There's no point in having ambition; it doesn't pay off.
You endure an abusive relationship and you go through life
    thinking— If I keep myself small and invisible,
    nothing bad will happen.
Your husband cheats and you go through life thinking—
    Looks are all that men care about.
Your wife cheats and you go through life thinking—
    Money is all that women care about.
You experience a natural disaster and you go through life
    thinking— We are never safe; you can never let down your
    guard.
You get conned and you go through life thinking—
    Everyone is looking out for themselves; no one can be trusted.
    It's safer to keep people at arm's length.
You take on a mortgage you can't afford and lose your home and
    you go through life thinking— I'm not smart enough to make
    my own decisions.

The TPAs listed above are just examples. It's not as if every possible trauma inevitably leads to the same TPAs. Whatever your TPAs are, they can have wide, sweeping effects on our lives. Barbara was the victim of a scam and lost nearly everything. She feels guilty and ashamed but is determined not to be taken advantage of again. In fact, Barbara is quite pleased with how savvy, street-smart, and aware she has become. She has a trauma-preserving assumption that everyone is trying to rip her off, and believe me, she finds ample evidence to prove that TPA true—from the pharmacist who shortchanged her by two pills to the billion-dollar Ponzi schemes in the news.

All this should make Barbara feel quite validated. But instead she is miserable. She came into therapy saying she is depressed and feels lonely, she's having marital problems, and she feels unsure about her bond with her kids. "I've been through so much and now it seems like everyone is pulling away from me," she says. Barbara didn't make the connection that her savvy TPA had built a wall of paranoia all around her—it had made her hard and judgmental.

Perhaps you can see a little more clearly, because we're talking about someone else, the effect that Barbara's trauma-preserving assumption has on her. First of all, you can see how her constant harvesting keeps her living in permatrauma. Every time we "prove" our TPAs true, we add another stick of kindling to the permatrauma fire. For Barbara, the harvesting proved that the scam wasn't just something that had happened once, but something that was happening every day—and so the feeling of being ripped off constantly gnawed at her, stoked by all the evidence she was collecting.

Harvesting turns a trauma-preserving assumption into a worldview.

It's no surprise that Barbara felt exhausted and irritable all the time; how could she relax when she constantly needed to be on guard against the possibility of someone taking advantage of her? And no wonder, too, that healing felt slow in coming when she was reliving some aspect of her trauma with every distrustful interaction.

Her most casual interaction was tainted by distrust and skepticism. Would you want to be friends with someone who is clearly keeping a tally of who's done what and for whom? Someone who always seems to suspect you of trying to rip her off?

When we harvest evidence to prove our TPAs true, they start to become a self-fulfilling prophecy. Knowing that every kind gesture would be scrutinized Barbara's friends and coworkers didn't bother to bring her a cup of coffee in the morning, and her neighbors didn't offer to water her plants when she was away. The people in Barbara's life felt they could never win with her, so they took their friendship elsewhere, while she ended up feeling lonely and misunderstood. So, Barbara's trauma-preserving assumptions not only cut her off from the kind of interactions that might have made her feel really good, but they led her to create a world where it really *did* seem like everybody was looking out for themselves.

TPAs make us see the world through what I call trauma-colored glasses. They keep us living in a world characterized by ugliness and distrust and fear, a world inhabited by people at their worst. Trauma-preserving assumptions make you look every gift horse in the mouth; as a result, they close the door on a lot of wonderful experiences, preempting them before they have the opportunity to occur. Maybe her husband's coworker who wanted to invest in their new business idea was really a good guy. Maybe the friend who offered to take her kid to the carnival really wanted nothing in return but friendship. Barbara may have gotten ripped off, but she was much poorer for all her harvesting. Nobody was cheating her as much as she was cheating herself.

"But My TPAs Are True!"

Now, you may feel compelled to jump in here: "But my trauma-preserving assumptions are true!" You probably want to tell me how the rules you made in the wake of your trauma keep you safe and how well they actually hold water. And you're probably willing to document your convictions with every piece of evidence you've ever harvested.

You're not wrong. It may be true that there are tons of lousy, cheating guys out there. And scammers. And hurricanes. And plane crashes. Indeed, one of the problems with our trauma-preserving assumptions is that they can be very convincing. In point of fact, they are no more right than they are wrong—after all, a half-full cup is also half-empty. Jeffrey is at least partially correct when he says that it's not safe to drive at night. But that assumption isn't right all the time, because many people do drive after dark without anything happening to them. And while this rule gives him a feeling of control, it's illusory: unfortunately, many people get into accidents during daytime hours as well.

Arguing the validity of your trauma-preserving assumptions is not my intention; in fact, it's something I really ask my patients *not* to do. My point is simply that if you are harvesting negative evidence to prove your TPAs correct, then you could *also* potentially be finding evidence to disprove them. Regardless of how much evidence you can amass to prove that they're true, I promise you that there is just as much evidence to prove that they are not. For every cheater there are many trustworthy men and women. For every plane that crashes, there are even more that don't.

I'm not insisting that you abandon your TPAs; I'd just like you to drag them out into the open, so you can see what they are, how they impact the way you live, and how they discolor the way you experience the world. To put it another way: if you had an unconventional tennis serve and came to me for a lesson, I would be obligated to first point out that the way you serve puts strain on your elbow and that there is another way. Ultimately, it's your decision: you may continue to hit the ball the way you've always done it. But it would be terrible, in my opinion, to go through life without realizing that your serve is why your elbow hurts.

As you'll remember, Alison, still smarting from her ex's infidelity, is harboring a TPA that all men are cheats. She's been telling herself that if the right guy came along, he'd be able to win her over. But she made the men she dated feel like they constantly had to prove their innocence, and a simple glance at another woman was enough for her to tell them to take a walk. Alison was snoopy and suspicious, accusatory and rejecting—no wonder very few of her suitors asked to see her again.

Initially, Alison was prepared to argue the validity of her TPAs, and she had a lot of evidence to "prove" to me that men can't be trusted. "If you keep looking for evidence, you will keep finding it," I told her. "But there's a price you pay for this harvesting—and that price is a second date."

> The best-case scenario of proving your trauma-preserving assumptions true is that then you have to live in the ugly world you have created.

Once you see the consequences of your successful harvesting my guess is that you won't want to accept the inevitable results.

Try Something Different: Harvesting Goodness

Ten years ago Bonnie's child fell ill with meningitis. The incident was understandably terrifying for her, although her child made a full recovery. Now she is an avowed germ freak and can't understand why everyone else is in denial about the hazards of infection. She has *chosen*, albeit unconsciously, to preferentially harvest evidence to support a trauma-preserving assumption that humans in general, and children in particular, are immunologically frail. She has no trouble harvesting evidence: newspapers are full of stories about swine flu, bird flu, mad cow disease, and an unimaginably terrifying array of bioterrorism agents. But every single day, Bonnie is *also* surrounded by healthy children who thrive despite picking their noses on the subway and drinking warm lunchroom milk. There is abundant evidence to prove both things: that children are frail, and that they are hearty. But in choosing only to see the bad stuff, Bonnie is constantly and chronically reinforcing a worldview that gives her a tremendous amount of pain.

> **A trauma-preserving assumption cannot persist if we don't harvest evidence to support it.**

I'm not asking you to make a commitment to overhauling your whole belief system at this point. But since you bought this book and committed to reading it, why not try the theory on for a while and then decide? The truth is that we can find lots of evidence for whatever we look for. Our emotional responses might be habitual, but they are not inevitable, and the surest way *out of* feeling like a victim is to regain control of our thoughts and feelings. Since you have a choice, why not harvest those things that will make the world seem a little less dangerous, cold, and unfriendly, instead of the ones that make you feel like a victim?

A researcher named Barbara Fredrickson has examined the function and effect of both positive and negative emotions, noting how each impacts our worldview. She observed that negative emotions, being associated with danger, narrow our response range; they make us focus and allow us to act with haste (presumably to avoid whatever dangerous thing caused the emotions). Conversely, positive emotions (presumably because they indicate that we are safe) encourage us to broaden our options and to build upon them.

Fredrickson calls this the "broaden-and-build" theory. While negative emotions give us an evolutionary advantage in the present by keeping us from getting killed, positive emotions give us an evolutionary advantage in the future. They encourage us to broaden our horizons, to experience and learn, all with the promise of a payoff in the future.

Fredrickson is not speaking about trauma, but I believe that the broaden-and-build theory is one with tremendous application to survivors, because it suggests that if we are about to embark on a journey of change it behooves us to get ourselves some positive emotions to help open our minds.

So I'm not merely advocating positive emotions because they feel good. I am likening them to getting a good night's sleep before a game. They will help you do your best as you endeavor to make life changes.

> **Our TPAs interfere with our ability to feel essential positive emotions: Lovable. Lucky. Blessed. Healthy. Vigorous. Vital.**

Your challenge is to create and harvest **TPA remedies.**

We do this not to prove our trauma-preserving assumptions wrong but to get back in touch with the emotions our trauma-preserving assumptions have masked for so long.

For instance, Alison acknowledged that people who had not experienced the trauma of being cheated on by a spouse might believe the following statement: "Most men are *not* unfaithful." In fact, she acknowledged, before her husband was unfaithful she even assumed that many men were as appalled by the concept of infidelity as she was. Together we crafted a TPA remedy: "The vast majority of the men I will meet will be good guys, worthy of trust." And Alison agreed, for a day, to try this on for size.

She noticed a dad at the playground attentively watching his daughter, a young man carrying all the grocery bags for his pregnant wife. She passed a janitor who stopped hosing the sidewalk as she approached, so she wouldn't get splashed.

Then Alison happened to notice a guy at a restaurant who was really listening to his female companion. She saw how that woman basked in his interest and attention. She admired the ease with which the woman made eye contact and how relaxed she was, how he made her laugh. As she watched them, Alison remembered that feeling—and realized that she hadn't allowed herself to enjoy it in a very long time. When she did, something important happened for her—Alison allowed herself, even if it was just for a minute, to connect with the emotions that her trauma-preserving assumptions had made inaccessible to her. Her TPA remedy had hit pay dirt.

Alison put herself in that other woman's shoes, a position she had not permitted herself to occupy since the trauma. "What would it feel like to relax and laugh with a male friend or a lover again?" she asked herself. "To listen to what he's saying without looking for a subtext or for clues that he'll stray?" Suddenly she realized how much she missed that emotional state of trust and confidence and relaxation, and made the connection: This was not something she could feel while clinging to her trauma-preserving assumptions.

> **TPA remedies help us access emotions we buried long ago when our post-trauma rules started to dictate an ugly new reality.**

What would it be like if you were as aggressive about harvesting evidence to prove your TPA remedies true as you typically are about proving your TPAs? How would life feel if Bonnie spent her days noticing all the healthy, hearty, resilient children who were not succumbing to disease? How would it feel for Alison to take note of all the decent men that surround her? How might Barbara's relationships shift if she stopped looking every gift horse in the mouth and instead went harvesting evidence of generosity in her world? For successful survivors, this harvesting of nontraumatized alternatives becomes a rigorous daily practice.

Here are examples of some TPA remedies that one might create in response to a few of the trauma-preserving examples that began this chapter and how someone might harvest evidence to support these new peacetime alternatives.

Note that TPA remedies are not merely the converse of their paired TPA. They are designed to help access an emotion that was blocked by the old post-trauma rules.

TPA: I am not good enough to be lovable.

Remedy: Even if I am flawed or imperfect, lots of people are, and they still merit love.

To harvest: Find evidence to prove it true, whether it's that relatively unattractive couple holding hands who seem very fond of each other or the fact that you love your brother to bits even though he's a slob.

RESULTING EMOTION: I am lovable.

TPA: People always end up disappointing me.

Remedy: I don't have to go it alone.

To harvest: Find evidence of support systems, as well as people who are touched and flattered when you ask for their help. Note that a mentoring program for women entrepreneurs is being offered in the paper—and it's free! Someone took the time to organize and finance that in order to help. Reflect on the time you asked your neighbor for free financial advice and found him happy to oblige. Recall the time you were worried that your friend would be burdened by hearing about your relationship problems, but she listened and asked you to have coffee again the following week.

RESULTING EMOTION: I feel safe and supported.

TPA: If I keep myself small and invisible, nothing bad will happen.

Remedy: I can stand up for injustice without being punished.

To harvest: Look for all the times in your life when you have effectively stood up for yourself: last night, when you asked your husband to do the dishes because you'd done the cooking, or the time you picketed at work due to poor conditions and weren't fired.

RESULTING EMOTION: I have power.

TPA: I'm not smart enough to take risks.

Remedy: I have good analytic skills and make good decisions.

To harvest: Ask yourself, what are the risks you've taken that have turned out well for you? Think about the camp you chose that turned out to be great for your kids; recognize that choosing to lease instead of buy has proven to be a great decision.

RESULTING EMOTION: I am capable.

TPA: There's no point in having ambition; it doesn't pay off.

Remedy: The world is full of people who notice and appreciate a job well done.

To harvest: Notice all the parents who chipped in to buy a gift for the crossing guard who always shows up, rain or shine? Your boss might not notice or reward your hard work, but you did receive a thank-you note from a client who did. Didn't you see the people lining the street to cheer at the finish line of the breast cancer run on the news last night?

RESULTING EMOTION: What I do matters.

TPA: Everyone is looking out for themselves; no one can be trusted. It's safer to keep people at arm's length.

Remedy: The world is full of reliable people who keep their promises.

To harvest: Make a list of the people in your life who have kept their promises, large and small—the Cub Scout leader who refunded the money when the magazine subscription didn't come through, the car rental place that gave you an upgrade because they ran out of the car you'd reserved, the customer who could shop at a big box store, but who comes to your family-owned business out of loyalty.

RESULTING EMOTION: I feel trustful.

Now, this certainly isn't a comprehensive list of all the trauma-preserving assumptions that survivors harbor. Nor are these the only TPA remedies available. With these examples, I simply want to demonstrate how the process works—and perhaps, from these examples, you can see not only how it's possible to harvest whatever evidence you're looking for, but also what a relief it is to get off "high alert." You can find evidence of a kinder, gentler world—provided you have the discipline and courage to look for it.

TAKE NOTE: FINDING REMEDIES FOR YOUR TRAUMA-PRESERVING ASSUMPTIONS

When this concept is explained, many people know exactly what their trauma-preserving assumptions are. But if figuring out your trauma-preserving assumptions are proving tricky, consider that TPAs are often lurking behind things we are bitter or cynical about. They are buried in the things we think we've learned from our trauma, all the ways that we feel we have become savvy or street-smart. And because they rob us of feel-good soul food, they are often skulking around in those aspects of our lives that make us feel depressed, defeated, or victimized.

Sometimes it's easier to see other people's TPAs than your own; can you identify the TPAs of your closest friends and family members? Once you have done so, look them over and see if you might have made some of these same "rules" for yourself. After all, we often seek out the company of people who validate our beliefs, healthy or unhealthy.

Write one of your TPAs here: _____

Once you've identified one of your trauma-preserving assumptions, I invite you to invent a TPA remedy. Remember: the goal here is not to challenge your TPA, per se, or to prove it wrong. It's simply to come up with another way you might look at the world that enables you to access emotions that the TPA blocked.

Write your TPA remedy here: _____

Now your job is to suspend your inner Moodith and go out harvesting evidence to support this new alternative to your post-trauma worldview.

First look for evidence in experiences from your memory of the past weeks, then go out into the world and do some harvesting there. For motivation, tell yourself that it's just for one day, and imagine someone is going to give you twenty bucks for every piece of evidence you find. Make a game of it; pretend you are on a new reality show: you're not defending the integrity of your viewpoint but trying to make some cash—and you'll get paid only if you successfully harvest evidence to prove that TPA remedy true.

Write some of the evidence you harvested here: _____, _____, _____.

At the end of the day, how much cash did you make? But, more importantly, how did it feel to be engaged in the process of looking for evidence of good?

As you've probably gathered by now, I love to read real-life survivor stories and the memoirs of overcomers whom I admire. But I do have a gripe with the format in which many of them are written. What I'm referring to is that formula in which, after a whole book of struggle and heartache, the subject suddenly has some epiphany, after which their life magically gets back on track and we see them emerge triumphant. Books like that make me feel ripped off. Because it's clear that they are leaving out some crucial step that differentiates pre- and post-epiphany thinking.

The difference, it turns out, has to do with trauma-preserving assumptions. More specifically, the moment when a person becomes willing to challenge TPAs and open their heart to something better is a huge moment in the process of overcoming your past.

The best way to get yourself the kind of overcomer epiphany that you read about in books is to dare to challenge a TPA.

One of my favorite survivor anecdotes comes from a book called *Why I Wore Lipstick to My Mastectomy* by Geralyn Lucas, who was twenty-seven years old and living a life straight out of *Sex in the City* when she was diagnosed with breast cancer. The gift that Geralyn gives us in her memoir is that she is very transparent about what she is doing to battle feelings of victimization. She deconstructs her epiphanies, so we can see that what differentiates pre- and post-epiphany thinking has to do with the way she challenges her trauma-preserving assumptions.

One of Geralyn's TPAs is that no one will be attracted to her after her mastectomy, that her sexual power lies exclusively with the way she looks. As she puts it, "No one cares about a breastless woman." Right before her mastectomy, Geralyn decides to go out one last time, all dressed up, to get some male attention. By going out dressed in a provocative way, she is digging her claws into her trauma-preserving assumption, looking for evidence that people are only attracted to her because of her body.

Knowing she looks sexy, she is smug when she sees a cab swerve through treacherous traffic to pick her up. The driver flirts outrageously with her. His attention simultaneously flatters her old self while hurting the new one. Convinced that he would never flirt with the bald and breastless woman she is about to become, her irritation gets the best of her, and she shocks the cabbie by telling him that she's scheduled for a mastectomy the next day.

On the one hand, it seems like a very aggressive thing to do—she's looking to see if he'll be put off. But at the same time, it's also a very vulnerable act: by putting her trauma-preserving assumption out there, she shows that she's open to seeing it disproved as well.

As is so often true when you're brave enough to look critically at these painful assumptions, what happens next is amazing. The guy pulls over, music still blaring, and gets out of the cab to join Geralyn in the backseat. He takes her hand and kisses it, and then shares his own story of a bout with cancer that left him with only one testicle.

He tells her that he survived, and that she will, too, and the two of them sit swaying together in tearful, joyful community and gratitude in the back of his cab. Geralyn concludes: "If a one-balled man and an about-to-be one-boobed woman can somehow end up dancing in a taxi in a city of millions, and figure out this hidden truth within the span of a seven-minute cab ride, then somehow I will survive this ordeal."

Not only did Geralyn prove that a man could see past her tight jeans and bodysuit, but it turned out that this random cabdriver had exactly the soul food she needed—soul food that she would never have gotten if she'd stuck to her trauma-preserving assumption. For me, the take-home message is this one: you can dress provocatively and flirt with men and feel justified in thinking that they're pigs because all they care about are your boobs. But if you work too hard at proving that TPA true, you might not get to meet the cabdriver who shares his soul and his hope with you.

In that cab the seeds of a TPA remedy emerged: "People will value me for my humanity and my truth." As she embarks on her battle with cancer, Geralyn faces a choice: she can set out with the belief that even if she survives, she will be asexual and without value in the eyes of others—a TPA. And she will certainly be able to harvest evidence to prove this true. But she also has an alternative: she can start a new chapter of her life, believing that she has worth for some aspect of herself that is deeper and more profound than her sexuality. And if she opts to harvest evidence to prove *this* TPA remedy true, she will also find it.

Most important, take a moment to consider the emotional climate one would inhabit given both alternatives. Maybe you think this is the kind of epiphany that only happens in other people's stories. I can't promise a cabdriver will miraculously appear to validate your new beliefs. But there is a kind of magic that happens when you open yourself up to the possibility of a world not dictated by the rules of your trauma.

Creating TPA alternatives and harvesting for them won't cast a magical spell that changes you forever. Instead, it marks the beginning of a daily (sometimes hourly) practice, one that will eventually enable you to get back to the emotions that will make you feel great again.

Survivors like Geralyn Lucas, Viktor Frankl, and Nelson Mandela have all made a very conscious choice about the kind of thoughts they allow to inhabit their minds. Whether we are talking about Big-T Traumas or little-t traumas, the people you see getting back to their lives are exerting a mental discipline to *not* allow their minds to amass evidence that they are still in danger, that they are still at risk, that all is lost.

> **Resilient survivors are people who are actively harvesting hope and happiness.**

As you live with this new understanding, you will come to see how your beliefs, even ones that feel savvy, can limit your horizons instead of expanding them, how they curtail your options instead of increasing them. There's a much wider world out there for you to enjoy and experience. And, as Geralyn Lucas's story shows, there are things out there that could help you heal, that would nourish your soul instead of starving it. But first, you'll have to let them in.

6

A Balanced Emotional Diet
Emotional Junk Food vs. Emotional Soul Food

TRADITIONAL THERAPY OFTEN FOCUSES ON *behaviors* that patients no longer allow themselves, and so the whole point of therapy then becomes
an exercise to get you back on the horse. You may have been mugged
while jogging in the woods, but I'm not going to focus on getting you
jogging again. I am much less interested in your reclaiming activities
that you now avoid, preferring to focus instead on the *emotions* that
you are now missing out on. In the last chapter we discussed ways
in which TPAs make certain emotions inaccessible. In this chapter
we will take an emotional inventory so that you know clearly which
emotions you already have an excess of and which you need more of.

In order to get optimal nutrition, you need to eat a rich variety
of phytochemicals and nutrients, and you can only get those from
a variety of sources. Nutritionists often counsel their clients to "eat
the rainbow"—red tomatoes, green asparagus, purple eggplants, and
orange sweet potatoes. In the same way, you need to experience the
full spectrum of your emotions.

Since this is a book about taking control of the thoughts and
emotions that you allow in your head, you will need to recognize

when you are experiencing emotions that you already have too much of (emotional junk food) and cultivate ways to introduce healthier options (emotional soul food). To begin, I'd like to give you two tools. One will help you recognize when your thoughts have drifted reflexively to the negative; the other will help you understand what you need when that moment happens.

TAKE NOTE: YOUR EMOTIONS LISTS

Get two different colored pens—a red one and a blue one. Keep them close as you read through the following list of emotions:

stressed	antsy	enraged	drained	spent	revengeful
scared	vulnerable	fragile	entitled	empowered	composed
delighted	silly	giddy	gleeful	trusting	fit
blessed	spiritual	adoring	tender	passionate	vibrant
brilliant	gifted	content	still	receptive	in-charge
defeated	timid	joyous	overwhelmed	euphoric	expansive
creative	abundant	reckless	unlovable	ugly	gorgeous
cursed	undefeatable	included	rejected	wounded	damaged
healed	grandiose	confident	private	needy	clingy
safe	snug	blue	weepy	pessimistic	hopeless
hopeful	eager	excited	quiet	energized	alive
purposeful	validated	faithful	triumphant	furious	vicious
shameful	undeserving	proud	mortified	miserable	desperate
frantic	hunted	haunted	liberated	delicious	charming
precious	sexy	sensual	seductive	desirable	worthy
valued	keen	strong	commanding	indispensable	submissive
panicked	suicidal	aggressive	observant	paranoid	invigorated
restful	serene	inspired	lovable	curious	nurturing
brave	protective	insightful	resourceful	just	adventuresome
resilient	trustworthy	decent	gracious	attuned	self-reliant
in control	forgiving	grateful	optimistic	funny	grounded

kind	soft	gentle	fierce	diplomatic	loving
curious	eager	thoughtful	inspirational	humble	dignified
reserved	dedicated	trusting	empathic	driven	determined
maternal/ paternal	considered/ not impulsive				

On this list there will undoubtedly be emotions you are familiar with and some that aren't part of your emotional repertoire. And there will be some that you were once familiar with but that seem "gone" since the trauma.

LIST #1: YOUR PERMATRAUMA EMOTIONS LIST

First, I'd like you to make one list, using a blue pen. This is a list of the emotions that you experience when something leads you to reflect back on your trauma. One minute you're fine, chugging along through your daily life, and then *wham!*—something takes you back, and you find yourself drowning in a whole sea of emotions. This list includes the whirlwind of feelings that takes over when you unexpectedly bump into your ex, or when you stumble upon a movie on late-night TV that transports you to an emotional place where you didn't intend to go. Maybe you experience these feelings when you hear a particular song, or visit your family, or after you attend a support group, or when you spend long periods alone in a car with your thoughts. Maybe you are flooded with them as you sit with your checkbook trying to pay your bills. I'm not just talking about how you feel immediately after experiencing whatever triggered you but the lingering dark cloud that hovers for hours or days.

I call this "feeling trauma-y." One of my patients, a firefighter not known for mincing his words, prefers to call this "feeling shitty," and his may be a more accurate diagnosis, but I'll leave what you call it up to you. You'll notice that "trauma-y" isn't a feeling on the list of emotions above. That's because I want you to *break down* how you feel: *what makes up that trauma-y feeling for you?*

As we spiral into depression and hopelessness, or rage, or anxiety, it's all too easy to forget that there are alternative emotions on the menu. What typically happens after your trauma is triggered is such an automatic and rapid cascade of thoughts that we may not even realize how they led you to feeling lousy. We often don't even know how we got from a sad song on the radio to feeling trauma-y all day.

Being armed with a list of emotions that you typically feel when you are feeling this way is a very useful tool—it allows you to engage in what is called metacognition, or thinking about your thoughts. When we are familiar with this list, we are better able to rise above the experience of the emotions themselves and take control to alter them.

So, without getting pulled into your past, recall the last time you were unexpectedly thrust back into a world that felt dangerous and out of control, and write in blue the emotions that plagued you afterward, referring as necessary to the emotions list on pages 82–83.

This blue list is your permatrauma list. Set it aside for a moment; it's time to make another list.

LIST #2: YOUR "LOST EMOTIONS" LIST

As I have said previously, when I work with trauma survivors, I often note that they appear to be in mourning. They are mourning a cherished belief system that feels like it no longer holds water, a comfortable sense of self that has been damaged by what happened to them.

In order to take productive action, I prefer to speak of these losses in terms of the *emotional states* that accompany them. Trish is a former high school athlete and marathon runner who developed multiple sclerosis. She used to think that taking care of herself would mean that she stayed healthy. So not only is she contending with her diagnosis (which would be enough), but her whole worldview has been rocked: rules she thought she could count on have gone out the window. In my view, it is *this*—not the illness—that is her trauma. Without her healthy-lifestyle rules as organizing principles to structure her day and her identity, Trish is floundering. She is actively mourning the loss of the confident Trish, who believed that eating clean and training hard would keep her well.

While Trish could easily and understandably get lost in a chorus of "why me," there's no point. It's hard to grapple on philosophical terms with something random like contracting a debilitating illness despite a life of choosing the salmon and getting up early to run, and in my experience, people rarely get satisfying answers out of it. Instead, I find it more productive (and ultimately, more comforting) to speak in terms of the *emotional toll* the trauma has taken, because you can stay quite concrete about the actual emotions that took a hit and focus on what to do about it.

What are the emotional states that Trish is missing now? She's missing feeling powerful and strong, energized and capable. She's definitely missing a sense of control. So Trish might choose those words out of the list above.

Which would *you* choose to describe the emotional toll your trauma has taken on you? In particular, what emotions used to make you feel happy and vibrantly alive? What beliefs did you have before that you don't have anymore? On a separate piece of paper, using your red pen, make a list of emotions that now feel inaccessible or out of reach to you. It may help to construct a sentence like "I am no longer a person who is_____," or "I used to be so _____," and to go through the list, substituting each word for the blank. I guarantee that you will feel it in your heart when you land upon an emotion that you are truly mourning.

You may find yourself wanting to add words or concepts to the list. For instance, Trish might want to add one that gives a sense of "body integrity"— the idea that your physical body is trustworthy and hardy and that it is serving you well. I wish we had a word for this in the English language, because this sense of one's body/self is a treasure that is often damaged by disease, accidents, and physical violence. It's hard for trauma survivors to rebuild a sense of something we don't even have a word for! So if there's a feeling-state (this one, or any other) that you can only describe with a phrase or a private word that makes sense only to you, feel free to add it.

Please bear in mind that this is not an exercise in mourning or wallowing; we are merely making a list that will be a launching pad for exercises to come.

So move through the list swiftly, resisting any temptation you may feel to daydream in a way that makes you feel bad. Then set it aside: this is your list of "lost" emotions.

We know two things about the emotions you placed on your red lost emotion list. The first is that they are emotions that you value. Each one of those words represents something worthwhile to you, something you liked and respected about yourself. The second thing we know about those emotions is that they feel like they are gone.

These emotions feel lost because your post-trauma rules, your trauma-preserving assumptions, have steered you away from them. Trish, in an attempt to be a good patient, to accept her diagnosis, and to do what her doctor tells her to do, has embraced a TPA that she is no longer in control of her body, her disease is. But it's no surprise that she's mourning the loss of feelings like being strong and in control. These emotions represent emotional soul food. Pushing them away means that we neglect the needs of our hearts and souls.

Trish's trauma may be her disease, but the take-home trauma is that she has given up a sense of personal power and efficacy. She's trying to force-feed herself an identity as a sick person, one whose doctor knows what's best and whose disease is calling the shots. Every time the scrappy marathoner in Trish rises up, her Moodith slaps her down again: after all, she was naïve and stupid enough to think that living healthy would mean that she'd stay that way. So when I suggest that Trish incorporate her usual juicing routine into her new medication regimen, she scoffs at the idea with disdain on her face; her Moodith mocks the girl who thought that stuff mattered.

We sacrifice who we are and what makes us happy for what we feel will make us safe and for what Moodith tells us is true. So like Trish, we give up activities and belief systems that used to give us a sense of wellness and pride.

Let's take a look at the kinds of statements people make when they have taken various soul food emotions off the menu.

"I'll never be able to believe another woman." (This is a person who has lost trust.)

"What's the point in doing anything? Nothing I do makes a difference."
(This is a person who has lost a sense of personal power.)
"With what I've seen, how can I unwind?" (This is a person who has
lost a sense of safety.)

My patients present these emotions to me in very final terms because
that's the way they feel, like these feelings are dead and buried. But the key to
healing is in understanding that these emotions are not gone forever. In fact,
you must recover your ability to feel them in order to heal. They are the soul
food you need.

> **Your lost emotions are not really lost; in fact, they're your
> guideposts on the way back to life.**

This probably feels like an odd insight. But the reason we struggle with
permatrauma, the reason that the aftermath of trauma continues to perpetuate
the injuries that were done to us, has less to do with what happened than with
the fact that we are now missing our soul food. These lost emotions nourished
an important part of you, a part that's going hungry these days because you're
not giving yourself the opportunity to enjoy them.

Every one of us had dreams for ourselves, hopes for the future. Those
plans got derailed by our traumas, which is why I hear: "I wanted to be married
with children by now; how's that going to happen when I can't even date?" or "I
love that apartment, but I can't buy it; my whole life is on hold until I know the
cancer is gone for good." We grieve the fact that realizing those dreams now
seems impossible; we grieve for the person who once believed that they could
come true. And we are suffering a kind of emotional malnutrition, the result of a
diet that is skewed toward unpleasant thoughts.

But you're undoubtedly already getting better at not getting lost in the
emotions those thoughts can trigger. You've learned to replace the negative,
critical voice of Moodith with survivor's pride and to think a little more critically
about the rules you have adopted in the wake of your trauma. So it's time now
to look at your lost emotions and to recognize that you can have those things in

your life, if you are willing to insist that they still have a place at the table.

The emotions on your red list are a bread crumb trail back to how you want to feel; in fact, they're the precise antidote you require when you feel overwhelmed and need to banish the emotions on your permatrauma list.

Together, your permatrauma list and your list of lost emotions represent a kind of yin and yang. In traditional trauma therapy, the focus would be on getting you to feel *fewer* of the emotions on your permatrauma list—less panicky, less hopeless, less angry—or at least to turn down the volume on them. If you could get your level-7 anxiety down to a level 3, many would consider that a great success. But in my experience, this is very slow going. Yes, you can do relaxation exercises to feel less stressed. But what do you do when the stressor is still present, if only in your mind?

I find that it is much easier to replace a bad feeling with a different one than it is to simply turn down the volume on the bad one. When you're feeling anxious, for instance, it is much better to pursue another emotion entirely than it is to try to feel *less* anxious. What you will replace your permatrauma feelings with are those so-called lost emotions.

The Metaphor of the Vase and Stones

In my practice, I use a metaphor to help drive home the concept of replacing negative emotions with emotional soul food. Here is the premise.

Imagine a glass vase filled to the brim with liquid. The vase represents a day's worth of emotions.

All day, without our even realizing it, we are thinking thoughts that make more sadness and stress drip into this vase. Every time Moodith whispers in your ear—more liquid drips.

Every time you harvest evidence to support a trauma-preserving assumption—more liquid drips into the vase. Since trauma survivors habitually tend toward sadness, pessimism, and fear, you can be sure that your vase is full. Our habitual—and often unconscious—tendency to think thoughts that make us feel bad keeps this vase filled to the brim.

> **If you could learn to be less sad, less hurt, less pessimistic, then less liquid might drip into that vase—but then all you'd have is a vase that's three-quarters full of bad feelings.**

I have a better plan.

If you were to drop a stone into that vase it would displace its own volume, overflowing the liquid. The more stones you drop in, the more of that bad-feeling liquid you displace. The liquid in the vase represents the emotional junk food that you already have too much of. And the stones represent the soul food you need more of.

Many of these stones will represent a lost emotion. Your stones might stand for the sense of power you feel you have lost, the confidence that eludes you now, a generosity of spirit that feels difficult to access. Maybe for you, there's a stone for "sexy" or "serene" or "grateful." Perhaps you can see words carved into each stone, like "pride," or "trust," or "hope." By definition, these emotions are incompatible with your permatrauma emotions; you cannot feel pride and shame at the same time.

> **Our goal is to fill your vase up with good-feeling emotions (stones) and displace as much bad-feeling emotions (liquid) as possible.**

We will explore ways to get back in touch with these good-feeling emotions because certainly recapturing them is going to entail more than procuring a rock with "hope" written on it. By using exercises and concrete actions you will craft stones to symbolize the emotions that are most helpful in displacing negativity. Your stones are your own; what helps you feel better will be different from what helps someone else. But once you identify a handful of emotions that pack a punch for you, you can create rituals to help you "work that stone" and displace your old, painful ways, just as the stones displace the liquid in the vase.

Notice that this is a very active approach. You cannot simply wait until good things happen. You will have to figure out what your stones are, understand how to get yourself a dose of that feeling, and try to access that feeling when trauma-y emotions arise.

Using your lost emotions to counter trauma-y feelings is powerful medicine. As we continue, we will return to the metaphor of the vase and stones to help you create rituals that enable you to displace some of the bad feelings that currently darken your day. When you notice that you are feeling trauma-y and choose to actively engage in such a ritual, I call this "working a stone."

Reaching for the Emotional Carrot Instead of the Cupcake

When we look at our heroes, it is tempting to put them on a pedestal or to make excuses for ourselves by imagining that our heroes were born with gifts that we lack, that they never struggled and never failed. But to do so robs them of their humanity and robs us of the chance to learn from the way they overcame.

It is also tempting to imagine that we could be like them, if only *some external thing* would happen—if only the right man came along, if only we got the right job, if only we could get out of the situation we're in. It would be easy to say that all we need to get back to life is a change in circumstance. But that's not how it works.

Your heart doesn't heal from the trauma of war simply because you are home. You don't feel whole again simply because your physical wounds have healed, and you don't learn to trust again simply because some Prince Charming shows up. When we study our heroes, we find that no external force came along and fixed their problems for them, either.

Your emotional repertoire has to change first so that your life can change—not vice versa.

Earlier in this chapter I wrote that it may take some work to figure out how to reclaim your lost emotions. I want to make it clear that I am not talking about abandoning your trauma-preserving assumptions so that you can walk down a dark alley in a miniskirt oblivious to all potential dangers and feeling "safe." Safety *is* an emotion worth feeling—not, perhaps, amid gunfire on the streets of your unsafe neighborhood, but someplace in your life where you have crafted a corner for it. Vulnerability *is* worth feeling—not in the presence of someone threatening you, but in a safe place of your own making.

Finding a place to reintroduce these emotions often requires that you create a small corner of your world where you can experience that lost emotion safely. And at first that corner might be a very small place. Maybe you will have to lock yourself alone in a room with ten dead bolts on the door in order to feel relaxed enough to enjoy a feeling of serenity. That's a fine start. If you can't find safety in the arms of a trustworthy human, perhaps you can sense it in the presence of a deity. Maybe you can't feel it with an adult, but you *can* feel it when you hold a baby. Maybe you can't conjure the emotion yourself at all, but you know a song that can kindle that feeling for you.

These emotions are like atrophied muscles. First, you have to remind yourself how to move the muscle—only then can you build it up and come to rely on it. But I will guarantee you one thing: when you start to reexperience these lost emotions, you will feel like the once-thin air suddenly has enough oxygen again.

In time, you will be able to claim more real estate for these lost emotions. I predict that a fleeting taste of them will be so delicious that you'll find yourself making life choices that give them more space.

We have a choice to fight back against the constant drip that fills our days with negative emotions. Once you know what emotions will displace that negativity for you, we will work to find ways to reliably get you a dose of them by "working a stone." Many resilient survivors use a version of this displacement technique to help them get back to life, and your stones will do the same for you. It is this work that we will tackle in part III of this book.

7

Avoiding the Crash Site
Detouring Around Your Trauma

"OKAY," YOU SAY. "I'M READY to move forward with my life. I'm sick of Moodith. I'm on to my TPAs. I know my signature strengths and the underlying values that fuel me. I know how I feel when I am trauma-y. And I know the emotional soul food that I have been missing. So what is this feeling that still stands in my way?"

You may find that it all sounds good to you, until you try to apply the theories to yourself, and then you find that your internal BS indicator light starts flashing and won't stop. In this chapter, we'll talk about some of the obstacles that prevent us from reclaiming lost emotions.

One factor that can make it difficult for trauma survivors to get back in touch with these lost emotions is that . . . well, we are trying *not* to feel. Feelings of being overwhelmed by emotions are often what drive people into therapy in the first place. Part of their therapeutic goal is to *stop* feeling things so powerfully. These clients often say things like: "I have to work out more because I hate feeling like a wimp/weakling all the time," or "I just want to forget about relationships and dive into my work." "All I want is to just get away from this place, to leave this all behind." None of these patients are people who want to be feeling *more*.

But bear in mind that I am not asking you to experience more of the emotions that plague you. I am suggesting you use other emotions to displace your excess of negative emotions. To refer back to my metaphor of the vase filled with liquid, we are striving to find great-feeling stones to replace the lousy-feeling liquid that you already have too much of.

These tools are designed to help you maintain your sense of emotional control. And remember, I am not asking you to revisit your trauma. We will not be opening that Pandora's box of emotions, so you don't have to worry about feeling overwhelmed by what flies out. In fact, even if the "lost" emotions in question disappeared from your life when you went through what you did, that doesn't mean you have to go back to the crash site to get yourself a dose of them.

What we are doing here is taking a detour, one that will get you to the same destination without forcing you to drive past the site of the crash.

You probably know—all too well—what will trigger a flashback, a nightmare, or a whole day's worth of blues; by the time we're done, you'll be equally aware of how to trigger joy, peace, righteous anger, and forgiveness. These feelings won't reappear magically—you will have to cultivate and harvest them, and do so with commitment.

Just as in traditional therapy, you will have to stay aware, and you may have to adjust your behaviors. But I think that you will find that it is much more enjoyable and rewarding to reclaim a rich rainbow of emotions than to engage in the sad, stressful, and often painful work of cataloging one's symptoms and recounting the past.

Even if your trauma left you with some tangible deficit, or the loss of something that truly cannot be replaced, there is still a way to craft a stone that allows you to feel the emotions that used to be your soul food. The particular dream may be lost, but the emotions that accompanied that dream are still accessible to you—even if you have to find an alternative route to getting to them.

If your emotional repertoire is like a diet, then your goal is to achieve balance. There are a lot of fads out there that tell you that you can lose weight by eating nothing but rice or grapefruit. But none of these is a good long-term plan. At heart, we all know that moderation is the key. Carbs are not bad, and neither is fat; we just can't fill our plates with them. Angry and sad are not the enemies; you just can't have a day full of them. The occasional snack of anger or sadness won't hurt you; on the other hand, if you know that "you can't eat just one," then don't invite a spiral by opening the bag.

Despite the fact that this technique is supposed to feel good, the simple truth is that trying on a new way of thinking requires a leap of faith. That's why I love the title of Barack Obama's book *The Audacity of Hope.* It acknowledges something very real: that to find hope in the world is a choice, one that takes a tremendous amount of courage. In our lives, we are often called upon to decide between cynicism and something better. To hope, or not to hope? To love, or not to love? To trust, or not to trust? To look for evidence of good in the world, or to allow your eyes always to come to rest on the negative? If you cite the cruelty of the world as your excuse for giving up hope of healing, I offer you the words of actor and Parkinson's disease activist Michael J. Fox: "Which is crueler, to not have hope or to have hope?"

So How Exactly Does This Detour Work?

The theme of reclaiming lost emotions without passing the crash site permeates Elizabeth Edwards's writing. You may be familiar with her story: she and her husband, the politician John Edwards, lost their teenage son, Wade, in a car crash. She subsequently developed breast cancer, which has since metastasized. And in the midst of dealing with her cancer, she was subjected to a tremendous amount of personal pain and public humiliation when it came out that her husband, a nominee for presidential candidacy at the time, had had an affair with another woman, fathering a child with her. Edwards is no stranger to adversity. Her second memoir is called *Resilience*.

Edwards admits that she spent the year after Wade's death cocooned in his old room. When something pressed her buttons—a song on the radio, the ham he used to like to eat—she says she "fell willingly into the grief." She acknowledges that grieving in this manner made her feel close to her son.

But in most people's lives, there comes a moment when we get fed up. We miss our old life and our old self, and we realize that whatever we have been doing to cope and to grieve has helped as much as it's ever going to. Edwards eventually realized that she needed a better way of connecting with her emotional need to parent than communing with her son's spirit in the room he no longer inhabited.

As she says, "You don't leave the need to parent just because the child left you."

In the year after Wade's death, she was mourning the loss not just of her son, but of her ability to experience maternal love for him. But spending her days in his old room fingering his clothes was the equivalent of going back to the crash site in search of that lost emotion. Instead she built a computer lab in her son's memory. Hanging out with the kids who used the lab gave her a place to parent; when she taught them a search engine trick that Wade had taught her, she felt she was keeping his memory alive in her heart in a healthy way.

Resilience is like the human immune system. When your body is exposed to a foreign pathogen, it responds in two ways: first, it makes an antidote to fight off the invader, and then it makes a template, so that if it encounters that foe again in the future, it can whip out a response even more quickly. (This system is the basis for vaccines; you're exposed to a little bit of flu so that if your body is exposed to the same agent later on in larger doses, it can fight back with quick vigor.)

Edwards's loss of her son was no microdose, but it did teach her a thing or two about what helps her cope. So when she was hit with subsequent traumas in her life, she moved swiftly into action, applying coping techniques that her past trials had taught her. In large part, what helped her cope was to identify the emotions she had lost and get herself a dose of this soul food. When her husband's affair made her feel emotionally adrift and spiritually homeless she crystallized the exact emotion that she felt she had been robbed of: a safe and cozy sense of home. In search of this lost emotion she made a career move no one would have anticipated from a lawyer and activist with her background: she opened a furniture store. There, without having to rely on any other person who might betray or disappoint, she was able to create for herself a sense of sanctuary and home.

Edwards offers us powerful examples of the way we can find ourselves the emotional soul food we crave and yet not pass the crash site. You can be betrayed and still find a sense of shelter, even if you do not do so in the arms of the husband who betrayed you. A child may die, but nurture is still accessible to you. You might lose your job, but you can still find ways to feel capable and secure and to enjoy a sense of providing for your family. A divorce might leave you feeling that your life lacks focus, but there is undoubtedly still a way to structure your days so that they have meaning.

TRY THIS: A PRESCRIPTION FOR HEALING

I'd like to leave this chapter, and this section of the book, with an audaciously hopeful gesture. Go back to the list of emotions on pages 82–83 and, using your red pen, circle any emotion on that list that appeals to you—

even if it's *not* one that you feel like you had access to before your trauma. Be greedy on your own behalf: is there anything there that you would like to experience, even if that feels completely impossible from where you're standing right now? After all, if you're going to be reclaiming emotions, why not go for it and aim for a wider range than what you might otherwise have had? Let's seize the opportunity to deliver you now to a life that is richer and fuller than anything you might have dreamed of, even before your trauma.

Return to your list of signature strengths and refresh your memory of the ones that "lit up" for you. As you read through the list of emotions, look for those that resonate with your core values; these are emotions that will pack a lot of juice for you. Add the emotions you have just circled to your lost emotions list.

Now cross out the title at the top of the page that says "lost emotions" and rename this list "Rx emotions."

Your lost emotions list is your new Rx.

These emotions, unique to you, are a prescription for you to use when you feel trauma-y. With this Rx list, we will figure out how to craft stones for you. Your stones will be like nonpharmaceutical remedies, an emotional pill to treat what ails you. It will be up to you to recognize when you are in pain, when you are feeling trauma-y, when you are spiraling. In these moments you will need to remember that you have a prescription ready to go in your pocket: your Rx emotion list. But like all prescriptions it doesn't work if you just keep it in your pocket. You've got to fill it, and you've got to remember to take it as prescribed. You've got to work your stones.

Just as you can count on relief from a headache when you take a pain reliever, having these tools will help you overcome the obstacles that have prevented you from feeling better in the past. Knowing that you don't have to pass the crash site, but have a detour, will reassure you when you fear becoming overwhelmed. Getting back to life takes courage and audacity, but it is a leap of faith that I know you are ready to take.

PART II | Changing What You Do

8

Acquiring Resilience
Bouncing Back in the Face of Adversity

OVER THE COURSE OF MY PSYCHIATRIC CAREER, I have worked in a variety of "trenches," and I have learned a great deal about the meaning of resilience from my patients that textbooks and teachers never taught me.

Our training taught us to accept that in psychiatry, helping often falls short of curing. Curing, I was told, was the domain of surgeons, not psychiatrists. I learned to be a realist, and not to expect miracles but to focus on damage control, harm reduction, helping people endure.

Over time however there were certain patients who defied all expectations about recovery and those patients taught me that perhaps my training had led me to set the bar too low, that maybe my initial indignation at a lousy outcome was in fact a better and healthier response than the one I'd been trained to have. Because always, despite the odds, there were those who were able to surmount the unthinkable and do so with a measure of grace.

Had I not been a psychiatrist, privy to their thought processes and to the incredible efforts these patients made, I might have thought that these people had an innate ability—a gene, maybe—that allowed them to right themselves when life and events conspired to knock them down. I found myself remembering a toy I'd had in childhood called a Weeble. It was a crazy little egg-shaped thing that always found its roly-poly way back to upright, no matter what you did to it. The slogan was: "Weebles wobble but they don't fall down."

But these patients didn't have a weight in the bottom of their egg-shaped self. They had **resilience,** an oft-referenced but ill-defined skill set that, along with hard work, allowed them to right themselves—often quite heroically and in the face of daunting foes. That same skill set is what enables some people to rise to the occasion in the face of a relationship crisis, parenting crisis, or work crisis—while others are left reeling.

> **Resilient people are those who have experienced trauma and yet find it possible to bounce back.**

Resilience theory is a relatively new therapeutic field, one that has emerged over the last twenty years. It stems from studies of at-risk children who thrive despite the odds, but it has much to teach all of us about the skills needed to bounce back from misfortune.

I have distilled the many traits and habits of resilient people into five skills. Over the course of this part of the book we will look at them one by one, considering how they relate to survivors and how we might try them on for size.

My successful patients all had several of these traits that enabled them to beat the odds. They saw their failures as learning experiences and weren't easily discouraged. They railed against their powerlessness instead of accepting it. They set their own bar higher than others might have told them was possible. They believed in their own ability to change their moods and to make themselves feel better. They felt a sense of self-efficacy, which led them to believe that they'd be able to achieve their goals. They had a tendency to focus on the positive even in a bad situation and to do whatever might be necessary to move themselves from a dark emotional place back into the light. They were resourceful and flexible and able to call upon others for the resources and the support they needed. These are the characteristics of resilient people. And when you carry these beliefs, your actions wind up being different from what they would have been had you not had them as a foundation.

The good news is that even if you don't have resilience, you can study and practice these skills and you will improve. Sometimes all it takes is a good role model to help you see how you might be doing things differently. I remember a period of time while I was working in a New York City psychiatric ER when it seemed that attacks by patients on the staff were occurring one after the other in rapid succession. There was hardly a week where our staff wasn't threatened or scared. One afternoon I found myself in a conflict with a patient who was angry because I wouldn't write him a prescription for a drug I knew he was abusing. When he extended his hand to "make peace," I foolishly extended my own, and he crushed it. I spent weeks unable to write, my wrapped-up mitten of a right hand a constant reminder of that bad decision.

I played the scene over and over in my head, wondering what I might have done differently. Ultimately, all this ruminating left my confidence in my professional skills and decision-making abilities badly shaken. I was frightened and jumpy at work and at home. Maybe, I thought, I wasn't up to working in such a rough environment, especially given my apparently poor judgment.

Shortly afterward, my friend Jane, the best psychiatric nurse I have ever known, was also badly hurt at work. A young boy admitted for violent and oppositional behavior had been in our ER for days, waiting for a bed to become available. To ease his boredom, Jane had offered him crayons. But when he used them to color the walls, Jane reminded him that he knew better and took the crayons away. The boy responded by lunging across the room and badly bit-ing her arm. I'll spare you the details, but it was bad enough that I didn't expect to see Jane at work for a while. But the next day there she was, charting away despite the huge bandage. "Look," she said, "losing his temper, trouble with authority, lousy impulse control—that's why he's here, right? He needs help."

I couldn't believe that Jane could feel empathy for the same kid who had so recently been violent toward her. But she was right. There he was in his Spider-Man pajamas, playing with a Game Boy in a cold cell of a room, on a plastic mattress surrounded by hospital rails that he might or might not get strapped to, depending on his behavior. He was just a boy, a boy with a problem. More importantly, as Jane pointed out, "This stuff happens in psych. If you're going to let it put you on disability for a month, then you shouldn't be in psych." With her characteristic smile she added, "It hurts like hell, but it would hurt like hell if I was home watching the Nature Channel, too."

Jane's ability to bounce back and function normally after what could have been a very upsetting incident was a testament to her resilience. The attack had not altered her view of the world as a safe, compassionate place. It hadn't shaken her self-esteem or made her feel like she was unfit to do her job. It hadn't turned her compassion into cynicism or anger. So there she was, back on the job, getting the support she needed and keeping her spirits high.

On a very personal level, her resilience served as a model for me. It forced me to look at her reaction and compare it to my own. What skills was she utilizing that I wasn't? What thoughts was she preferentially focusing on, and how did they differ from the ones I'd chosen to obsess about?

What It Means to Have Resilience

We have already discussed the fact that resilient survivors don't spiral into Moodith-style thinking. And they don't abandon their values in favor of trauma-preserving assumptions that don't hold water. In addition, resilient people can pick themselves back up and get on with their lives because they know they have the tools to soothe themselves, and they would much rather use those tools to feel better than to stay in a bad-feeling place. Resilient people believe all problems have a solution and believe in their own ability to find those answers and to see them through. They don't anticipate that their lives will be problem free but take comfort from knowing that, having surmounted past obstacles, they are better equipped for the future.

By contrast, someone who lacks resilience doesn't know how— or even *if*—she will be able to overcome life's obstacles. She becomes upset at problems, even minor ones, mostly because she doesn't have a lot of faith in her ability to change a situation or to make it different. She ruminates, replaying events over and over, exacerbating her bad feelings. She is reluctant or unable to do the things that might make her feel better, whether that means making time to see friends who make her laugh or saying no to an obligation so that she'll have time to relax and recharge.

Perhaps most importantly, people who lack resilience are sure that their current situation is carved in stone and will never change. When someone who lacks resilience hits a setback, she becomes depressed and defeated. As a result, she often feels discouraged, cynical, jaded, indifferent, or hopeless.

In order to grow up with resilience, we must be raised in an environment where people believed in us, saw the best in us, and assumed that we could solve our own problems. We need to have been allowed to make mistakes and supported in finding our own answers. We need to have had role models who demonstrated the emotional feat of pulling themselves out of a bad mood, people who modeled positivism for us. Not all of us were so lucky. Thankfully, there is an enormous movement afoot in the world of education, parenting, and psychology to raise children with resilience, so that they don't have to learn it as adults.

The rest of us can cultivate this skill. Sometimes, in order to do that, we need a little help from role models who model survivorship and the life skills necessary to bounce back.

I believed everything Jane had said in the wake of her traumatic experience. I too had gotten into psychiatry to help people. I knew, deep down, that I was good at my job and that my judgment was sound most of the time. I knew that the people we were working with sometimes acted in ways that were outside of their own control, let alone ours. And yet I was allowing events that were clearly out of my control to determine how I felt about myself and my professional capabilities.

My coping style seemed fine until I held it up against Jane's. She simply wasn't going to let herself stay in a bad place, and so she gave herself the mental medicine she needed. She knew that nursing was a great way of exercising her signature strengths and that performing this value-based activity that she was good at would help her retain her sense of self-esteem and not feel like a victim. By putting herself face-to-face with the kid who had injured her (and by reminding herself that he was, after all, just a kid in Spidey pajamas), she was preventing a series of dangerous trauma-preserving assumptions from taking root in her mind—that patients were dangerous, for instance, or that she was unfit for her job.

Jane's example showed me a more resilient way of coping; she had gone to that place naturally, and I could follow her, even though I had initially chosen to follow another course. I, too, needed to connect with my colleagues for support and sympathy and understanding; I also needed to get in touch with everything I loved about being a psychiatrist. I needed to see the people we were treating, and I needed to remember that I could help them. I needed to look my trauma-preserving assumptions in the face and see that they were just broken cognitions—no truer than the TPA remedies I'd forgotten to harvest, but much more damaging to my own sense of competence and safety.

Try On Something New

Resilience theory is not typically applied as a technique to aid trauma survivors. This surprises me, because resilience has everything to do with how people experience and bounce back from life's hard knocks. It would seem that studying those who know how to overcome with grace should provide a foundation for all trauma therapy.

What are people with resilience doing differently than the rest of us? In this section of the book, "Changing What You Do," I will invite you to jump into the head of some resilient heroes, to see what the world looks like through their eyes. We're accustomed to a variation on this idea because it's a fairly common sociological experiment—we've all read about the intrepid reporter who dyes her hair for a month to see if blondes do have more fun, or when hidden cameras follow a daytime TV host in a fat suit to show what it's like to move through the world carrying a hundred extra pounds.

What I am proposing that you do in this section is to try on the attributes of resilient people in order to see what it feels like to be more empowered in the face of your own past. How does the situation look through their eyes? How do they reassure themselves? How do they achieve that seeming invincibility that we so admire?

When we embody the resilient people we admire—be they heroes or role models—our outlook changes, our psychological posture changes, and then our response to the crisis changes. When I "tried on" Jane's approach, I found it easier to cope emotionally and easier to function at my job.

Thinking and acting like a resilient person is not going to feel natural at first for someone more used to listening to Moodith's voice. Moodith doesn't believe in resilience—and she certainly doesn't put much stock in your ability to bounce back. But I encourage you to give it a try.

9

Resilience Skill #1: Flexibility
A Fully Stocked Toolbox

MOST COPING MECHANISMS (and the emotions behind them) are appropriate *some of the time.* It's when one coping style is applied universally that it can start to cause issues in our lives.

The problem is, after you've been through the kind of challenge that you've been through, there is a tendency to return to the same coping method over and over again, even when it's not the best choice for the occasion. But war tactics don't serve us very well in peacetime, which is one of the reasons that life after trauma is so incredibly difficult: how can it possibly be otherwise when you're bringing the rulebook you crafted in the worst moments of your life to the slow-moving line at the grocery?

Resilient survivors understand that in the midst of the trauma they had one set of challenges and tasks, and that today requires a different set of skills and behaviors; they acknowledge that the trauma is not ongoing, and they do not live today as if they are still in it. Most importantly, if something's not working, they don't keep doing the same things expecting a different result. If a response is effective, a resilient survivor will use it; if it's not, she has an armamentarium of potential approaches up her sleeve.

Say your boyfriend drops his carrot-spirulina energy drink on the ground and instead of cleaning it up properly, he uses an old T-shirt to kind of mop it around. Then the phone rings, and he ends up leaving the rest of the spill along with the T-shirt on the floor—presumably for you to clean up. Two days later it's still there.

There are a variety of ways one might respond. You might flirt, charm, and cajole your boyfriend into mopping up his orange and green glop in exchange for kisses; that's a nice trick and a very effective way to let him save face while still getting him to clean up his yuck. Another viable option would be to furiously point out how inconsiderate he's being and insist that he clean up his own disgusting mess. Then again, if he comes home and tells you he's just lost his job, you might just find that the "right" response is no response at all, at least for the time being.

Our coping skills are at their best when we have a wide range of feelings and responses at our disposal. Sometimes this means using your sense of humor, other times it means accessing your righteous indignation. Sometimes it means demonstrating the generosity of spirit to quietly clean up someone else's mess because they're having a much worse day than you are.

Resilient survivors are able to access a wide array of emotions, which enables them to react in a manner that suits the occasion.

What's Your Coping Style?

Knowing what you *usually* do is a good place to start when you're thinking about doing something different.

In general, I have found that there are four basic types of emotional responders. As you will see, I have named them after the animals they most remind me of. (The idea that there are four basic categories of coping style is hardly an original observation; many psychiatrists and psychologists use similar categories. In fact, Laura Day has written a book called *Welcome to Your Crisis*, in which she relies heavily on the construct of four very similar personality types; I recommend it if this concept is of interest to you.)

It's pretty rare for someone to fit squarely into one category or another: you might be one type at work and more of another type at home. What I'm looking for is how you respond under pressure or stress—when you feel "trauma-y."

TAKE NOTE: WHAT IS YOUR GO-TO EMOTION WHEN YOU ARE TRYING TO COPE?

Think back to an event that happened over the last week or two that engendered a strong emotional reaction in you. For our purposes, try to keep this light; while it *should* be something that upset you, it *shouldn't* be something that triggered deep-seated trauma feelings. I'm thinking about events like being cut off in traffic, interrupted by your spouse, misunderstood in a business meeting, or finding out that you've been volunteered for something you don't have time to do. It *should* be something that got under your skin: even though it happened at nine A.M., you're still feeling a need to process with your spouse at ten that night, or to retell the whole thing to your best friend the next day.

The fact that you can't let it go is a clue suggesting that the way you responded wasn't satisfying to you. In fact, the fantasy you have about how you might otherwise have acted is very valuable information. Take note of both the way you actually responded as well as the way you *wish* you'd responded.

Write down both the incident that comes to mind and how you wish you'd responded.

Keep those responses in mind as you read through the four emotional types below. Again, there's no judgment here; each one of these coping styles is completely appropriate some of the time: there's a time for Rocky and a time for Rocky Road. Ultimately, the goal is for you to be able to dip into all of these, depending on what's most fitting.

As you read, if you see yourself in a particular coping style, make a star next to it. But just as importantly, if a particular style reminds you of someone you know (your spouse, your mom, a friend, a former boss, or an ex) write their name in the margin. Having a real live template for each coping style will be useful to you later.

THE TYPES
The Mouse

When something hits one of your trauma triggers, you retreat into your thoughts—and we're not talking happy thoughts. Let's say a huge guy comes barreling down the sidewalk and bangs into you, causing you to drop what you're carrying. You say nothing but pick up your things and rush home, feeling hurt and scared. Other adjectives that might feel familiar to a triggered Mouse are "exhausted," "overwhelmed," "hopeless," "powerless," "in need of rescuing," or "in need of escape."

Mice tend to ruminate and spiral into negativity, so something like being bumped on the sidewalk can ruin your entire afternoon. If you are a Mouse, you believe in the value of processing and expressing your emotions, so you may have dabbled in art or writing. You are likely to be found at a support group made up of people who have gone through something similar; hearing their stories makes you feel like you are not alone. You're in touch with your emotions, but they can overwhelm and define you.

What we can all learn from the Mouse: The Mouse is capable of a tremendous depth of emotion; they feel a lot, and easily. They're complex, acutely sensitive to meaning, and are as moved by the tremendous beauty of the world as they are by its sadness. They're great at intimacy and connecting with other people, and they're not at all afraid to feel their emotions, or other people's.

What it's like to live with a Mouse: Living with someone as sad and fragile as the Mouse can be exhausting. Because the people in your life love you and want you to be happy, they may invest much of their time trying to take care of you and neglecting their own happiness. They may feel it's inappropriate to be light, silly, or joyous with you, so it's not uncommon for your support system to feel overwhelmed and burned out. As a result, they may pull away from you when you need them most. And while Mice may be masters of emotional endurance, they are not good at modeling distraction or containment for their children; after all, these are things the Mouse can hardly do for him- or herself.

The Mouse's challenge: Unlike some of the other coping styles we will learn about, you don't run from negative or heavy emotions. But you would benefit from learning to contain them, from stopping yourself when you feel like you're wallowing in negativity or destructive thoughts. You need to get out of your own head, and involving yourself in the world outside of it is a good start.

Feeling angry is a sign of progress for you. Your lost emotion list contains many of the traditional happy feel-good ones; in fact, it may be hard for you to have and to sustain positive emotions, instead of the highly negative ones you trend toward. You will need to cultivate handfuls of feel-good stones that allow you to reintroduce and bask in good feelings again, and you can often do that by harvesting evidence of beauty and joy.

Because you spend too much time in your own head, *doing* something is good for you. Change venue, get outside, be around others. Taking action is not your natural inclination, but you need a break from yourself. Use your gift for connection to get the support you need, but stay mindful that too much "heaviness" can deplete those around you.

The Bull

Nothing enrages you more than seeing someone innocent victimized. You consider yourself a defender and protector. In your world there is a right and wrong, a way things *should* be done. And the consequences seem pretty black and white. Your coping reaction is best described as anger. Your fuse is short, and you're often cranky or irritable.

You harbor rancor for past slights and fantasize about revenge: God help the guy who bumps *you* on the sidewalk. It feels good when someone gives you an excuse to scream at them or to curse. You itch for a fight and have to hold back from taking a swing at someone who has pissed you off.

People are disappointing to you; they frequently don't live up to your expectations. Although your sharp words can sting others, you know that deep inside, you're a softie. Unfortunately, you feel that very few people warrant the softness you harbor at your core.

What we can learn from the Bull: You're a fighter, someone with seemingly endless tenacity and persistence; you don't back down. You don't let imagined consequences prevent you from acting to defend yourself. You feel passionately about things in a way that helps you take action. You are a natural doer, not a thinker-feeler like the Mouse. Your ferocity makes you feel safe, so you're not threatened by very many people, which means that you don't shy away from conflict when it's appropriate—standing up for someone else or for yourself.

What it's like to live with a Bull: The people who know you well see the good inside you, but they still walk on eggshells. Your tough exterior makes people feel they can't share their own softer side, so even though you can feel great compassion for others, they may not share their secrets with you. And, because you have a temper, you may find the people in your life collaborating to hide things from you, or to sugarcoat things, so that you don't blow up. It can be lonely being a Bull.

Helping others gives you great pleasure, but your tendency to be a fixer gives the people in your life (especially your children) the impression that they can't take care of their own problems.

The Bull's challenge: Your lost emotion list contains such things as vulnerability, safety, and tenderness. It is hard for a Bull to trust others—and *not* to react in a rageful or rejecting way when you feel others are not treating you well or disrespecting you. Something in your past made you feel powerless; it hurt you or made you feel unprotected. But even though discharging your negative feelings in the form of anger might satisfy you in the moment, it also causes you to alienate people who then become unavailable to support you.

It's not uncommon for Bulls to turn to unhealthy outlets—hitting the strip club or buying something extravagant that they can't afford—because it makes them feel like they are back on top of their game.

Your goal is to put away bitter cynicism, blame, anger, and disappointment, and to find ways to experience other emotions, especially the hard ones for you: joy, sadness, vulnerability. Take time to think without action and to experience things more profoundly. (Things *other* than rage and indignation, that is.) Remember that even if there was a time in your life where you were powerless, that time is not now.

Cultivate stones that allow you to accept a sense of openness and safety, to reconnect with gentleness and vulnerability, even if you have to be alone to feel it. Seek opportunities to let someone else take charge or to allow someone else to defend you. You may need to harvest evidence that you are safe in the world. You may need an outlet for sadness that doesn't overwhelm you, a place where you can have strong feelings and see that you are still in control of your life.

The Bee

You respond to upset with a whirlwind of activity; busy, busy, busy is your motto. You're a doer, full of zest and life, vigorous and aware. Aware, that is, of everything that's happening and needs to be done, but not particularly aware of how you are feeling just beneath the surface.

You get more done in a day than most people do in a month; Bees are often highly accomplished. But when people try to comfort the Bee by offering reassurance, taking over, or trying to solve her problems, it's often met with irritation: The Bee feels that others simply do not understand the complexities of the situation as she does. If you are a Bee, you tend to get yourself worked into a lather over the details (many of your own creation) while losing sight of the big picture. This is why the Bee can't and won't delegate.

People like to be with you and seek you out because you're often funny and usually setting something exciting into motion. But a hundred miles an hour is your only speed: quiet times make your mind race. You have trouble sleeping, or even sitting still; you crawl the walls just thinking about a meditation class. In fact, if you're forced to sit still in one place, like when you're driving for long periods alone, you often find yourself tearful or getting overwhelmed by anxiety.

All this action is a distraction. But from what? You feel that if you're not on guard all the time, things might implode. Lists, spreadsheets, and itineraries keep you from feeling panic—which is what happens when you feel disorganized or passive. So if someone bumps you on the sidewalk, there is no time to think, just a to-do list: of spilled things on the sidewalk that will need reorganizing in your handbag, some ripped pants that have to get to the tailor stat.

Constant action acts as a buffer against grief and hopelessness. But it also means that you're not really feeling anything—you become, as they say, a human *doing* instead of a human *being,* jumping around from task to task instead of soothing yourself.

What we can learn from the Bee: The Bee doesn't stay in her emotions: she gets out of her head and gets things done. You are a master of distraction, and you use your gifts wisely. Bees leave a legacy. Bees are the earthmovers, lawmakers, and situation changers. They pursue justice. The skills of the Bee, practiced in moderation, are excellent containment skills for all people who tend to become emotionally overwhelmed.

What it's like to live with a Bee: All the action you demand of yourself may make people in your life feel that you never have time for them or are too preoccupied with other things to care. (You won't find a Bee going on a long, silent, companionable fishing trip with his son.) Those around you may ultimately feel they couldn't hold your attention, that they were never good enough, or that it "was always all about you."

And because you're so self-reliant, you rob those around you of the ability to nurture you, to exercise their own compassionate signature values.

The Bee's challenge: Since absolute stillness is so difficult for the Bee, I often recommend a consuming but still activity like knitting—not because I'm angling for a muffler, but because it forces you to sit down and focus in a relaxed but concentrated way. Anxious people can't do the relaxation exercises recommended in so many trauma workshops; they end up panicking, or making to-do lists, or spiraling into catastrophic thinking. To break the cycle, you're going to have to expel some of that extra energy—to wear yourself out a little. Sports can help; so can sex. Both of these are sensory experiences that you can get completely consumed and lost in.

Ultimately, your challenge is to allow yourself to feel emotions like anxiety, fear, and a lack of control, and to know that they are a part of life and not dangerous or unhealthy, in and of themselves. Slowing down means feeling more, and this can be frightening for you. Try to remember that even though it feels scary, it's not lethal; after all, if you do end up feeling overwhelmed, you can always use your gift for distracting yourself to pull yourself out of it.

The Bee may find that emotions like serenity, safety, gratitude, and peace are on her lost emotion list. But so is the good kind of recklessness that comes from skiing fast or letting your bike fly down a hill. Chaos without fear and speed without danger are enlightening for a Bee who tends to brake and zigzag, just to prove to herself that she still has control.

Another stone for a Bee might be allowing someone else to do something for you without butting in or taking over; try instead just basking in the feelings of gratitude that come with letting someone else take care of you. A foot massage, for instance, is good medicine for the Bee, whose trauma has taught him to fear both physical and cognitive stillness while allowing a trusted person to take control.

Allowing yourself a deeper emotional repertoire will strengthen your connections with others, as well. People will always be drawn to you because you're fun and always at the center of the action. But the Bee needs to gain awareness of what all the buzzing is covering up. The Bee may need to harvest evidence that a serene, safe, and meaningful world exists just beyond his buzz.

The Wolf

When everything goes to hell in a handbasket, the Wolf stays calm, cool, and in control. You rarely lose your temper, and you'd never dream of bursting into spontaneous tears. What you've gone through has made you thick-skinned and unflappable; life goes on, right? Above all, your trauma taught you that the only person you can count on is yourself.

Like the Bee, the Wolf is often a workaholic. Certainly, you don't make a lot of time for fun or relaxation. When you have hobbies you approach them with the vigor and discipline of an Olympian. And while you don't think or talk very much about your trauma, you don't always sleep so well either; all those feelings have to come out sometime.

What we can learn from the Wolf: You're steady and consistent. A lone Wolf can always function, which bolsters your sense of being capable. If you get bumped and knocked down on the sidewalk, you won't mention it to the friend you were on your way to meet; it doesn't occur to you, because you've already moved on. To be honest, it's unlikely that a Wolf is reading this book, unless someone in his life bought it for him. Wolves rarely come to therapy; they are not plagued by their emotions because they simply don't indulge in them.

What it's like to live with a Wolf: Unlike the Mouse, other people's moods or the sadness of their circumstances *don't* rub off on you, making you well suited to jobs others couldn't handle—a paramedic, for instance. But these same skills can also isolate the Wolf.

Although you may feel compassion for others, you generally feel that they indulge themselves too much in their feelings. Without realizing it, you may be projecting a "buck up" message that devalues the pain and process of those in your life. And while keeping a lid on your own feelings is a practical tool, it also means that you cut yourself off from people who might help or offer you support, depriving yourself of closeness and denying others the opportunity to help you.

Even when you're "there," you're a little absent: your partner can feel lonely; your children miss you. Others think of you as solid and dependable, but they may also find you forgetful, uncaring, or numb. People in your life may feel they are constantly trying to prove their trustworthiness to you, which robs them of the feeling of unconditional love or healthy communalism.

The Wolf's challenge: Trust, healthy interdependence, and a host of fuzzy mushy feelings are all on your lost emotion list; by resisting emotions both good and bad, you've thrown out the baby with the bathwater.

Your challenge is simply to *feel*. When emotions arise, your knee-jerk reaction is to delve back into work or another compulsion to escape whatever is making you so uncomfortable. (You are especially afraid of your anger, sadness, and sense of dependence.) The Wolf needs to carve out rituals in life that allow him to feel deeply and safely. You may have a secret love for sad movies or country music. While the Mouse is advised *not* to indulge in these triggers, you should! Seek out people who make you feel emotions outside your typical range, and note not only that you like them, but also that they are able to feel strongly and still function.

Your greatest challenge is to believe that you are safe with people, that others want to know you, and that your emotions and true self are a gift to them. If you can cultivate stones of courageous authenticity and trust, you will find that people are kinder than you expected. The Wolf needs to harvest evidence that it is okay to be emotional.

There is nothing inherently "right" or "wrong" with any of these coping styles—they all have their place. But each represents *just one way* of going about things. Each one has benefits and shortcomings. Nobody has to tell a Bull to stand up for herself, the way they might with a Mouse. On the other hand, nobody has to tell the Mouse to ask others for support and companionship, the way they might with her lone-Wolf counterpart. Distracting yourself the way a Bee does *is* a good response when you're spiraling into melancholy, but there are times when it might be better for the Bee to sit quietly with his feelings, as the Mouse naturally would.

TRY THIS: WHAT WOULD _____ DO?

Be as specific as you can about which category you feel you fall into and when, taking note especially of your characteristic coping style when you feel trauma-y. Then, think back to the incident with which you began the last exercise. You know how you reacted at the time—now imagine what would have been different if you'd used a *different* coping style. Go through each coping style. How might a Wolf have responded? A Bee? A Mouse?

Think about the way that using a different coping style might have been received. And think about how reacting differently would have made you *feel*.

Here's how it might look, except *you'll* fill in the prompts. I took the liberty of filling in (*in italics*) what the grid might look like for a Mouse who was bumped into while walking on the sidewalk. But fill in the chart for your own type reflecting the incident you chose on page 110.

INCIDENT: *I got bumped on the sidewalk.*

TYPE	TYPICAL RESPONSE	EMOTIONS ACCESSED
I am a *Mouse* and my usual response would be:	*Call my friends and tell them about it*	*supported, expressive, validated*
In this same situation, a *Bull* would:	*Yell*	*entitled, safe, strong, empowered*
In this same situation, a *Bee* would:	*Keep busy, distract themselves, go to work and accomplish things*	*purposeful, indispensable, valued*
In this same situation, a *Wolf* would:	*Move on without letting it affect their day*	*in control, grounded, composed*

Of course, if you're a Mouse, then you don't need more of the emotions you already easily feel. But is there something on those other lists that you do need? Return to your Rx emotion list to see which, if any, of those emotions might have been accessible to you if you had chosen to cope in one of the other ways. Could you reclaim one of the emotions "lost" to you by behaving a little differently? Could you try on the coping styles of one of the other types on the list and make the emotions that drive them yours once again?

In her memoir *Celebrity Detox,* TV personality Rosie O'Donnell beautifully describes how reaching for a coping style other than your own can connect you with Rx emotions and help you problem-solve when your usual coping style has run you into a roadblock.

Rosie survived the dual childhood traumas of sexual abuse and the death of her mother. In neither circumstance was she offered the opportunity to share her emotions and have them supported; in fact, silence and denial were the unspoken rule. So it's no wonder that Rosie as an adult is a combination of tough Bull, busy Bee, and lone Wolf.

If you are familiar with Rosie, you know that one of her heroes is the singer Barbra Streisand. Streisand's music connects Rosie to her signature strength of appreciation for beauty. In Rosie's poetic descriptions of the way Streisand's music transports her, we see how it offers her an almost spiritual transcendence. If the lesson of Rosie's childhood was to keep her vulnerable emotions bottled up, we can see how Streisand's passionate delivery could leave her awestruck. Streisand excels at the very thing Rosie struggles with. She is the Mouse to Rosie's Bee, Bull, Wolf.

Again and again Rosie describes how she reaches for Streisand's music as a stone when negative emotions start to dominate her day. At one point, Rosie describes a conflict with the producers of *The View;* she wants to change the content of the show to include topics that speak more to her values. But she comes at them with her Bull persona and is not successful.

So she literally asks herself, "What would Streisand have done?" Using her knowledge of her Mouse icon, she can answer her own question: "she would've worked with what was in front of her, tuned and tuned, tweaked and tipped, until her touch transformed." When her own Bullish coping strategies fail, Rosie borrows the patience, persuasion, and perseverance of her hero to try a different way.

Notice that when you dabble in other styles, your response changes. And these new responses may help put you back in touch with lost emotions. In fact, that's why many reality television shows featuring people in crisis often end with a survivor engaging in some symbolic act—a former "victim" donning boxing gloves and punching a heavy bag, for instance. Nobody thinks that she's walking away from that punching bag healed. So what's the point? Well, if she is a Mouse, then trying on a different set of responses—in this case, acting like a Bull—may help her reclaim her anger and energy, so that she can experience a world in which she is no longer helpless and powerless.

When the raging teen finally tearfully agrees to go to rehab, we see a Bull become a Mouse. In curbing her anger, she is able to feel her family's fear for her and see the pain she is causing them, and this allows for a different response.

The reasons these shows can be powerful—not only for the participants, but for those of us who watch them—is because they illustrate how significant an experience it is to cope differently and how profound the effects can be.

> **Trying on an alternative coping style is like staging your own rescue intervention.**

TRY THIS: BORROWING THE TOOLS OF YOUR HEROES

We can use the examples of our heroes—and other people in our lives whom we admire—to help us explore alternative ways of responding and coping with challenges.

Imagine one of your heroes coming to rescue you in a time of crisis. One of my patients had gotten into financial trouble. She was feeling depressed and defeated, her confidence was shot, and she was overwhelmed by the sheer volume of the paperwork and bills. In her rescue fantasy, the personal-finance guru Suze Orman suddenly swept into her house and took charge. Spreading all those bank statements and overdue notices out over the dining room table, Suze figured out exactly what the problem was and came up with a manageable payment plan.

Your fantasy rescuer scenario (and your hero) will be specific to you. But pay close attention to who your imagined rescuer is—what they represent for you and what they do for you. How is their coping style different from your own? My patient in financial trouble was feeling trapped and acting like a Mouse, while Suze Orman was the ultimate Bee: someone who could put her emotions aside in order to spring into action, taking charge of the situation. And right there, my patient found her prescription: in order to rescue herself, she would have to borrow some skills from the Bee toolbox. The Rx emotions that acting like a Bee help you tap into? Feeling capable. Feeling in control.

Next time you find yourself ruminating about how a conflict or crisis played out, ask yourself if the way you are coping is reinforcing one of your trauma-preserving assumptions. Is there another way of coping that might broaden your emotional repertoire, that might add some leafy greens to your emotional diet? Would acting more like a Bull or a Bee or a Mouse help you be more like the rescuer you have been fantasizing about?

I suspect you'll discover that it's very empowering to act differently, to prove to yourself that you're not constrained by a way of behaving that doesn't serve you. Every time a Bull shrugs off a slight as a Wolf would, or a Bee takes a moment to luxuriate in her feelings like a Mouse would, you prove to yourself that there are ways of reacting differently, that you can change and grow, and that you are doing so before your very eyes.

This idea of "trying on" requires some practice and a willing suspension of disbelief.

Each type faces its own resistances to responding in an uncharacteristic way. Mice have to rise above a low-energy state combined with the feeling that doing something different won't work. They have to battle the concept that they are somehow dishonoring or devaluing their own emotional experience by allowing and encouraging alternate emotions.

Bees have to fight the belief that things aren't happening fast enough or that things won't get done right if they don't react in their characteristic style. They have to master ways of tolerating anxiety and chaos and accept that terrible things may not happen just because they let down their guard.

Bulls must battle their desire to react. Remaining passive and allowing a perceived slight to roll off their shoulders may push some emotional buttons, making them feel vulnerable or weak.

And Wolves have to remind themselves that feelings aren't facts and that emotions won't kill you or make you crazy. The fact that you were disappointed by the neglect of someone in your past or left to deal with hard emotions on your own doesn't mean that there aren't others in the world who might be there for you and love you, emotional frailties and all.

The emotions your coping style was constructed to mask don't just go away when you try on other coping styles. So let's take a moment to at least understand what it is about those emotions that may be distasteful to you. You may find that there is a trauma-preserving assumption lurking in your reluctance to try on a different response pattern.

Do you believe that if you dip into your emotions you may never get out? Do you feel that only sissies let themselves get pushed around? Do you feel that letting your guard down makes you an easy target? Are you afraid that if you step out into the world in an unvictimized way that it will somehow erase what happened to you?

When you act assertively, stick up for yourself, or get angry, do you feel that you are behaving in a way that is unattractive, out of control, or too similar to someone who hurt you?

Once you have a better understanding of why you resist trying on a new style, take a moment to see whether or not this is the trauma talking or if perhaps you have embraced a value system that is preventing you from harnessing the power of anger. Does your cultural heritage or gender dictate how you *should* be acting? These societal values can be cripplingly limiting: after all, we have all these emotions so that we can feel them and use them.

TRY THIS: RESCUING YOURSELF IN THE REAL WORLD

Pretend that you've been hired to star in a movie, and the character you're playing has a very different coping style than your own. If you're a Bee, you've been hired to play a Wolf; if you're naturally more Mouse-like by nature, then your job is to play a Bull.

Now, leave your house and go out into the world at large in your new, assumed character. You must go somewhere—to the grocery store, to the gym, to a public place of some type. And you have to stay in character, no matter what. For the purposes of this experiment, cameras are rolling.

That means reacting to events and other people exclusively with the coping style your character would use in all aspects of everyday life. Say your persona of the day is a Bull. When you pick up a newspaper ask yourself, "What would a

Bull think about this headline?" Consider a health problem you are having and ask yourself, "How would a Bull respond?"

Now, the point of the experiment isn't to get you punched in the nose or to teach you to emulate the most extreme, antisocial aspects of other coping styles. The goal is to help you access the emotional and behavioral repertoire of someone who is dealing with life in a very different (but nonetheless viable) way than the way you're used to.

If you find yourself at a loss for how your character would behave, it's helpful to have identified Bulls and Mice and Wolves and Bees from your own life, whether they're heroes, friends, family, or acquaintances. It will help if you have a person in mind when you ask yourself, "What would a (Bee/Bull/Mouse/ Wolf) do?"

Interview them if you'd like, and ask them what goes through their mind as they confront the cabdriver who shortchanged them so that you understand their motives and their inner world. Did they feel afraid as they spoke up for themselves in that taxi? If so, what enabled them to defend themselves anyway? If they weren't afraid to speak up for themselves, why not? Were they feeling entitled, or mad? Were they motivated by a sense of justice, or did they simply really want their five bucks? Or watch a movie that features someone modeling Bull behavior to get you in the right frame of mind.

The person you emulate doesn't even have to be someone you universally admire. Maybe your Bullish ex was a jerk, but that doesn't mean you can't channel him to your advantage when the auto body shop returns your car with the same rattle it had when you dropped it off.

If I were the director in this movie we're pretending to make, I would do a bunch of takes; I'd have you replay the same scene in different characters. But in this exercise, you may have to play the different roles on different days. The point is that not only do you get to write the story of your own life, you also get to decide how you play your part.

Behaving differently can truly be an epiphany, one that you can take out and use to take yourself in a new direction emotionally. And every time you do it, you rescue yourself. Try it, and you might stumble on something groundbreaking.

10

Resilience Skill #2: Accountability
Stop Feeding Your Monsters

EVERY DAY WE MAKE CHOICES about the things we expose ourselves to. The music we listen to, the people we spend time with, all of these choices contribute to our assumptions about the world. And yet we often don't pause to quantify the emotional impact of what we allow in.

I have found that many of my patients are making choices that only serve to further engrain the very emotions that they need less of. Patients prone to melancholy are the ones who tell me they spent their weekend watching tear-jerkers; the rageaholics spend theirs watching World Wrestling Entertainment. These choices nourish their trauma-preserving assumptions and reinforce their characteristic coping styles; I call this **"feeding your monsters."** I am also going to ask you to consider filtering the influences that you allow in your life.

Do the things you allow into your life hurt you? Do the things you do encourage you to step further out of balance? Or do they help you take steps closer to your ultimate goal, which is to feel more of the stuff you haven't been letting in?

We've already talked about shutting down your nasty unsupportive inner voice and messages from the culture around you that add to your take-home trauma. I'm about to introduce you to another three-headed monster you'll need to slay: toxic media messages, toxic work, and toxic people. The question we'll be asking in this chapter is: given what you now know about your coping styles, do the things you choose—your hobbies and activities, your leisure choices, and your friends—push you in the right direction or the wrong one? Are these choices adding to the already too abundant junk food in your emotional diet or the soul food that you need more of?

Question Your Direction

Resilient people aren't reactionary or impulsive. They are considered, which is a fancy way of saying that they don't let their trauma drive them. Your goal is to be conscious about the choices you are making. If exposing yourself to a person, place, or thing is going to add to liquid in your vase instead of adding to the stones you need to keep yourself balanced, then you need to pause to question your direction. It takes a little practice to stop and think about what you're doing before you act. But that effort can stop you from looking for healing in all the wrong places.

Revenge, for instance, is a classic Bull take on trauma; the typical Bull won't rest until someone has paid for what happened to him. But this position perpetuates a toxic stew of danger and anger. A similar predicament is also experienced when a person decides to put off closure until the court system gives them a sense of justice. If you are relying on something so precarious as the criminal justice system to make sense of something that was likely senseless, you are going to make the process of getting back to your life much more lengthy and complicated. A truly resilient survivor is going to consider whether that sense of justice or revenge is worth the protracted negative emotions.

The actions you pursue and the influences you continue to permit in your life may be exacerbating your take-home trauma. Although it is hard to hear that we ourselves may be contributing to perpetuating our own wound, the good news is that we are in control of these thoughts and actions.

Be Accountable!

Joey always wore a very expensive black sweatshirt emblazoned with a repeating gold pattern of brass knuckles, guns, and Hummers. I asked him once if he had ever been hit or threatened with brass knuckles; he said he hadn't. I asked if he owned any, and he said he didn't. Ever driven a Hummer? No. Ever been held at gunpoint? No, but he knew lots of people who'd been shot. Had that been a good thing? No. "Then what are you trying to say with that jacket?" I asked him.

"Girls like it," he told me.

"The Hummers, maybe—but why would a girl like brass knuckles?" I asked.

He finally admitted that he liked his jacket for the tough "don't mess with me" message it sent out, particularly to the other guys in his neighborhood. But he was right about something else, too: girls were noticing and responding to his sweatshirt. And the kind of girl who is attracted to a guy wearing a sweatshirt that's patterned like Louis Vuitton luggage except with weapons is not the kind of girl that Joey, who was trying desperately not to be sucked into the chronic violence that had already claimed too many of his friends and family, wanted to attract. "You get the wrong girl, and then you have to live up to her expectations," I told him. "And then you've got the wrong life."

I have had similar conversations with other patients over the years. (Pointing out these inconsistencies is both what shrinks are paid to do and the thing that is most likely to get them fired.) It is not a lack of empathy that leads me to point out when someone's actions are in direct conflict with what they say they want; if anything, it's the opposite—it's hard to watch someone hurting himself without realizing it. Resilient people hold themselves accountable for their actions and thoughts. They do not say one thing and do another—and when they do, they call themselves on those inconsistencies.

> **There has to be congruence between what you say you want and what you do.**

Resilient survivors do not expect to be exempt from rules, nor do they feel they are due special consideration because of what happened to them. This means that they don't use what happened to them as an excuse for why they are not working, why they are not in relationships, and why they are not pursuing their life goals.

Your Choices Are Affecting Your Take-Home Trauma

How are toxic messages, toxic people, and toxic media affecting your trauma-preserving assumptions? Unfortunately, it doesn't take very much to "prove" to yourself that the world is dangerous, that people are untrustworthy, that violence or pain lurks around every corner. We're harvesting *all the time*.

As an example, consider the news. Watching is a habit that's so deeply ingrained in many of us that it goes unquestioned. And yet, the news, especially American television news, is designed to support many trauma-preserving assumptions. There's a killer germ in your sandwich, a pervert teaching at your public high school, a terrorist on your commuter train, a tsunami just lying in wait for your next vacation. Fear-based media reinforces every single one of a trauma survivor's worst fears and suspicions about the world.

And it's stimulation that is completely out of your control, unless you use the remote to turn it off. How can you tell what terrible story is just around the corner? You're relaxing, getting a pedicure with one eye on the TV and the other on your gossip mag, and suddenly you find yourself ambushed by an image of pallbearers carrying the tiny coffin of a child beaten to death by his stepfather. Did you ask for that information? Did you sign up for it? Was there a warning or rating that might have protected you from seeing something sure to trigger a host of unwanted memories for the rest of that day?

"But I want to stay informed," you say. Okay. Fine, but I have to turn it around and ask you: How many epidemics have you been warned about that never affected you? How many storms were predicted that turned into flurries? What good does it do you, really, to know that a little girl has gone missing in a suburb two thousand miles away from where you live? If you won't be able to help in a material way, and if knowing about her won't help you keep your own child safe, why are you choosing to let this harmful piece of information support your understanding of the world as a frightening and hostile place?

This is where the metaphor of the vase and the stones is very helpful. It invites us to be aware of whether our daily choices are resulting in more liquid (representing the habitual flow of negative emotions) or more stone (representing the healthy balance of feel-good emotions that most people reading this book need more of). Asking yourself this question as you picture the fluid-filled vase encourages us to be accountable for what we choose; how many fluid ounces of anxiety, worry, weariness, or sadness will that news story dump into your day? Because, let's face it, it's hard to get the news without inadvertently also getting a hefty serving of misery.

TRY THIS: NO NEWS IS GOOD NEWS

I sometimes ask my news-junkie patients to do the following awareness exercise.

In Homeland Security's national threat level system, green means there's a low risk of attack; red means we need to be on high alert. What I'd like to ask you to do is to watch the TV news or go through the newspaper with a set of highlighters—keeping your trauma-preserving assumptions in mind. Ask yourself, "How does what I'm reading make me feel? Does it support a worldview in which life is frightening and dangerous?" Every time you read a story that supports one of your trauma-preserving assumptions, mark it in red. (If you're watching television, make a red or green mark for every story.)

You'll soon see: pretty much everything is red. The news is designed to resonate with our trauma-preserving assumptions. Occasionally, they'll throw in a green story—a fireman rescued a kitten!—but for the most part, the news plays to a fundamental misconception: that knowing about these potential threats protects you.

My city has been on orange alert for ages. And while I'm enormously grateful for the men and women protecting us who know what to *do differently* because of our alert level, the rest of us have the challenge of going about our daily lives without being too panicked to function. Red and green rough-surf flags by the lifeguard stand on the beach—helpful. Red and green terror threat alert—not so much.

The theory that constant awareness of all potential risks is protective is a fallacy of the news media and also happens to be the reason why we feel our TPAs are protecting us. But in the end, the news—like your TPAs—fosters terror and insecurity grossly out of proportion to your actual daily risk.

Once you realize the extent to which true journalism has been twisted in the interest of scaring you, you may feel angry. One client of mine who witnessed firsthand the collapse of the Twin Towers proposed a class-action suit after a major network repeatedly showed images of bodies falling from the sky. Every time he unexpectedly saw that image while he was getting his morning coffee, our progress was set back a couple of weeks.

I frankly wish that there were safer ways to obtain objective news without risking being emotionally hijacked by manipulative scare tactics. But the current offerings make you realize how hard you're going to have to work to harvest evidence in support of your TPA remedies, because the media intends to bombard you with messages that support your TPAs—and provide you with a few you hadn't yet thought of.

Once you're onto what they're doing, you stop being a passive victim. You can finally say, "No, thank you—I want news that's newsworthy."

Another one of the questions I always ask people is what television shows they regularly watch. According to Nielsen, the average American watches more than four hours of TV each day. And, if my patients are any indication, a lot of us are tuning in to shows that promote our trauma-preserving assumptions.

I see any number of people who have been wronged by the justice system and yet never miss a crime show. Sometimes shows like that do give us what the real world can't; it can be very satisfying to watch the perpetrator of a crime get what he deserves, especially when, in your own experience, there was no closure. But sometimes, on those shows, the perpetrator gets off on a technicality, and your TPA that no one cares or that there is no justice gets reinforced.

On the other hand, sometimes seeing someone else get fairness when it was denied to you creates yet another wound, forcing you to speculate: "What did I do wrong? Why didn't it work out that way for me?" For trauma survivors, these shows are an invitation to spiral. Turn them off.

Television and the news—these are just two examples of choices we make over the course of our daily lives that strongly affect the way we feel. The music we listen to, the books we read, the people and family members we surround ourselves with, the plays we go to—we're sifting through all of these things to find either evidence of good or evidence that supports our TPAs. Deciding what television show to watch probably doesn't feel like an important decision with consequences for your general well-being. But it is.

TAKE NOTE: WHAT DO YOU LET IN?

It's sometimes difficult to make a connection between our actions and the way those actions make us feel. In the interest of having greater congruence in our lives between what we do and what we say we want . . . let's make a chart. Many diet books ask you to do a similar exercise and call it a food journal. In it you record everything that you eat for a day, so that you can see what your problem areas are. I'd like to suggest that you look through how you spend your days. Answer the following questions:

What do you do for a living?

What types of things do you usually do in your leisure time? (Consult your datebook or PDA for accurate info.)

What music do you like to listen to? (List favorite bands or songs.)

What are your favorite TV shows?

What video games do you play?

What movie genres do you like to watch?

What sporting events do you follow?

What plays do you see?

How do you get your news of the world?

Who are the people that you spend a significant amount of time with? (People you talk to or see more than once or twice a week.)

What podcasts do you download?

What blogs do you read regularly?

What Web sites do you visit almost every day?

How You'll Know What's Hurting You

I wish I could create hard-and-fast rules, that I could tell you that Bulls should always stay away from violent, first-person shooter video games and that Mice shouldn't watch Lifetime movies. But many of my Bull patients find that a safe, controlled release for their anger and aggression makes it easier for them *not* to discharge it on the people in their life. And there are some Mice who find real relief in a good, hard, two-hour-long cry. So it's not that simple.

There's only one way to tell, and that's to stay aware. The only barometer you have about whether something is helpful or hurtful for you is *how it makes you feel*—how you feel when you're watching or doing it or being with that person, and how you feel *afterward*.

Ask yourself the following question:

> **Is this exposure reinforcing my TPAs,**
> **or is it helping me get on with my life?**

Will knowing this information or being with this person affect my worldview in a positive way or in a way that will reinforce my trauma-preserving assumptions? Is my choice to expose myself to this getting me a dose of my Rx emotions, or is it turning up the volume on trauma-y emotions I already feel too much of?

TRY THIS: HELPING—OR HURTING?

Using your answers from the previous exercise, ask yourself the following questions, filling in the blank with each item, person, or activity:

When you _____ (talk with your brother on the phone, watch
that crime drama on TV, peruse the headlines, go to a community
board meeting), do you feel better or worse?

Does it/he/she make you feel emotions from your Rx emotions list or
your permatrauma list?

Did your time spent with this person or on this activity make you feel
more empowered, or did they/it make you feel more powerless?

Is this activity or person reinforcing your trauma-preserving
assumptions or helping you harvest more feel-good, healing
emotions?

This exercise can be enlightening. First of all, in a media-saturated world,
the sheer number of the messages we receive every day is staggering. Most
of us are not aware of how much evidence we're harvesting. We're often not
aware of how many times we're triggered. All we know is that we wake up in the
morning with a terrible emotional hangover; without help, we'd never connect
it to the hours we logged in front of the TV the night before. It's time to get
honest about what we're consuming—and then to decide how much of this we
want to continue consuming, given how it makes us feel.

We assume that we do the things we do and hang out with the people we
hang out with because they make us feel good. Nobody deliberately goes out
looking for ways to hurt themselves—do they? And yet, we do it all the time:
we say we want to lose weight, and then we go out for ice cream. We say we
want to move past the trauma and heal, and then we spend an entire afternoon
going through old love letters. We are not pleased with the fact that we feel so
cynical and bitter and yet we choose to have lunch with our girlfriend who is,
that's right, cynical and bitter.

You are at the helm. The people and things you surround yourself with are
choices—choices that inform the way you think about the circumstances in
your life.

Toxic Work

What if you chose a career path that perpetuates your sense of danger and unhappiness? Vivian endured an abusive childhood and emerged as an adult with a trauma-preserving assumption that if she could just master the art of always appearing tough no one would mess with her. Of course, in order to have ample opportunities to harvest evidence to prove this TPA true, one would have to put oneself in harm's way with regularity. So it's no wonder that Vivian became a prison guard, a job that afforded her daily opportunities to prove to herself that she could hold her own with violent people.

But for Vivian, real healing didn't mean getting numb in the face of violence—instead, it meant realizing how scary violent people are and how unworthy of her time. For real healing to begin she would have to begin harvesting evidence to support a TPA remedy that she was fundamentally safe and in control of whether violent people had access to her. Clearly she couldn't exercise this new way of being or try on new ways of coping when her job placed her in the line of fire. After a great deal of thought and discussion, Vivian took a pay cut to switch to an administrative position.

Of course, changing jobs is a luxury that not all of us can afford. But that doesn't mean there's nothing you can do about a workplace situation that triggers trauma feelings in you. Debbie was a subway conductor whose train ran over a child who had accidentally fallen on the tracks. After a year on disability, Debbie knew she had to go back to work but needed to find a way to feel less vulnerable, fragile, and frightened while on the job. Rather than feel passive in the face of potential tragedy, she developed the habit of counting subway runs that went smoothly. She said hi to people on the platform, reassuring herself that most of them were alert and careful about not standing too close to the edge.

When foolish schoolchildren played stupid games on the platform, she took a moment to intervene, sharing with them how she learned the hard way the dangers of their behavior. "People get killed playing those games," she told them. "Respect yourselves and your families; think of how they would feel if you got hurt." The words didn't come easily, but she simply could not remain passive in the face of her fears. In speaking up when she saw kids placing themselves in danger, she felt that she had made their world and her own a safer place—even though she was still working in the same place where her trauma happened.

If your work is pushing your buttons and triggering trauma-y feelings, or if it is giving you ample opportunities to support a TPA that doesn't need more support, consider what changes you might make to allow yourself an opportunity to experience fewer trauma triggers.

Toxic People

The people we surround ourselves with can also be a major feeding ground for our monsters. We turn to them for support—but often, they're not supporting us as much as our negative assumptions about the world. Are you in the habit of calling your uncompassionate sister when you feel like no one cares? Your rigidly perfectionist friend when you feel you've fallen short? Your friend with the Ph.D. in victimization when you feel someone's done you wrong? While speaking to them may validate our preestablished assumptions, how does their influence affect your emotional landscape? What emotions do you feel when you're with them? What emotions do you feel afterward?

As an aside, I do advise my patients to be careful whom you share the details of your trauma with. It's not like what happened to you is a secret, to be unearthed only to those who know the secret password. But it's not nothing, either, and you can protect yourself from a lot of inadvertent toxic messages if you pick and choose carefully who you trust with this information. People don't know what to say, and too often, they say the wrong thing—comments that make you feel doubted, or invalidated, or guilty, or blamed.

In addition to making conscious choices about whom we spend time with, most of us could benefit from better interpersonal boundaries around our trauma. There is hardly a survivor of interpersonal trauma who wouldn't benefit from a crash course in what I call "traumassertiveness" skills.

Honing Your "Traumassertiveness" Skills

Be directive and specific: "I'd prefer not to talk about medical issues when we're together," you might say to your hypochondriac aunt, who's sure she can relate to your multiple miscarriages because of her botched bunion surgery. "Let's focus instead on everything else we have in common."

If she doesn't listen, say it again, repeating your *exact words*. Even if she doesn't stop after you've repeated yourself, doing this takes you out of a victim mind-set. It reminds you that you aren't the passive recipient of all these messages about trauma. You have the right to an opinion and to control your own reality. You can say no and have it respected. And when she fails to get it after you've repeated the same exact sentence five times, it becomes very clear who has the problem.

Set clear limits: You may have to set an even clearer boundary with Auntie, and with even firmer language: "I'm not comfortable talking about this; if you persist, it's going to become difficult for us to stay in contact."

Ultimately, if she doesn't get it, you may have to determine whether or not she's someone you want to have in your life, given how she triggers you.

Avoid feeling that you have to explain your reasons: If your impulse is to try to educate and inform the toxic people in your life, cool your jets for a moment and consider how that usually unfolds before you act.

Here's what *not* to do: *Don't* sit Mom down and explain to her how it makes you feel when she talks about how none of this would ever have happened if you'd gone to Sunday school and married a nice girl like your brother did. *Don't* challenge her or try to reform her. She's going to be embarrassed and defensive—and then she's going to say something even worse. Chances are you are not going to have success in enlightening the toxic people in your life. Sometimes it's best to leave well enough alone.

Sometimes you just have to say no: Even with a better understanding of their motives, I still think it's wise to limit exposure to certain people. If they make you feel like the trauma was your fault, like it wasn't that big a deal, like it might not have happened at all, or that your recovery is taking too long or going too slowly, limit your exposure.

If the message is truly toxic—"Rape? A man can't rape his own wife!"—then you have a choice to make. Do you try to limit the extent to which they can rub salt in your wounds, or do you eliminate them completely from your life—at least until you get back on your feet?

Get your support from people who are best able to give it: In general, I'd suggest that you don't try to morph the faulty support system you've got, but instead find one that can champion the mission you're on. Focus your energy on finding people who don't belittle or blame you.

You may already have some of these positive supporters in your life; seek them out and spend time with them. Learn from their reactions—and note your own resistances. You may find that when you encounter the kind of empathy, concern, or anger on your behalf that you have always dreamed of getting, it makes you feel uncomfortable. If so, you may have been unconsciously avoiding or pushing away the very types of supporters that you need and deserve. It's time to let those people in and allow the healing to begin.

What messages do supportive people send you about your trauma? What if you felt that way about yourself? Being around people who believe you, who sympathize with you, and who believe that you can overcome what you've been through is soul food, not junk food.

TRY THIS: LIMITING THE INCONSISTENCIES

Let us look at the inconsistencies you highlighted in the previous exercise. What's hurting you, and what can you do about it?

As I've said, it's one thing to turn the television off—but not every monster is so easily starved. If it's impossible to completely avoid the activities and people who cause you pain, you may have to limit them—or at least their impact on you.

For example, there may be activities or rituals you can incorporate into your work schedule that help minimize the extent to which your job reinforces your trauma-preserving assumptions. I'm always curious to know what my patients do on their lunch breaks, and I often recommend that they try replacing the break-room gossip session with something that contributes to a sense of peace and well-being. Eat lunch in the park, call someone who makes you feel great—even watching a puppy cam seems like a better choice than dining with someone who makes you feel lousy.

Take a moment here to imagine some creative ways that you can limit (if not eliminate) the damage done by the people and activities on your list.

Despite the restrictions you impose, you may still have a certain amount of negativity flowing into your vase. Once you have a handle on the unavoidable toxic influences in your life, at least you have a sense of how much positivity you are going to have to cultivate to displace it.

Permatrauma is a lifestyle. In order to move on to something better, some things just have to go.

Yes, there's a strong element of personal responsibility here. A trigger isn't a foregone conclusion: it's called that because it triggers something in you—and chasing that rabbit is something you have to abstain from. Set boundaries with yourself, and if you are ambushed by something that upsets you, don't go home and ruminate about it. You're never going to be able to prevent the culture from tossing you that ball, but you don't have to catch it and run with it.

Does it seem extreme to restrict or eliminate people and things from your life in order to feel better? If so, talk to anyone who has struggled with and overcome an addiction and they will tell you that in order to create a new life, many things from your old life may have to go.

Some big changes are going to have to occur. If you want to feel safe, you're going to have to be brave in the face of potential danger. If you want to feel lovable, you're going to have to take a risk on being vulnerable in order to find love. If you want to relearn what it's like not to feel damaged and ruined, you cannot live as if you are preparing to die. It's time to stop hurting yourself.

11

Resilience Skill #3: Self-Efficacy
You Are at the Helm

MANDY WAS BORED AT SCHOOL until her parents decided to push the board to develop a gifted and talented program. They made the argument that bright kids had special needs and needed specific services: if the jocks had gifts special enough to warrant coaches, uniforms, buses, equipment, and fields, they argued, then the bright kids deserved no less.

Mandy watched as her folks raised awareness, got others involved, raised money, and spoke at school board meetings. There was some push-back, but no one laughed them off the block, like Mandy would have expected—and finally, they were able to start the program.

Flash forward twenty years. Mandy is now mother to a sweet, shy girl who, along with her friends, is being targeted by the "mean girls" in their class. There are prank phone calls and e-mails, and an upsetting incident on Facebook that her daughter will not discuss. Mandy calls the parents of the other bullied kids and is shocked to find how complacent they are about it. "It's just a part of life," they say. "They'll grow out of it. There's nothing we can do."

Mandy knows better. "Let's meet with the principal to find out what the school is doing about this. There should be harsher punishments, parental involvement, an anti-bullying curriculum," she says. The other parents protest: "The school board decides the curriculum. They're not going to change what they teach because a couple of girls can't get along. Even if they do implement some kind of wrist-slap, it's not going to happen in time for our kids."

Undeterred, Mandy attacks the problem with the expectation—and, indeed, the knowledge, given to her by her parents—that things can and do change. She builds a coalition, the school administration gets involved, and the problem is eventually resolved.

What characterizes Mandy, in contrast to the other parents in her daughter's class, is a sense of **self-efficacy.** This is a sense of personal power, the knowledge that you always have the skills and where-withal to help yourself. And it is one of the defining characteristics of resilient people.

Redefining Power

The concept of self-efficacy was developed by the psychologist Albert Bandura, who defined it as our belief in our ability to succeed in our goals. Note that this is different than effectiveness. Efficacy pertains to your perceptions, not the actual outcome of your efforts. Bandura observed that the way we view our own efficacy has a profound impact on how we approach our ambitions, tasks, and challenges. In particular, people with a high sense of self-efficacy (like Mandy) are likely to approach a difficult task as if it is something they can master—as opposed to something that is hopeless and should be avoided.

When researchers look at kids in troubled situations, one of the biggest indicators of whether or not they will be able to overcome the challenges of their environment is their own sense of whether or not they have power. Unfortunately, the word "power" is often misinterpreted. For instance, if I were to ask you if you felt you had power, you might say, "No, I don't have a very prestigious job," or "No, I don't make a lot of money," or even "No, my kids never listen to me." But in this context, what I mean is *personal* power—the power to speak up and be heard, to have an effect, to make a change.

We all have the potential for power. But whether or not we exercise that power depends largely on *whether or not we think we will get the desired outcome.* And for most of us, that depends largely on the life experiences we have had and our assessment of whether or not we have been effective in the past.

Trauma directly attacks our sense of self-efficacy: a bad thing happened, and it was completely beyond your control to do anything about it. Indeed, sometimes, all it takes is one shock—especially if we were young, or under circumstances in which we were afraid for our lives—to teach us a lifelong lesson that there's no point in trying to help ourselves. And when the blow is unexpected or comes out of the blue, it is even more likely to leave us feeling helpless. We learn to expect that we won't have efficacy, and so we don't try.

Many scholarly works have been written about the benefit of a sense of self-efficacy. Like most of the traits in the skill set of resilient people, it can be cultivated and enhanced. By setting goals for ourselves and achieving them, our successes accumulate at our base, making us increasingly more untippable, like the Weeble toys of my youth.

There are two kinds of efficacy—what I call **internal efficacy** and **external efficacy.** External efficacy is the belief that one has power and can get things done in the outside world, that you can be heard and have the power to change things for the better. (This is essentially the gift Mandy learned from her parents.) Internal efficacy is the belief that you have control over your *internal world,* the understanding that you are at the helm of your own emotional journey, so to speak.

These two bubble up from the same place, although they aren't always twinned in real life. You can certainly have one without the other. And the way internal and external efficacy manifest can be very different.

But a truly resilient person has both. I might even make the argument that internal efficacy—the belief that you can control how you feel—is the fuel that powers external efficacy. This chapter will be dedicated to the concept of internal efficacy, while the next chapter will focus on external efficacy.

Let's return to Mandy as an example. When Mandy first heard what was going on in her daughter's class, she felt a whirlwind of emotions: disappointed in her daughter for not standing up to her bullies, murderously rageful at the kids who dared to taunt her child. But her sense of internal efficacy led her to the belief that she could control those emotions. She knew that she didn't have to stay in this emotionally dark place, and she knew that she didn't want to. She took charge of her emotional state and morphed it into one that better served her. She swapped feelings of violent rage and helplessness for feelings of loyalty, protectiveness, and entitled anger.

This, in turn, made her better equipped to exercise her *external* efficacy, her belief that she could march into that school and talk to some people and get the rules changed. Mandy's sense of internal efficacy laid the groundwork for her external efficacy: she would never have been as effective in dealing with the other parents or the principal if she was coming from a place of rage and helplessness. Had she not been able to take control of her emotions she most likely wouldn't have made any moves at all.

Both internal and external efficacy are important resilience skills, and both take a tremendous hit after trauma. But internal efficacy is where it all begins, so let's start there.

Internal Efficacy

Ben's girlfriend repeatedly lied, cheated, and stole from him; she routinely belittled him in front of his friends. So why in the world was this person still in his life? With a dreamy look on his face, Ben raised his shoulders in a shrug and said with a sigh: "You can't help who you love."

Ben had romanticized the notion that love is out of our control. And his sense of powerlessness extended to all of his other emotions as well—betrayal, loneliness. Ben believed that his moods were like the weather: when they descended upon you, you just had to wait them out.

Now, if your moods don't and won't change, no matter what you do, there is a distinct possibility you are suffering from major depression or mania or an anxiety disorder. Part of what differentiates a mood from a mood disorder is the fact that in the former, we can do things to change the mood, whereas in the latter we cannot.

Fortunately, most of us who think our moods are beyond our control are not suffering from a psychiatric disorder: we just don't have a lot of experience in internal efficacy. In fact, our moods are malleable. A state of mind, whether good or bad, can be very quickly altered by something as simple as a comment, a song, or a distraction. In the course of a therapy session, a TV show, or a subway ride, you can experience a whole medley of moods. But it is not uncommon, especially among people who have been through what you have, to believe what Ben does: that we can't control the way we feel.

In reality, Ben was exercising *a lot* of control over his feelings, electing to spend whole afternoons thinking about how beautiful and mysterious his girlfriend was and how unworthy he was of her— instead of how controlling and abusive she was.

I don't accept that we are the powerless passengers on a runaway train of our emotions and thoughts. But if you insist that you are powerless in the face of your emotions, I will also insist that you at least acknowledge that these thoughts represent an underlying goal. If you, like Ben, are steadfast in selectively focusing on how beautiful, sexy, and special your abusive girlfriend is, then you must at least admit—to me, and to yourself—that your goal is to continue to experience love for her. That way, at least you're giving yourself credit for the fact that you are at the helm of your own ship, even if you are choosing to steer it to a place that makes you feel bad.

In truth, you may be rusty at controlling your emotions. But you can make yourself feel almost anything.

Your emotions are at the mercy of your thoughts and your thoughts are under your voluntary control.

Just as you have the capacity to go indoors when you get cold, you can take yourself to another emotional climate if the one you're in becomes uncomfortable. That means you can pull yourself out of a slump or a rage. You can reintroduce feelings even if you have spent a sizable portion of your life numb. And, if need be, you can fall out of love. Resilient people believe that they can—and should—make themselves feel better.

An essential part of being able to do this is knowing when you feel bad. Resilient people are aware—they know when something has pushed a button and they've ended up feeling trauma-y. And instead of just being adrift in a sea of emotions, they have the ability to say, "Hey, I'm in a bad mood, let me do something about it." They know when they're off balance. And knowing that you're off balance isn't so scary when you're resilient, because you have internal efficacy—the knowledge that you'll be able to make yourself feel better.

Whether they need soothing and comfort, or some distraction, or a little physical activity, or rest, resilient survivors feel confident that they'll be able to change their moods by taking action; they know that they can restore their natural equilibrium.

Indeed, what is remarkable about resilient survivors with regard to their sense of internal efficacy is that they not only believe they are at the helm of their own emotions, but they have a willingness to do something about it—to put on a different song, for instance, and to let their emotions be changed by it. They grab an emotion off of their Rx emotions list, and they do what they have to do to get themselves feeling that way. Taking positive action helps them move from defeated to empowered.

> **Resilient survivors have the mental discipline to move out of the shadows and into the light.**

TRY THIS: ASSESSING YOUR INTERNAL EFFICACY

Everyone's beliefs about their own efficacy lie on a continuum. Some of us feel we have a lot of control over our feelings and others don't. Undoubtedly your family, your life experiences, and your culture come into play in determining where your beliefs lie.

Do you feel that it is reasonable to ask a person to try to change their emotions? Have you helped someone else out of a bad mood? Have you ever tried to help a person out of a bad mood but found that they seemed to be stuck or unable to shake it?

Have you had success in pulling yourself out of your own bad moods? Is there anyone that you know who has a real knack for helping you feel better, for offering a fresh perspective, or for trying to distract you? Have you ever experienced resentment toward someone who was trying to help you out of a bad mood?

Can you recall a time when you were feeling bad but then made a conscious choice to shake it off? Maybe you called friends and went out; maybe you went to the gym or to church. Maybe you just decided to let it go. How does thinking about that episode make you feel about internal efficacy?

Today, as you experience the events of your day, experiment with trying to intentionally direct your feelings, instead of being subject to them. Perhaps you feel grumpy and irritated that you have to make an appearance at one of your spouse's professional events. See if you can choose to move into the sunlight by connecting with a positive, empowering emotion. Can you feel pride in his accomplishments or flattered that he wants you by his side? Note what resistances come up for you. These are valuable clues about your internal efficacy belief system.

Boosting Your Internal Efficacy

There are a lot of ways that a person can grab the wheel of his emotions and steer to better-feeling terrain. Some people do it by focusing their attention on something that evokes a better feeling for them.

A combat veteran at a Fourth of July celebration might feel panicked and overwhelmed by the sound of the fireworks, but might take control of his emotions by looking at his son's rapt face on the picnic blanket next to him and consciously replacing his fear with a sense of wonder. He might listen closely to the soaring music and note the peacefulness of the scene to reconnect with the patriotism that drove him to enlist in the first place.

If you feel skeptical that resilient survivors are using techniques such as this one, I'd refer you to a story from a memoir called *Golden Bones: An Extraordinary Journey from Hell in Cambodia to a New Life in America* by Cambodian refugee–turned–ambassador to the UN Sichan Siv. When he is finally safe in America, he attends his very first Fourth of July parade. Like our veteran, he finds himself overwhelmed, but he steers himself somewhere better. He relates the moment: "The image of a little girl dressed as the Statue of Liberty in a red wagon pulled by a golden retriever stuck with me. I said to myself, 'This is a beautiful country.'" Even with panic pulsing in his veins, Siv has the audacity to find an image that makes him feel liberty and encourage his heart to follow his eyes.

In our lives we really do get second chances. But all too often our emotions keep us prisoners of the past. Are you willing to surrender your feelings of victimization in favor of something more positive?

Can you conceive of a time in the future when you will be able to let these feelings and beliefs go? When you feel trauma-y, can you convince yourself to look for a way to try to feel better? Will you agree to try to distract and soothe yourself?

Let's go back for a moment to the metaphor of the glass vase filled with negative emotions and the stones of positive emotion that we cultivate to displace the liquid. A stone is like a tool that you can grab on to when you feel lousy to try to direct your emotions to a better place. In this way, stones can be like a nonpharmacological pill, something you can "take" to alleviate distress.

Here is an opportunity to see how you might craft a stone using something you can count on: music.

Music as a Tool for Feeling Better

Music is some of the most powerful medicine we have at our disposal. Isn't the *Rocky* theme song enough to get even the laziest of us up off the couch? The right song is proof that moods can in fact be changed and that they are under your own control. So music can be a valuable tool in helping us move away from a bad feeling and get ourselves a dose of an Rx emotion.

Civil rights activist Rosa Parks described how she turned to music to rebuild her spirit on the day she learned Martin Luther King Jr. had been assassinated. Filled with an aching emptiness, she wondered if America's civil rights era had just ended in defeat. But then she put on a record of one of her favorite songs, Sam Cooke's "A Change Is Gonna Come," which features the refrain, "It's been a long, a long time coming, but I know a change is gonna come."

Rosa later credited that ballad with saving her sanity. "His smooth voice was like medicine to the soul," she recalls. "It was as if Dr. King was speaking directly to me." Later that day, she boarded a plane to Memphis to resume the work that King had been working on when he was killed. If Rosa had a stone labeled "Keep the Faith," she might have worked that stone by listening to Sam Cooke, or to her *other* favorite inspirational melody, "We Shall Overcome."

TRY THIS: MAKE A PLAYLIST

Once my patients have identified emotions they want more of in their lives, I encourage them to make playlists of songs that help evoke that feeling. Which emotions you need (and which ones you should avoid) is individual to you. The beauty of music is that we can use it to access straightforward emotions like serenity, sexuality, or gratitude, or we can create a playlist of songs to help us access complex emotional states. I have playlists of songs that evoke faith that it's all going to work out after a tragedy and playlists of songs that celebrate a sense of well-being and abundance. You can make playlists that offer very specific antidotes to your particular dark places. If you were betrayed by a lover, you might want to put together a playlist of songs about people who stood up for themselves in love and decided that they weren't going to take it anymore. If you know you would benefit from having more of a sense of humor, assemble a list of songs that celebrate life's ironies.

Maybe you have iTunes or a big music library that you can go to in order to look for songs. (To view my playlists, including song titles, please visit aliciasalzer.com.) You can also simply do an Internet search of "songs about _____" and listen to what you come up with. There are even search engines used by DJs, such as the Green Book of Songs. For $4 you can subscribe for a week. Then you simply type in an emotion and Green Book gives you lists of titles. You can listen to almost any song on YouTube and find lyrics easily on the Internet by typing in the name of the song and the word "lyrics." In an hour at your computer, you can assemble a substantial playlist of songs about almost any emotion you choose.

As you assemble these playlists, take note of how each song affects you. Observe whether the song is reinforcing your old trauma-preserving assumption (you'll want to avoid those) or helping to connect you with a lost emotion.

This exercise is not just about making playlists, it's also about demonstrating to yourself the phenomenon of internal efficacy. As you listen to the songs you will notice your ability to change your mood. As you choose one song over the other, you will notice how some songs are better than others at getting you to the emotion you are seeking.

Many of us feel it dishonors or discredits the memory of what we endured to move our emotions to a positive place. But I will offer you this: you may find yourself better able to feel empowered about what you overcame if you are willing to exert your internal efficacy and steer your emotions to a more positive place. Cambodian-American Sichan Siv could have very easily rationalized staying in a sad and fearful place on that Fourth of July instead of training his eyes on a little girl dressed as the Statue of Liberty. His mind could have drifted to his painful past and gotten stuck there. Instead, he chose to latch on to more positive emotions and use that strength to become an activist and advocate for his fellow countrymen. Your circumstances have changed, and neither your emotions nor your experiences need to stay stuck.

12

Boosting Your External Efficacy
Being the Agent of Change

INTERNAL EFFICACY, BELIEVING THAT YOU are at the helm of how you feel, can fuel your sense of *external* efficacy.

Moving our emotions to a place of empowerment primes us to be optimistic about what we can accomplish. And when we see that we can accomplish even small things, we accumulate proof that we are not helpless. This in turn boosts external efficacy, giving us optimism and confidence about our ability to be agents for positive change.

As we will see in this chapter, believing in your external self-efficacy is a critical component of resilience skill #3.

The Power of Small Goals

As I've mentioned, resilience theory was initially developed as a way to understand how some children can grow up under highly adverse circumstances and still thrive. What researchers have learned from those children is now widely applied to other at-risk kids, to teach them life skills that will help them navigate their way out of their situations and into healthy and productive adulthood.

Much of the programming targeted toward these kids has to do with helping them develop external efficacy by establishing small goals with concrete outcomes—projects that they can take pride in when they are successfully accomplished.

When a kid participates in a clean-up-the-playground day, she learns how to constructively overcome obstacles instead of giving up, getting mad, or getting even. And when she votes to repaint the slide purple instead of green, she experiences agency and learns that her opinion matters. These opportunities make her feel that she can make a difference, that she can make choices and see those choices reflected in the outside world.

The seeds of a resilient adult are sown when a child accomplishes something she thought she couldn't do. That usually happens when someone believes that she can pull off something that she considers impossible or unimaginable and points her in the direction of the tools she can use to get there.

The flip side of this type of self-efficacy, unfortunately, is that if you have repeatedly tried and failed or are relentlessly discouraged, eventually you stop wasting your time. If the adults around a child tell her that the playground is a dangerous dump and nothing can be done about it, then their sense of powerlessness amplifies her own. And if that type of thing happens often enough, then she will grow up believing that nothing she does will make any difference. In this way, our sense of external efficacy (or the lack of it) can be learned vicariously.

And we're not just talking about children who are poor or disadvantaged; a child can be robbed of the opportunity to develop resilience by overprotective and privileged parenting just as easily as by a life of hardship.

Efficacy is not the same as effectiveness. It has more to do with our *expectation* of our effectiveness.

Our sense of efficacy affects our daily decisions in ways large and small. A good example of this is the decision not to vote. Now, there are a lot of reasons that a sensible person might conclude that one vote doesn't matter in a country as big as our own. But since we are trying on the habits of resilient people—and, in particular, trying to understand how they conceptualize their own efficacy—let's take a peek at how the actor and Parkinson's disease activist Michael J. Fox sees the act of voting.

Anyone who has used stormy weather or a cold as an election-day excuse should read Fox's account of the obstacles he faces as he goes to the polls. In his memoir *Always Looking Up,* Fox describes the physical battle he faces just trying to get to his polling place. The tremors of his illness make it a challenge to dress, walk, ascend the stairs, flip the toggles for his candidates, and pull the lever. "Then it's done. I've dropped my pebble in the ocean, and hopefully, throughout the course of the day, millions of others will drop theirs in, too. No single one of us knows which pebble causes the wave to crest, but each of us, quite rightly, believes that it might be ours. An act of faith."

When you look at the world through Michael's glasses, you see that his sense of efficacy is not delusional or his impact overestimated—he knows his ballot is a mere pebble in the ocean. Yet his words are so passionate. Voting makes him feel he is a part of something that really matters. It makes him feel he can make a difference, which is understandably essential to a man in his circumstances. In the face of an illness or experience that threatens to rob you of your sense of power, knowing that you need not be a passive victim of outside circumstance is a gorgeous sensation.

Efficacy is powerful medicine.

If what you went through made you feel helpless or hopeless, or that you have no power and your actions don't matter, then exercising your sense of external self-efficacy may be a stone for you. You may find that you are able to feel much better by accomplishing even small tasks that move you in the direction of your goal.

TRY THIS: HOW MUCH EFFICACY DO YOU HAVE?

Is there a defining moment in your childhood when you observed to your amazement that someone, yourself or someone else, was able to achieve something you had thought impossible?

The efficacy message I got from this experience was:
I am powerless and helpless 1 . . . 2 . . . 3 . . . 4 . . . 5 I have efficacy

What were the early messages about efficacy that you got from your caregivers? Did you observe that *they* had efficacy—at home, in the workplace, and in the world at large (their area politics or religious community)?

The efficacy message I got from this experience was:
I am powerless and helpless 1 . . . 2 . . . 3 . . . 4 . . . 5 I have efficacy

When one parent had strong feelings about something, were they able to make themselves heard to the other one?

The efficacy message I got from this experience was:
I am powerless and helpless 1 . . . 2 . . . 3 . . . 4 . . . 5 I have efficacy

When there were problems in the neighborhood, did you observe your family doing something about it, or was it accepted as inevitable? Was there a way to talk about it, improve it, negotiate compromises, or improve conditions?

The efficacy message I got from this experience was:
I am powerless and helpless 1 . . . 2 . . . 3 . . . 4 . . . 5 I have efficacy

Can you remember something you did in your childhood that represented a real triumph in terms of your own efficacy? Was there a project you undertook and then saw through to completion? Do you recall voicing an opinion and seeing adults take it seriously enough to make a change?

The efficacy message I got from this experience was:
I am powerless and helpless 1 . . . 2 . . . 3 . . . 4 . . . 5 I have efficacy

Did you have a role model whom you can identify as someone who believed that one person could make a difference? This person can be someone you knew personally or an icon of your time.

The efficacy message I got from this experience was:
I am powerless and helpless 1 . . . 2 . . . 3 . . . 4 . . . 5 I have efficacy

What about now, in your current life? Are you a person who accepts what life deals you as a given, or do you believe that one person's voice and actions matter?

Many of us weren't lucky enough to be raised in an environment that taught us resilience. And, even if you were, events like what you went through can do a real number on a person's sense of external efficacy. That's why it's important to realize that this feeling of a lack of external efficacy does not necessarily have to be a permanent condition. Even if there isn't anything in your childhood experience to suggest that you can take control of your environment and what happens to you, you can readjust your expectations.

> **All it takes to reverse a trauma-preserving assumption telling you "there's no point" is a few powerful experiences that prove to you that there *is* a point.**

Trauma survivors often have trouble recognizing and appreciating their own efficacy. But often, we aren't keeping accurate accounting. In the same way that we preferentially see evidence that supports our trauma-preserving assumptions, we may be biased toward seeing evidence of our helplessness and ineffectuality. (Our own lack of agency in our lives is perhaps the biggest trauma-preserving assumption of all.) You may say that you're helpless, that everything you do fails, that even great stuff turns to garbage in your hands. But I know that if I were to follow you around, keeping tabs on all the things that happen in your day, a different picture would emerge.

Letty's emotionally abusive first husband seriously sabotaged her self-efficacy. In order to make himself feel like "the man of the family," he told Letty what to wear, when to be home, and what to cook. He was insulting, controlling, and dismissive of her feelings. Even after the marriage was over, Letty was left with a wounded self-perception—she felt stupid, powerless, and ineffectual.

One day, as we rescheduled an appointment, I looked over Letty's shoulder at her date book. There, in her neat printing, was all the substantiation she could possibly need for her self-efficacy claim. Her calendar was crowded with scheduling for her busy children, religious responsibilities, household maintenance, financial obligations—she was gracefully performing hundreds of important tasks every day, and the record of her efficacy was right there in that book.

But when I asked Letty to comment on her sense of power and

control over her life—a question about how she perceived her self-efficacy—she delved into a discussion of her inability to control the way the men in her life treated her.

"I have no luck with men," she asserted. Hopefully, by now, you can see that the phrase "I have no luck with men" is unrealistically passive. "Men" are not something that happen to you. There's no bingo hopper in the sky that doles out lousy abusive guys to the unlucky, while everyone else gets a dreamboat. Letty had chosen the wrong man to marry; that was true.

But there were some other truths she was ignoring. First of all, the problems in her marriage had much more to do with her husband's issues than with her own. And while there were reasons that she had chosen a man like him, she was catching on to the pattern and was making better choices already.

But why was Letty's whole sense of efficacy dictated *exclusively* by a historic lack of effectiveness in relationships? In gathering evidence about her self-efficacy, the material she should have been giving preferential attention to was her date book—not her marriage. The entries in that book were proof that on any given day, Letty had accomplished many difficult tasks, tasks that required patience and intelligence and the cooperation of others. This woman was managing a family while dealing with a marital crisis and maintaining her career. She had more efficacy than most of us—she just wasn't keeping an accurate score.

If, like Letty, you are basing your sense of efficacy on a perceived lack of power or effectiveness, it's likely that you are looking in the wrong places. You may need to take a closer look at what you already do and what you have already accomplished, giving yourself credit for what you achieved—and without expecting perfection.

"Our cable TV has been out, and despite spending an hour on the phone with tech support, I still couldn't get it working," you might say. But when that's the way you tell the story to yourself, you're neglecting some very important information. You made the time to call tech support. You followed their irritating prompts without throwing the phone across the room. You articulated the problem. You juggled your schedule so that the technician could come next week. Eventually the problem will be solved, and you will have been responsible for most of the effort required to do so, while the technician who visits takes care of the final 10 percent.

Don't forget: partial triumphs count! Efforts that got you halfway to your goal are still valid sources of self-esteem. If you don't believe this statement, perhaps you've never had a lawyer who charges by the hour. Mine keeps tabs on every phone call she's made, even if she doesn't get through. She notes every Google search, even if she didn't find what she was looking for. Her bills sting a little, but the reality is that she deserves to get paid for her time. So do the guys who have been digging up my street for several months, even though they still haven't fixed the sewer line problem. The same is true of the lab that did the test that suggested that my daughter might have an illness that she thankfully turned out not to have.

> **In life, people get paid for their time and effort—not for the outcome.**

It's high time you started keeping more accurate track of your own billable hours.

It's All in How You See It . . .

Okay, so resilient survivors create small goals and let their achievements fuel the fire of their sense of self-efficacy. And they give themselves credit for partial successes. But what do resilient survivors do when their efforts flat-out fail? How we interpret our failures, it turns out, is just as important as how we interpret our victories. And resilient people have a very interesting take.

When I was in medical school, I had a good friend who failed an oral exam. While I would have promptly tucked my tail between my legs after such an occurrence, he marched directly into the dean's office demanding a retest. "I am paying a fortune for my education," he said, "and I do not intend to have my career undermined by the fact that my examiner chose to focus on an obscure piece of medical minutia." It was true that the illness he had been drilled on was so rare that it was likely none of us would ever see a patient with that diagnosis, but I couldn't believe that a person could feel so confident after failing a test!

What my friend did was to take credit for what he had done right (he knew that he had studied hard and knew his stuff) while deflecting blame for what had gone wrong (he had a poor examiner). It turns out that this strange tendency is quite common among resilient people!

Because resilient survivors tend to take personal responsibility for what goes right but deflect responsibility for what goes wrong, they aren't saddled with the bad emotions that typically accompany failures. In characteristic optimist style, my med school friend did not see his failure as personal, permanent, or pervasive. He did not generalize, personalize, or catastrophize. He chose instead to see the failure as systemic and something that could be fixed. And yes, my friend did get to retake his oral exam.

TRY THIS: TAKING CREDIT FOR WHAT GOES RIGHT— AND DEFLECTING WHAT DOESN'T

The resilience trait we are trying on here is that resilient people tend to take personal responsibility for what goes right and *not* take it for the things that don't.

Let's look back over the past month or so of your life. Think about something you tried for and failed at—a job you didn't get, someone you dated who ultimately didn't like you as much as you liked them, a candidate you wanted to see elected who lost. It should be something that discouraged you, something that bummed you out and made you want to give up. It will be something you've been kicking yourself over, replaying the sequence of events in your head and wishing you'd done it all differently.

STEP ONE: TAKE CREDIT FOR THE GOOD STUFF

Even if the effort wasn't ultimately successful, take a moment to look at all the things you did right. Or, to think about this a different way, if things *had* gone your way, what would you have patted yourself on the back about?

Let's say that your outfit for the interview was well-chosen, your conversation was interesting and relevant, you were attentive to unspoken cues, your résumé showed ample experience. Or that you registered several hundred voters and handed out thousands of brochures and stickers. You were on time, showed perseverance, and kept a positive attitude. Make sure your list includes both actions you executed as well as character traits you embodied. And don't be lazy here; I want ten things, minimum.

This is where you get to tabulate a more accurate record of your "billable hours."

STEP TWO: DEFLECT BLAME FOR THE BAD STUFF

Now list the things you feel you did wrong, all the things you find yourself ruminating about at three o'clock in the morning. The person you were dating broke up with you, and you think: "I dressed too provocatively, so he didn't take me seriously as relationship material." The candidate you supported doesn't get elected after you spend months campaigning on his behalf, and you think: "I didn't have my facts in line, so I wasn't convincing when talking up my candidate to voters who were on the fence." You blew an important interview and you think: "I didn't realize that the guy who welcomed me in the waiting room was my potential future boss, so I didn't make a good first impression."

Now go through and rewrite each of the negatives, placing the responsibility on something *other* than you. Note that we are not inventing ridiculous and false blame; this is a perfect example of how the glass can simultaneously be half-full *and* half-empty. Perhaps there were things that went wrong that *were* your responsibility or your fault. But those aren't the things your resilient heroes focus on, so dig deep and find a reasonable reason why what happened might *not* have been your fault.

Instead of deciding you dressed too provocatively and scared that man away, try "I'm a passionate person who needs a guy who isn't intimidated by a woman who wears her sexuality on her sleeve. He wasn't right for me." Instead of faulting your pitch for your candidate, try: "The other candidate was better funded; there was no competing with the amount of publicity he had." About the job: "It was tricky of my interviewer not to introduce himself; I value directness in the workplace. It probably wasn't the right place for me."

STEP THREE: LEARN, AND MOVE ON

If there was anything to be learned from the experience, make note of it here. What would you do differently next time that might result in a better outcome? Maybe you do need to crib those talking points so you feel sharp when you're building a case for a candidate in unfriendly territory. Maybe it is a good idea to Google your interviewer so that you recognize him on sight; then at least you won't have handicapped yourself, and if the job's not right for you, then you can decide whether or not to take it.

List what you might have done differently—then chalk it up to a learning experience, and allow yourself to move on.

After completing the exercise, take a minute to note whether you have a different sense of your self-efficacy with regard to the incident. Usually, it's very effective to recast an event this way. This one failure isn't indicative of a life of failure; it's merely one event. It is neither permanent nor pervasive. You did many things right. And some other things happened that were either not your fault or beyond your control. Viewed in this manner, our "failures" leave us better able to succeed next time.

> **Resilient people do not linger where they are powerless.**

In 1955 Rosa Parks made history by refusing to give up her seat to a white person on a bus. But did you know that twelve years before that, the same exact bus driver, a man named James Blake, threw her off his bus? What did Rosa Parks do after this demoralizing event occurred? Nearly every day for twelve years, when driver James Blake pulled up to the stop, Rosa opted to walk or wait rather than board his bus. But she did not remain passive or avoidant about racism. She took her considerable skills to the offices of the NAACP, where she worked and applied her talents where they were more likely to have effect.

The story, as it is told in her biography, *Rosa Parks,* highlights why it is equally important for us to study the failures and defeats of our heroes as it is to admire their victories. How do our heroes pick themselves up and dust themselves off? Resilient people may believe in their own internal and external efficacy, but if they find themselves in a position where they lack power they aggressively move to the places in their lives where their efficacy is optimized. So not only are they at the helm of their own ship, but they use the wheel to steer toward the light.

Applying Efficacy from One Area of Your Life to Another

We all have areas in which we are effective and areas in which we are not. What types of things do you accomplish with ease? Which ones give you more trouble?

Are there certain types of tasks and accomplishments that you avoid because you are afraid of failure or of being hurt? Getting back on the dating circuit after a series of bad breakups, for instance, or aggressively going after more money and responsibility at work after working under a bad boss? These are your low-efficacy areas.

What tasks and accomplishments do you feel proud of? Are

you a self-starter, someone who is able to motivate yourself without difficulty? Are you a team builder, someone who can make the people who are working on your behalf feel good? Are you quick on the uptake and even-tempered at work? These are your high-efficacy areas.

Tease apart the different facets of your life in which you either *do* or *don't* have a strong sense of efficacy. You may have a strong sense of efficacy at your daughter's school but not in your workplace. Or you may have a good sense of efficacy in the realm of local politics but not in the realm of health.

These things may seem unrelated, but they are not. In fact, your efficacy skills are transferable. To demonstrate how this works, allow me to share with you an area in which I have a lot of efficacy, and one in which I have less efficacy than I'd like—and what I do about it.

One of the reasons I admire almost all of the heroes I mention in this book is that they didn't lose their spirit or their sense of efficacy in the face of obstacles. In the realm of making the world a safer and better place for victims, I tend to feel low efficacy. I just don't have a lot of faith that those in power will ever care about the underdog, or that laws can change, or that the situation will improve. Instead my mind fills with the stories of people like Susan B. Anthony, the suffragist who died before her dreams came to fruition.

This is me harvesting evidence to prove my own trauma-preserving assumption that no one cares about oppressed people and that nothing can be done about their plight. This is Moodith telling me that there's no point in fighting, my misguided mind trying to protect me from disappointment. It is an ugly little TPA, and one that I am committed to fighting tooth and nail for the rest of my life.

So when I am feeling powerless in the realm of human rights activism, I need a stone to work. I need something hefty to toss into that vase of liquid negativity in order to prove to myself that I can have efficacy in this realm. To do that I borrow a skill from an area where I *do* have efficacy, both internal and external: my work.

In the realm of my work, I am bold about taking on challenges, even when they require a lot of delayed gratification and endurance. One of the things that I have often said to myself in my professional life, when I have embarked on challenges with very uncertain outcomes, is: "What would you attempt to do if you knew you could not fail?" In my work, I have good *internal* efficacy, because I am easily able to mobilize this belief. And I have good *external* efficacy in the work realm as well. (Who would ever write a book if they didn't believe that someday someone would read it?)

So I use an efficacy skill from a high-efficacy area of my life (in this case, work) and apply it to a low-efficacy area of my life (civil rights). If I am fighting for the rights of battered women, or bullied children, or the mentally ill, and I find myself feeling overwhelmed by blue-list permatrauma emotions, I dose myself with some transferred efficacy by asking myself, "What would you attempt to do if you knew you could not fail?" It bolsters my strength and allows me to tap into muscles that I can easily use in one realm of my life but not in others.

I confront myself on the inconsistencies in my sense of efficacy. As a result, I am able to set a goal and follow through. I don't just go to a rally and stand in the shadows, I make a sign to carry and I bring it. I don't just *attend* a fund-raiser for a domestic violence organization, I approach the head of that organization as she stands in line at the bar and—heart pounding—I share my perspective.

In other words, I do something small and achievable that increases my efficacy, both internal and external. I allow myself to believe not just that I *can* make a difference but that I *will* make a difference. I act as if I cannot fail. It is an act, but it works: it makes me feel good, and it enables me to get the job done. With practice, we observe from the accomplishment of these small goals that we have more efficacy than we had previously thought.

Perhaps it was the transferred sense of self-efficacy that Rosa Parks gained while working at the NAACP offices that eventually gave her the courage to reboard that bus twelve years later and "sit down for her rights."

TRY THIS: WHERE DO YOU HAVE EFFICACY?

Below, you will find a list of a variety of life realms. Read down the list in the left-hand column (feel free to add an area if there's a significant area of your life that you don't see represented), and evaluate both your internal and external efficacy in those areas. Put a "+" or a "−" in the appropriate **External Efficacy** column, depending on whether you have high or low efficacy in that area. Next, put another "+" or "−" in one of the two **Internal Efficacy** columns, depending on whether you feel you have high or low efficacy in these areas.

	EXTERNAL EFFICACY		INTERNAL EFFICACY	
	High I am good at getting things done in this realm. My actions matter, and I can have a positive impact on the outcome I am pursuing.	**Low** I am *not* good at getting things done in this realm. My actions *don't* matter, and I *can't* have a positive impact on the outcome I am pursuing.	**High** In this realm of life, I am at the helm of my own emotions.	**Low** In this realm of life, I am *not* at the helm of my own emotions.
Work				
Home				
Spouse				
Church				
School				
Health				
Community				
Money				
Kids				
Parents				
Men				

Women				
Group				
Solitary				
Friendships				
Strangers				

Once you've finished with your "+"s and "−"s, look back at your low-efficacy areas and see what they have in common. Look for ways that what you went through has negatively affected your sense of efficacy in areas that remind you of it.

For example, maybe your botched investment and embarrassment in front of people who gave you their cash explains why you feel low efficacy in the realms of work, friends, and family, but not with the kids or strangers. Can you notice trends among the realms that give you trouble?

Letty, the patient with the abusive ex and the packed day planner, found she had low efficacy in the home and with men but a lot of efficacy in many other realms. In her high-efficacy realms Letty noticed that she was a real take-charge kind of gal, one might even say a control freak. She diligently researched and considered things before making decisions and when she did decide, she did so with gusto, knowing that her decisions weren't hasty.

The exercise above will help you borrow skills from areas in which you have a lot of efficacy to bolster up those areas where you don't.

> **You can improve areas of low efficacy by utilizing the skill sets and beliefs taken from the areas of your life where you *do* have efficacy.**

Going forward, your job is to figure out what gives you so much confidence in your high-efficacy areas and apply that to your areas of low efficacy. For Letty, I recommended that she make a list of all the guys she knew, ranking them according to whether they'd be a bad or a good choice for a partner. She let her inner control freak see what it felt like to take the wheel in the man department.

Doing this helped her get back in touch with her own sense of control; it taught her that she could use the discernment borrowed from the high-efficacy areas of her life and apply those same skills to her low-efficacy areas.

From this vantage point she could see that stable, sensitive Drew from accounting would be a better choice than handsome, volatile, often-hungover Steve in sales. But the point of the exercise is not to decide whom to invite to the office holiday party; the point is to enforce a reality check. The truth is that Letty is in charge of *all* aspects of her life, and she has the ability, the efficacy, the intelligence, and the judgment to choose her men wisely. Choosing Drew over Steve has nothing to do with luck.

Efficacy as a Life Force

A human is supposed to be indignant, angry, and passionately empowered in the face of something that challenges his efficacy. This is a natural and healthy response. Our innate drive to right ourselves when tipped is as natural as a plant leaning toward the light.

We tend to forget that many of the world's movers and shakers, the richest moguls, the most accomplished role models, were motivated to accomplish what they did because they were touched by a trauma that robbed them of their sense of efficacy and they wanted to take it back. Mandela wasn't born a freedom fighter; he became one because he could not tolerate feeling a lack of efficacy in the realm of civil rights. This was his knee-jerk response to a culture of racism and oppression that tried to rob him of his efficacy. Michael J. Fox also rose to the occasion when an illness undermined his sense of efficacy.

If what you went through robbed you of your sense of efficacy, perhaps there are actions you need to take to reclaim an optimistic sense of your own personal power. Don't let feeling low efficacy stand in your way.

What would *you* attempt to do if you knew you could not fail?

If you still find yourself at a loss for what actions will pack a punch for you, refer to your signature strengths and the heroes that embody them for you. Your core values are the essence of who you are and what makes you tick, and they may provide you with clues as to what will help you feel confident again.

If your signature strengths have to do with justice and leadership, maybe you will follow in the footsteps of Parks and Mandela and be a political activist. If your signature strengths involve authenticity and kindness, then maybe, like Rosie O'Donnell, you will choose to be the voice of children who cannot speak for themselves, or will devote yourself to raising a child and bestowing upon it the acceptance and freedom to express feelings that you were denied in your own childhood. If your signature strengths lie in the areas of courage and perseverance, then perhaps, like Michael J. Fox, you will boldly share your experience, raising awareness and searching for solutions. If you are a person who deeply values perspective and wisdom, then maybe, like Elizabeth Edwards, you will share what you have learned about resilience so others can benefit from your experiences.

If I told you at the beginning of this book that you were going to learn to be like your heroes by listening to an inspirational ballad, talking to someone at a fund-raiser, or listing eligible bachelors in your office, it would have sounded simplistic and ridiculous. I hope you realize now that we're not talking about just any song or any dating game. If power or efficacy or hope are lost emotions for you—and I would dare to say that they are for most of us—then listening to feel-good music, making a sign for a rally, or taking an active stance in romance is a radical act of defiance in the face of a trauma that has been trying to rob you of your life. The steps you are taking to experience greater efficacy represent real progress toward healing.

Don't skip these exercises or dismiss them. There is much to be learned from the way our heroes cope. Heroes are not people who do what you cannot do. Heroes are people who show you what *can* be done. I have had the privilege of knowing a few heroes in my life. And the difference between them and those who admire them is often as simple as the choices that they make in times of hardship.

Resilience Skill #4: Rosewashing

MY MOTHER HAS A NAME for the world's naturally positive, happy people. You know: the people who are always in a good mood, who naturally bounce back, who always see the cup as half-full.

She calls them golden retrievers.

While I found this trait extremely endearing in the dogs we had while I was growing up, I was highly suspicious of human "golden retrievers." I assumed they were happy because they had just been blessed with lives in which nothing went wrong.

On closer inspection, most of the golden retrievers of the world go through all the same trials and agonies as the rest of us. The only difference between us and them is their admirable, enviable gift for resilience and optimism. I know now that behind nearly every happy-go-lucky person you meet is a soul not unlike yours, with a plateful of challenges—and a steely resolve to stay on the sunny side of the street.

The Work of Optimism

I've spoken quite a bit about the glass being simultaneously half-full *and* half-empty. Life is like that—a mixed bag. People are like that, too: there are almost always aspects you admire about them and aspects you disapprove of. Jobs are a mixed bag, too. The joy of working for yourself can sometimes give way to loneliness. A job that requires a lot of boring repetition might also offer security in a precarious economy.

Most of us acknowledge that there's good and bad in all aspects of our lives. But many of us still feel victimized by our lives, as if we don't have choices. We take the good for granted while giving ourselves the unlimited right to whine about the bad stuff.

Resilient people, on the other hand, acknowledge that their life is of their own creation: the result of their choices. But even more than this, they make a mental commitment to focus on the good stuff.

I watch my spouse, an ER doctor, do this all the time. It's not easy to head in for what you know will be a sleepless and frantic overnight shift, and it's even more difficult when it means saying good-bye to a household just settling into the couch for a cozy evening movie. In those moments, you *could* feel bitter—or you could kiss everybody good-bye and leave the house telling yourself, "I may save a life tonight," or "I'm glad to know that I'm the reason my family feels so safe and secure."

It sometimes seems that optimistic people are looking at the world through rose-colored glasses. Are they born that way? Sometimes you'll find someone who happened to be born with a sunny outlook or who was lucky enough to grow up with a good model for these skills. That's not impossible. But most of the time, you find someone who is aggressively harvesting positivity, someone who has brought their very best weapons to the battle against negativity and fear and trauma.

In most cases, this is not effortless but something they really work on, every single day—and they work even harder when times are tough. Once you realize this, the word "optimistic" seems a bit insulting and definitely inaccurate; it's too passive to be descriptive. It negates years of hard work and accomplishment on the part of the people who are able to pull it off. After all, just because something looks effortless doesn't mean it comes easily.

One of my patients says that there are two kinds of sober: the kind where you don't drink because you never have and the kind where you don't drink because you almost lost your life to alcohol and had to wrench it back, and now have to fight every day to keep it. And that's the best description I've heard of what you find when you scratch the surface of these "golden retrievers" who have survived trauma.

Rosewashing Your Life

Now, I recognize that it's not fair of me to say that resilient people are optimistic and that you should be, too. You would be left feeling—rightfully so—that the instructions were missing. So let's look at what these resilient survivors do.

I have already mentioned how much I loved a memoir by Geralyn Lucas, a young woman whose fun, glamorous, cosmopolitan life as a journalist was interrupted by a breast cancer diagnosis. The title of her book, *Why I Wore Lipstick to My Mastectomy,* tells you everything: this is someone who is dedicated to fighting to see herself as something other than a cancer victim. By wearing lipstick to her surgery, she is saying, "I am not my symptoms. I am not my diagnosis. I am not a victim." Geralyn is a *fighter,* and her battle with cancer was real combat. She shares every tactic, every maneuver, and every foxhole prayer with her reader. She never stints on the "how"; instead, she lays the process bare.

The technique that Geralyn relates is nothing less than the rigorous discipline of mind control. She believes that there is a positive way of interpreting even the most frightening events and she insists on finding it. When her phobia of scalpels and needles kicks in, she actively replaces those thoughts with ones of gratitude for the existence of the very medical technology that may save her life. When she is afraid that her doctors will make a mistake, she shifts gears by reassuring herself that she is in a room full of experts. Instead of hoping that her anesthesiologist will know how to comfort her as she is put under, she writes a note to herself for him to read to her as he puts on the mask. Even as a tumor in her breast is trying to kill her, she focuses on the other breast and how it will someday nurse a baby.

To do this—to trend toward the positive with this kind of relentlessness—takes a tremendous amount of internal efficacy, the belief that you are at the helm of your own emotions. And it takes a tremendous amount of willpower, too. This is something that we hear overcomers say again and again. In every single autobiography I have ever read of every successful person I admire, there is a line that reads something like this: "I simply do not indulge in the luxury of negative thinking."

Resilient survivors don't let themselves stay in a negative place.

Instead, they know how to apply a coat of what I call **rosewash** —like whitewash—that allows them to see the world through rose-colored glasses instead of through trauma-colored ones. Every single time that Geralyn finds herself confronting something scary, or depressing, or traumatic, she forces herself to rosewash it. She moves from a place of helplessness to a place of efficacy. Those dark-colored glasses keep finding a way back onto her face, and she keeps ripping them off and replacing them with the rose-colored ones.

Theorists Soygüt Gonca and Isik Savasir have described how we both "construct and construe" our environments. Reality is highly interpretable, and we are constantly using our belief systems as a sounding board, looking for the overarching patterns that make life look consistent. When you go out into the world carrying these schemas, it changes the way you act—it changes *what you do.* This is obvious, right? When you treat people like you're expecting them to take advantage of you, it brings out the worst in people, which fortifies your belief that people are mean, ugly, and selfish. And so the cycle goes.

But what resilient survivors realize is that *the opposite is also true.* And so they make themselves do that rosewashing, even when they don't want to. Even when it feels like spin or delusion. They stand at the fork in the road and choose to wrap their head around the viewpoint that makes them feel better.

Consider this scene from Geralyn Lucas's book. It is the week before her surgery and she is struggling to maintain some sense of her identity in the noncancer world. Her family takes her out to her favorite French bistro, but the sight of the white linen tablecloth takes her back to the hospital sheets in the radiology suite, and she freaks out. Even though she is in a bistro with her family, her nostrils are filled with the smell of the alcohol swab used before she gets a needle full of contrast dye to prepare her for a scan. She begins crying uncontrollably, having what appears to be a flashback.

Remember chapter 1, where we talked about not losing sight of the car behind your dent? The thing that moves me about Geralyn is that even in this lowest of moments, *she is working hard to notice things around her that aren't her trauma.* She focuses on the smell of the food in front of her, on the fresh summer breeze, the smell of chocolate soufflé, of the warm baguettes the waitress has just placed on the table. She is grasping for affirmations of her aliveness, evidence that her body is made for sensual pleasures and that she is still capable of enjoying them. Miserable panicky liquid is flowing into her vase and she is grabbing stones representing the things she loves best about life, the things that define her, and tossing them in. She is determined to remind herself that she is not destined for a life of just antiseptic smells and painful sensations but one of beauty and goodness.

This is no small thing to be able to do in the midst of a panic attack, the week before a mastectomy. But even if what happened to you occurred a long time ago, you may still find it hard to exercise this kind of rosewash.

Why is it that we have a tendency to cling to negative feelings? There are moments when you may say to yourself: "Am I just asking myself to be in denial? Shouldn't some piece of me be accepting the possibility that the worst may happen so that at least I can be prepared for it?" Expecting the worst has a built-in benefit: should the worst come to pass, at least it doesn't catch us unawares. There are real comforts and satisfactions in the default negative position.

Practicing resilience skills can feel like going out on a limb. Additionally, as I've said before, many of us suffer from a value bias toward negative emotions. There is a real predisposition in our culture toward thinking that negativity is normal. It's not at all unusual for someone to say they have been stressed or depressed all week. But when someone says they have been feeling great all week you can't help but wonder who spiked their breakfast cereal. We don't see a lot of positive role models demonstrating golden retriever behavior; instead, characters like this are considered marginal, simplistic, unsophisticated—the "dumb friend" on the sitcom.

And that's too bad; I think resilience should be taught in schools and fostered where it is found. (In my opinion, learning to be happy will take you much farther in life than learning algebra will.) But we've been taught that our negative emotions are "more real" than their positive counterparts. Maybe you feel that there's no point in trying to feel anything different because your negative emotions will claim you in the end. Maybe you're someone for whom these positive emotions cause anxiety, like someone's setting you up for a fall.

If so, these are beliefs that need to be challenged. The reason that I feel trauma survivors need to hear this message, more than anyone else, is because we, of all people, should know better. We have looked real negativity in the face. We know exactly how fragile and precious life is. Of all the people in the world, trauma survivors should know better than to waste life being glum merely because no one has taught us, trained us, or modeled for us how to appreciate all the good there is in life.

Giving Yourself a Break

Searching for the silver lining won't turn you into a Pollyanna; what it will do is give you a break, so that you have the reserves to take on some appropriate sadness when the situation demands it.

One of my patients was constantly overwhelmed with grief and fear. "Oh my God," she would say at the start of her session, "can you believe what happened?" And we'd go through a week's worth of celebrity deaths and betrayals, ending up with the terrible thing that happened to the daughter of the principal at her son's school, a man whom she'd met twice in her life. Why on earth did she want to spend her therapy session talking about terrible things happening to people she didn't even know?

This patient had so much empathy for everyone and everything else that every news story and interaction with the outside world left her completely depleted. She prided herself on what a compassionate and caring individual she was, but in reality she was a person hobbled by her compassion. If this patient could have given herself permission to care *less,* she would have been able to care *more;* if she'd allowed herself to recharge, then she could have done something to take on one of the issues that so disturbed her. With a little respite from the crashing sea of her emotions, she could have made a difference; as it was, she was spending all her energy trying to stay on her feet, as wave after wave of negativity smashed her into the sand.

> **Resilient people don't eliminate negative emotions completely; they bolster themselves with positive emotions so they can tolerate and endure the other stuff.**

This is another example of why it's so important to insist on a balanced diet of emotions. There are times when it is appropriate and necessary to feel negative emotions. But a balance of positive emotions in our lives is crucially important. Researcher Barbara Fredrickson showed that positive emotions like contentment and amusement *undo* the physiologic effects of stress, like increased heart rate and blood pressure, better than "neutral" emotions do. Fredrickson proved that something as simple and artificial as making yourself watch puppies has been scientifically proven to be an effective tool in returning fight-or-flight responses back to baseline. So all this insistence on searching out feel-good emotions isn't just a smoke screen. In this study, positive emotions were literally good medicine.

And when we are experiencing positive emotions, we bring a whole other set of skills to the task of problem solving. To quote Martin Seligman in his book *Authentic Happiness,* "A chilly negative mood activates a battle-stations mode of thinking: the order of the day is to focus on what is wrong and then eliminate it. A positive mood, in contrast, buoys people into a way of thinking that is creative, tolerant, constructive, generous, undefensive, and lateral."

This is true whether you are a resilient person or not. But what differentiates resilient people is that they are willing, in the midst of their stress, to show themselves the puppies. Like Geralyn Lucas, in the middle of a panic attack, they are willing to sniff for the smell of soufflé and baguettes.

Feeling these positive emotions not only helps our body undo the physiologic effects of stress, but it can also serve as a tool that we can use to "medicate" ourselves out of stress when we are ready to feel better. If all work and no play makes Johnny a dull boy, then all permatrauma and no pleasure makes it impossible for us to do anything but feel bad.

The Art of Savoring

We know that resilient people rosewash, looking for and focusing on the positive aspects of a situation. Well, here's another thing they do when something goes well: they juice it for all it's worth. Resilient people anticipate pleasure, enjoy it in the moment, and reflect on it afterward. They *savor*.

Two researchers at Loyola University, Fred B. Bryant and Joseph Veroff, have dedicated their careers to studying savoring, noting four key elements: **basking,** accepting congratulations and admiration; **thanksgiving,** in which we acknowledge the ways we are blessed and communicate our gratitude; **marveling,** reveling with wonder and awe, and **luxuriating,** deriving protracted pleasure from sensory experiences.

So the term "savoring," when used in the world of positive psychology, isn't just about slowing down to enjoy something—although that's part of it. Instead, it's something you do in the past, present, and future.

> **To savor, you (1) optimize your anticipation, (2) lose yourself in the moment, and (3) replay it for your own pleasure after it is done.**

Let's compare two women: both are going out on promising first dates. Michele forgets that she has plans until she checks her calendar midafternoon, and then rushes into the bathroom to wash her face and put on a little lipstick. She spends the cab ride reviewing a PowerPoint presentation. She has missed out on a variety of opportunities to milk the good feelings surrounding her date.

Camille, on the other hand, clears her afternoon work schedule so she can go home to shave her legs and change. She listens to sexy feel-good music. She gets dressed slowly, anticipating her date admiring her outfit and the sensual pleasures that might ensue. As she hails a cab, she feels lucky to be going out on an exciting evening adventure in this great city. The day after her date, Camille schedules a lunchtime workout with a friend so she can spill all the details—reexperiencing all the basking and thanksgiving and marveling that one can muster on a treadmill. In Camille's case, her preparation for and enjoyment of the aftermath of the date are as enjoyable as the date itself.

It's true that different people excel at different aspects of savoring. Some people find it easy to lose themselves in wonderful stories of the past but have trouble enjoying the present. Others get so excited about the planning and anticipation that the event itself always seems to disappoint. Some people are great at savoring in the moment but when it's over, it's over; it doesn't occur to them to replay the event in the days, weeks, or years that follow. When their boss publicly acknowledges their contribution at the annual Christmas party, they soak up the glory and accept the admiration without false humility, but they neglect to replay the moment later that night with their spouse.

How are you at savoring? When everything's going right, can you relax and enjoy it? Or do you start expecting a lightning bolt to strike you down or fantasizing that Mr. Right already has a wife and seven children in another town?

Most of us rein in our happiness.

Bryant noted that some of us are habitual savorers, while others are quick to undo the good. Of course, Bryant's findings are not a surprise: people who can savor are happier, more satisfied with life, and more optimistic.

Savoring leads to some great emotions, things like profound gratitude, passionate tenderness, serenity, safety, contentment. If we're lucky, most of us experience these emotions fleetingly. But, if you think about it, what would be so bad about lazing around in a gluttonous excess of serenity and tenderness?

We spend so much time in our dark moods! After a bad day at work, we spend our commute bathed in bad feelings: anger, anxiety, guilt, indignation, fear. When we get home, we replay every slight, mulling over what we might have done differently. We call our friends to unload. We toss and turn instead of getting a good night's sleep. Sound familiar? These are days in which you are juicing your *bad* feelings for everything they're worth.

Now imagine that same day—but with rosewash. Imagine spending the same amount of time that you spent obsessing about bad things and instead savoring positive ones. Picture yourself expending the same amount of energy trying to get to—and stay in—a good place. Imagine juicing those *positive* feelings for everything they're worth. Take each one of the day's accomplishments out to show your family, turning it around and enjoying it all over again. Call a friend just to tell her about a compliment you got from your boss, and then—instead of feeling like your self-indulgent three minutes are up and it's time to move on—ask your friend to tell you about everything that went well for *her* today.

Can you create a protracted moment that is about how great something is? Remember, savoring has three parts: a past, a present, and a future. You don't have to wait for something good to happen. It can be as much of a joy to recollect something good that has already happened or to plan something to look forward to: grab a photo album and reminisce, or plan a brunch with a bunch of friends you don't get to see enough of.

Reclaiming Pleasure

Why is it so hard to savor? Part of it, I believe, has to do with that cultural bias against positive feelings. But a lot of it has to do with a strongly puritanical vein embedded in our culture, which manifests in a disapproval of pleasure. I strongly believe that we must challenge the idea that it is somehow hedonistic, dangerous, or recklessly irresponsible to value, seek out, enhance, and bask in that which is pleasurable in life.

We must reclaim pleasure.

One of the very real ways that we can reclaim pleasure is in the physical world, in the world of our senses. Trauma survivors tend to get stuck in their heads, and we can benefit enormously from things that direct our attention once again back to the physical world. In part 3 we will explore ways of mindfully attuning your senses as a mechanism of responding to trauma-y feelings. The challenge is not just in remembering to do this when we feel badly, but in staying in a moment of sensual or physical pleasure without Moodith going off in our heads.

Savoring is one way to maximize pleasure that all of us can learn to be better at. If you think about it, this is what we tend to do when we are newly in love. We rosewash and we savor. And it feels great, right? This is a skill that resilient survivors apply outside their love life as well. When they accomplish things, they enhance their sense of efficacy by savoring their accomplishments.

Resilient survivors savor their own efficacy.

Resilient survivors keep their successes front and center in their mind, and they pull them out and savor them just as a less resilient person might replay a humiliation.

Staying in an empowered place and savoring our own efficacy is especially hard for women. We're socialized to modesty and humility. Think about how often you've heard guys boast each other up. "Rich here is our best new sales rep," "Bruce is an amazing guitar player," "Tom can kick my ass on the court." And what do Tom, Bruce, and Rich do in response to the compliment? They grin and admit, "Yeah, I really like what I do."

But say something like that to most women, and you'll see them backpedal or pass the compliment on to someone else: "Oh, don't say that! Susan's better than I am; I've just been doing it longer." We think it's tacky to brag about ourselves—even just to ourselves. This modesty makes it hard to savor our efficacy or to groove on our power. And this, in turn, presents a predicament. Because if we are going to be resilient, then we really need to keep accurate score of how powerful we are.

TRY THIS: USING SAVORING TO MAXIMIZE GOOD EMOTIONS

To do this exercise, first take notice of some discrete act that you think you did well. A good grade, the five pounds you lost, your peacekeeping ability when your kids started to bicker at the table. Alternatively, choose a sensory experience you recently had that pleased you, a work of art, a delicious meal, a view. Now go back and really savor, seeing how long you can stay in your appreciation and how much juice you can squeeze out of it.

Harder than you expected? Fortunately, researchers Bryant and Veroff break it down for those of us new to the concept. They outline five different ways to savor.

Share the experience with others: Buy five postcards at the museum shop and send them, describing what you saw there that took your breath away. Call three people you love, and tell them all about something great that happened in your life today. And the next time you know that you're going to be participating in or seeing something great, ask someone to come with you.

Build a memory: Take mental photographs, or actual ones; save a physical memento that you can use to reminisce with later. Create a scrapbook or shoebox of feel-great mementos. Write an article or poem about why the experience was meaningful, something that you can reread later to jog your emotional memory of the feelings you have now.

Congratulate yourself: Save your modesty for other aspects of your life. If you are savoring an accomplishment or a success, note how much others admire you, how long and hard you worked or waited for this day, how patient or disciplined you have been. Notice how deserving you are of this little joy and the various ways you have earned it. Remind yourself how lucky and blessed you are.

Sharpen your perceptions: We edit the world around us all the time; we have to, or we'd go mad. But it also means that we can spend a lot of time rushing around without ever taking the time to notice things. Savoring is all about noticing. If you're reading a novel, take the time to appreciate the craft behind a beautifully turned phrase; read it twice, or copy it out. Slow down to really taste the food you're eating.

Ask yourself: How you would describe the visual aspects of your experience to a sightless person? How would you describe the sounds and smells to someone over the phone? List the emotions you feel in the moment.

Savoring is all about editing, too. Focus strongly on the elements that give you pleasure, taking in all the details, while ignoring and minimizing others that are less pleasurable.

Absorption: Let yourself get totally immersed in the pleasure, and don't think about other things. Bees, this may be especially hard for you. Meditation teachers sometimes encourage practitioners to think about their minds like kittens or toddlers; if you catch it wandering off, gently redirect it back to the task at hand.

I would add one more thing to Bryant and Veroff's list. It is something that enables you to savor in advance:

Anticipate with delight: Of course, it's fun to do something spontaneous. But it's even better to spend the day in eager expectation, planning what you will wear, leafing through guidebooks and travel magazines, telling your friends about how excited you are, and packing the perfect accessory that will heighten your enjoyment of the event. Orchestrate what will please you. Plan it in glorious detail, and take joy in watching something you imagine come to fruition.

Dangle a Carrot

Savoring is not just a way to squeeze more juice out of pleasurable events. It can be used as a survival skill, a coping mechanism, an antidote to hopelessness. Even when tough times hit and they find themselves plunged into darkness, resilient survivors are not afraid to paint a picture for themselves of what things will be like when life is better. Knowing that they are agents of change in their own lives, they feel confident that things will not always be as they are, and they use that knowledge to tempt themselves with visions of a better future.

Resilient survivors encourage themselves through difficult times by dangling a carrot of hope in front of themselves.

Viktor Frankl did it in the concentration camps by imagining himself lecturing again. He imagined his dignity restored, being respected for his intelligence, enjoying the attention of his pupils. And he savored the details, right down to the warm, comfortable auditorium and the upholstery on the lecture hall seats. He dangled a carrot for himself, and an elaborately imagined one at that, laden with sensory experiences that stood in stark contrast to his current environment.

From his jail cell, Nelson Mandela imagined returning to the grassy hills of his childhood home to pay respect to his elders and celebrate the land where he had once experienced the naïve liberty of a boy. He, too, dangled a carrot, one that was steeped in his signature strengths and most closely held values to make it even tastier.

Geralyn Lucas got herself through the trials of her cancer treatment by dangling a carrot called motherhood. The hair loss, the vomiting, the terror—in her mind, the point of it all was to get her eggs safely to the other side. She had a choice. She might just as easily have felt filled with grief and loss at the very thought of motherhood. But instead she used this fantasy to give purpose and meaning to her suffering; dangling a carrot became an antidote to the senselessness of her cancer. This is essentially rosewashing something that hasn't happened yet, savoring it in advance.

Many of us wouldn't dare to go there. We're too prone to generalizing, personalizing, and catastrophizing to believe that anything good could ever happen to us again. From this spiral of negativity, it seems that the current crisis will last forever, that it will take over our whole lives. Obviously, this kind of pessimistic spiral is not congruent with losing yourself in all that glowy, orange carrotyness of your dreams. Dangling a carrot would be too painful: our inner Moodith would mock us for our hopefulness, and we would listen. After all, what's the point of torturing yourself with your most poignant longings?

The reality is that the longing is there anyway. Imprisoned for more than twenty years, Mandela must have craved the green hills of his childhood; Geralyn Lucas must have wanted a baby so badly she was frantic with the desire—especially because her doctors were telling her it couldn't happen. You have a choice: either you mentally discipline yourself to believe that someday the carrot will be yours, which serves as motivation, or the very same carrot (the same hometown, the same baby, the same auditorium) is a torture to you.

Resilient people insist on the rosewashing, even when it seems almost delusional. They convince themselves—despite considerable evidence to the contrary—that they will have the things they most desire in the future and they use that longing to tempt them through the tough times.

Resilience Skill #5: Community

WE HAVE DISCUSSED THE RESILIENCE SKILLS of flexibility, accountability, efficacy, and rosewashing. The final resilience skill we will discuss is community. Resilient people know they can't go it alone; their social safety net is a part of their daily life as well as their investment in the future.

We are all social animals, part of a global community. *We need other people.* And life is much, much easier and richer if we can see the opportunities for support that other people offer and feel comfortable utilizing that support.

But many of us who have been stung by trauma have also been stung by the people in our lives who let us down, failed to help, or otherwise fell short. So we struggle with trust.

In some cases, the people in our lives perpetrated the trauma themselves. Many survivors, especially those who have lived in abusive situations, have been taught by their experiences to be "people pleasers," forgoing their own needs in favor of those of others. So it may feel dangerous or unwise to lean on anyone else. Asking for help can make us feel like a burden. We don't anticipate that others may enjoy helping us, often because we have been lifelong victims of inadequate nurturing or because we have been sorely disappointed by those we needed in the past.

We don't always feel inclined to gather people together to help us through. Instead, we default to a negative position, expecting that people will fail us or that they'll reject us because we're unworthy of support. The threat of this disappointment, and all that it would imply about us, would be so emotionally devastating that it's not worth asking.

Add to that the sense of shame that cloaks so many of our traumas, and it becomes even harder to reach out to others when we feel vulnerable and trauma-y. Instead, we focus on hiding, putting up a front that we feel normal and that everything's okay. Clearly though, this stance is not conducive to honest relationships. If our friends and family don't know that we are suffering, how can they possibly help?

Learning to break these habits and to rely on others is an extremely important resilience trait, and it's crucial that we learn to approach it with the expectation of success. So in this chapter, we'll try on the social networking skills of some resilient survivors.

The Argument for Extroversion

More money, a bigger house, higher-achieving kids—these are all things people might tell you will make them happier and more satisfied. But in fact, once basic needs are met, there's very little correlation between money and happiness.

So what traits really are associated with happiness? Apparently, some of the most robust happiness predictors have their roots in our social interactions and our interdependence on others. You might be thinking, "Good for the extroverts, but I've always been shy." But there's considerable and compelling evidence to suggest that you should give extroversion a chance, even if you don't naturally trend toward it. In 2002, researchers asked introverts and extroverts to go out and do a range of activities while recording their moods. At the end of the three-week period, they found that *both groups* were happiest doing things that were extroverted.

If the exercises in this chapter are challenging, remember that the permatrauma mind paints an inaccurate picture of the world. The assumption that people are out for themselves, or that they won't want to help, comes courtesy of Moodith. But resilient survivors default to a positive position—they assume the best and anticipate their own success.

This chapter will help you experience what it's like when you assume the best of people. How might you hone your emotional intelligence so as to best match the people in your life to your various and specific needs for support? How might you become more aware of your effect on people so that you don't wear your support networks out? What would happen if you were able to drop the "I've got everything under control" act and allow people to know the imperfect mixed bag that you really are?

If you can do this, you will learn what resilient survivors know— that the feeling of being part of a community or tribe is a mighty antidote to the shame and isolation you may have been feeling. It's time to see how much better life can be when you have the courage to put yourself out there.

The Problem with Black-and-White Thinking

Black-and-white thinking is common in people who have been victims of interpersonal violence early in life.

When we are small, we have not yet internalized a sense of morality; we're still honing our discernment about what separates a "good" from a "bad" person. Fairy tales and comic strips feed this by offering up a steady diet of good guys and bad guys; if you haven't noticed, there's not a great deal of subtle character shading in your average Disney movie.

As we grow older, we're more able to recognize and embrace truths about human nature that are a little more complex. People, as most adults know, can sometimes behave in contradictory ways. Maybe your father was both a rageful alcoholic *and* a dutiful provider, hardworking and loyal to his family. Maybe your wife cheated and is an untrustworthy mate but she is *also* a loving and responsible mother. Maybe your friend is both a great listener *and* incredibly financially irresponsible.

When a trauma happens in childhood, we don't quite make it to this stage of development. Instead, we have a tendency to get stuck in black-and-white thinking: we see good guys and bad guys, without a whole lot of gray in between.

The resilient neither idealize nor demonize other people, but instead accept that all people (and things) have a mix of good and bad traits. Their ability to do this is one of the reasons they're so successful at relationships. This might seem quite minor to you, but it winds up having a profound effect both on how we interact with others as well as on how we feel about ourselves.

After all, if everyone is either good or bad, then you must see yourself the same way, right? Many trauma survivors are consumed by the need to maintain a façade of perfection. Much of the chronic interpersonal pathology of trauma victims comes from either shamefully hiding our bad stuff from others or from feeling that we have to overcompensate for our perceived flaws, lest the people in our lives discover the truth. This feeds Moodith, who's only too happy to perch on your shoulder, personalizing, generalizing, and catastrophizing away, using your character flaws as evidence that you're messed up and destined to mess up your whole life.

Perfectionism is nothing more than a life sentence of finding that we always fall short—and so does everyone else around us.

And it's a fundamentally isolated position. If you're supposed to be perfect, then it's very difficult to ask for help, isn't it? On the other hand, if you embrace the good and bad in other people and accept that you are also a realistic amalgam of strengths and weaknesses, then it's much easier to be vulnerable with someone else and to believe that the people in your life will still love you and respect you and treasure you, even if you're flawed, as all of us are. This brings a level of authenticity to your relationships that would otherwise be lost.

When you live your life pretending to be what you think you should be, or what you think others want you to be, you throw a real monkey wrench into your ability to love and be loved. You always feel like a fraud: how can you relax around other people when you think they like you under false pretenses? Whereas if you're willing *not* to be the golden child, but to let people see you—the real you, warts and all—you can achieve true intimacy.

Perfectionism, idealization, and black-and-white thinking are the enemies of intimacy.

Resilient people are able to reach out to and rely on others because they have rosewashed expectations of how others will experience them.

Expecting the Best

The resilient not only anticipate that people will see the best in them, but they see the best in others.

This is hard not just for people with antitrust trauma-preserving assumptions, but also for people whose family or culture supported the belief that others can't be trusted. "Your closest friends will stab you in the back." "Trust no one." "You'll never fit in." If such belief systems were a part of the family or social culture in which you were raised, or if trauma left you with these beliefs, cultivating a social network in the interest of becoming more resilient may not come easily. But I would like you to consider the possibility that people out there are considerably kinder and gentler than you are anticipating.

I am indebted to my friend Christina for opening my eyes to this. Christina has a tendency to see the best in people and has always befriended people that the rest of us might not have been attracted to—the shy and awkward, the badly behaved, and the unlikable. She has a gift for seeing through to the talents and dreams and wonderful attributes in all of us and is vocal in her recognition and appreciation of those wonderful traits. When someone behaves badly, she interprets their behavior in a forgiving psychological context that makes their actions understandable. And because she sees the best in people, she inspires the best in them.

Many saw Andy as playboy, but Christina saw a decent but insecure guy misguidedly flaunting his sexuality. She treated him like a gentleman and in her presence, he acted like one. Everyone in the building saw Nadia as a stingy slumlord, but Christina saw a weary hardworking immigrant who felt her tenants took her property for granted. She treated Nadia with gratitude and respect and the landlady revealed a warm nurturing side no one would have guessed existed.

To this day, Christina is surrounded by an amazing array of people and not surprisingly, she has an amazing network of support. Resilient people often have this kind of social safety net.

Constructing a social safety net is something that you simply cannot do while expecting the worst of people. Rather it comes from seeing in people the best version of themselves and allowing them to rise to the occasion. Resilient people don't just rosewash the events in their lives, they rosewash *people,* too.

Just as Moodith tries to protect us from repeated trauma, trauma survivors often make inaccurate generalizations about people that stem from a dark place. We're guarded, lest others take advantage. We anticipate meanness or selfishness, or interpret other people's shyness as haughtiness. An interpersonal paranoia of sorts is quite common in people who have been through traumas both big and small. When you've been badly burned by others you are at risk of living the rest of your life projecting a lot of ugly onto undeserving folks. And these expectations become self-fulfilling prophecies.

TRY THIS: FINDING THE BEST

In this exercise, you will be asked to try on some of Christina's skills for yourself.

To begin, make a list of the five human interpersonal traits that you most admire and value in people.

Perhaps you can complete the sentence, "The trait that is most important to me in a caregiver or nurturer is _____." (Loyalty, honesty, kindness—whatever you'd be looking for in an ideal mate, parent, therapist, or pastor.)

Pick the most important one to you. You will look for evidence of this trait in people throughout the day; your goal is to find as many examples as you possibly can.

Do whatever you have to do to motivate yourself to hunt for evidence that these traits exist in people all around you. Make a contest in which you're rewarded with $100 every time you find a person demonstrating this trait. Imagine a competition: if you don't find one person an hour, you won't make enough money to finish the "race."

What Makes a Safety Net Strong?

In chapter 10 I asked you to "stop feeding your monsters" by limiting your exposure to toxic people. Resilient people don't surround themselves with pessimists or people who burst their bubble, who bring them down or otherwise fail to help them be their best.

Indeed, they take it one step farther: they make a point of surrounding themselves with people who nourish them spiritually and emotionally, people who embody the traits they want to cultivate in themselves, and those whose values they admire. They invite relationships with people who allow them to be the best version of themselves.

One of the most powerful resilience traits associated with the success of at-risk children is their ability to find a mentor. The kids who seek out positive people and reel them in are the ones most likely to be able to rise above their circumstances. Resilient kids and adults alike surround themselves with boosters, with people who have positive energy and an optimistic attitude.

> **The people we spend time with are strong predictors of our mood and outlook.**

Are you choosing to surround yourself with people who make you feel good? Do the people in your life help you to model the behaviors you are trying to acquire or need to grow?

Accepting Support

Resilient people don't just build effective social networks; they *use* them. They are able to receive emotional comfort and concrete help from others. They are able to ask for assistance and can articulate—in a concrete way—what they need.

When a friend asks a resilient survivor, "What can I do to help?" a resilient survivor does not say, "Nothing, thank you, I'll be fine. Don't worry about it." The resilient survivor says, "Thanks for asking; I'm so glad you're here. *This* is what I need." (Someone to walk my dog, a casserole for the kids, some cash to tide me over.) When a trauma strikes a resilient survivor, they rally the troops and get everyone involved in getting them through it. This is not just a coping strategy that resilient people employ in times of crisis; it is how they live their lives.

> **Know what you need, and ask for it directly, with the expectation that the answer will be yes.**

Many survivors at the time of their trauma had to go it alone. Asking for help exposes us to the humiliation of seeming needy or weak; we feel that people are more likely to get behind us emotionally if we appear brave. But this stoicism starves us of the support we need and cheats the people who love us of the opportunity to help.

Unfortunately, when you start the race, you don't know how it's going to turn out; none of us do. But if you don't invite people to watch you run, no one will be there cheering at the finish line, and no one will be there to scoop you up if you wipe out halfway. This is true not just of your race but also of your chemo, your divorce, your trial, the anniversary of your trauma. Are you a person who keeps others abreast of the challenges you are dealing with? Are you inclined to bring people along on your journey?

Of course, in order to ask for help, we have to believe that help will be forthcoming. We have to believe that exposing this soft underbelly will not incite people to attack us or judge us, but to help.

And since in the midst of a trauma we don't always see clearly what would help, it pays to practice during peacetime.

I often invite my patients to float a test balloon by asking people for just a little bit of help. Borrow two dollars for a cup of coffee from a colleague you don't know very well; ask a neighbor for a corkscrew or a hammer. These aren't major commitments; they're more like conversation starters. Conversely, offer to help someone else; reach up and get the item off the top shelf for someone who's shorter than you are, even before they ask. It feels good to help, right? So why are we so inclined to anticipate that others will feel put upon or resentful if they are asked to help us?

TRY THIS: WHAT DO YOU BRING TO THE TABLE?

Because trauma survivors have so much trouble imagining that anyone might want to help them, it behooves us to pause to examine why someone would. Relationships aren't all about "What's in it for me?" but it can be illuminating to think seriously about what *we* bring to the table, and what *we* have to offer, in the interest of seeing what the experience of caring for us might feel like to others.

Make two columns. In the first, list all the ways that you might support someone in your life if they were in need. List everything you can think of that would compel someone to reach out to you for support. Why might someone want to be in your life? Because you're funny? Because you're a good listener and a loyal friend? Because you're a lawyer, and everyone needs legal advice sometimes?

In the next column, make a list of what you need to get from others, what you hope that other people in your life can provide because you're not so good at getting it for yourself. This column requires us to really delve deep. It's hard to look at our own shortcomings, but less hard if we anticipate that there will be others in our community of friends who will be able to fill those gaps for us. Maybe you don't have a family, so you need a strong tribe of friends who make you feel like you're a part of theirs. Maybe you're shy and ill at ease in social situations, so you like it when your friends are outgoing and engineer social opportunities for you. Are you someone who is poorly organized, who needs help with budgeting or staying on top of household maintenance? Are you a working single mom whose child would be lonely if not for your neighbor's bustling brood?

You'll notice from my examples that I'm asking you to be quite candid with yourself. I want you to list the good, the bad, and the ugly; no one is going to see this but you.

When you view these lists side by side, how do you feel about the balance of give and take? Are you comfortable with the entries in column two, or would you be ashamed to share them with someone else? Are they things you think you should be able to provide for yourself but can't?

Take a moment to think about how effective you've been in securing these things for yourself in the past. Have you been able to get your needs met? If so, how? If you're taking more than you have to give in certain areas, call yourself on it; that's a valid thing for you to work on. But I hope that your column A shows you that there are lots of ways that you can offer help and support to someone else in need.

If there are holes in your list—areas in which you might need support you aren't getting from the people you currently know—it might be time to fill in some of those gaps. There is no reason to feel guilty about cultivating friendships in terms of what people can offer you in times of crisis, especially when what you're offering is a two-way street. The woman next door with the bustling brood of kids might not mind your child hanging out after school every day because she is so grateful for the way you always troubleshoot her computer problems, set up her DVR, or know what's ailing her car.

We thrive when we know we have a safety net; knowing that we are surrounded by a group of people with diverse talents and abilities and gifts is precisely what being part of a community is. And part of the way that we earn our place in a social network is by knowing what we have to offer—what we bring to the table, in both good times and bad—and sharing those things liberally.

The Importance of a Diversified Safety Net

It's never a good plan to have only one savior, which is why resilient people create a *network* of mentorship, friendship, and support.

First of all, everyone has different strengths. If you get into a financial pickle, you're, of course, going to want help from someone practical and good with numbers. But it might also be helpful to be able to talk to someone compassionate and empathic who will understand how you got into this mess and who won't judge you for it. It's rare to get all your needs met in a crisis by the same person. The more people you have, the more strengths you will have to draw on.

It also means that, even if someone very important turns out to be a disappointment, you've got other people to fall back on. Expecting too much from one person is one of the reasons that trauma is often very destructive to marriages and other intimate relationships. It's not uncommon for a spouse or partner to react inappropriately or inadequately to their partner's trauma. One way to relieve some of this pressure is to make sure that you'll have several sources of various types of support.

Taking Stock

Great social networkers know what each of their friends will be able to do—and what they won't be able to do.

When my patient Eleanor's husband was in a terrible accident, her first reflexive impulse was to notify everyone. She didn't know how they could help, or if they could help, but her first instinct was to reach out. And it paid off. Her next-door neighbor had plans that night, but she told her babysitter to order extra pizza because Eleanor's kids might be staying over. Her colleague made arrangements to get Eleanor out of the presentation they were giving the following day at work. Her sister was stuck at work but asked her own dog walker to take her spare key and walk Eleanor's dogs. Her friend Bette was dating a doctor, and she offered his services to help "translate" the information Eleanor was getting from her husband's medical team.

In the end, Eleanor didn't need any of the help or services that her support net was offering. But that night in bed, she imagined herself on a trapeze, with her frazzled emotions a little bit out of control, and she felt blessed to have her friends gathered beneath her, arms interlinked, to provide her with a tightly woven safety net. No matter what happened, she felt, they would cushion her fall.

This is how social networking confers resilience. Just by making a series of phone calls, Eleanor not only got herself a whole wealth of practical support—child care, dog walking, medical advice—but she reassured herself at a difficult time that she and her husband were loved and supported in the world. As you might imagine, there is a tremendous amount of comfort to be taken from knowing that you are part of a community and that people are there to do the things that you cannot do.

One of the things I found interesting about this story is that practically everyone who offered something to Eleanor had some limitation—some "no" within the "yes"—that she very well might have read as a rejection. Her neighbor had plans; her sister had to work. This could have made Eleanor feel like a burden or imposition. Conversely, she could have concluded that she and her husband weren't important enough to warrant that her sister find a sub or her neighbor cancel her evening plans. But because Eleanor was wearing rose-colored glasses and not trauma-colored ones, she gladly took what her friends and neighbors were offering instead of focusing on what they couldn't. She rosewashed the situation and saw the best in them.

TRY THIS: WHO CAN HELP YOU—AND HOW?

Trauma survivors go to great lengths trying to protect themselves in ways that often don't really help. I am not an advocate of living in fear. I would discourage anyone from setting up a bunker in their basement in case of attack, and for the most part you will notice that my goal is to help you *not* live your life looking over your shoulder and preparing for the worst. But in the case of building a social safety net, planning ahead is a good thing. Since crises big and small occur in life with regularity, I think it pays to take inventory of what your social needs would be and stock your social circle with people who can support you, just as you would stock a bunker in your basement.

Imagine that a crisis is going to hit tomorrow. Fold a paper in thirds, to make three columns.

What do you anticipate your needs would be? List them down the left side of a piece of paper. These should range from the practical (someone to help with child and pet care, someone to take you to doctors' appointments) to the emotional (someone to be your advocate, someone who could tolerate you being sad and scared and who would let you cry, someone who could make you laugh and give you some perspective).

Down the middle of the paper, list all the people in your life who might be able to support you. (They don't have to line up or be matched in terms of who can provide what support. For now, just make the list.)

As you do this exercise, reach to imagine people at their best. Don't allow Moodith to get in the way of the people you list or what you would ask of them. Assume that everyone on the list has several things they could potentially contribute and list names freely and generously.

Now draw a line from each need to any and every person who might be able to help you with it. When you finish, go back to the first column, and see which items don't have someone to cover them. Try to think of resources that will help you cover everything. Add to your list organizations that might be of help, as well as people you don't know particularly well but who might just have some form of support.

Now it's time to fill the right-hand column on your paper. Whereas the first column was a potentially frightening account of your unmet needs, the third column should be a confidence booster. This column helps you see how much support you actually have, including the fact that you may have several backups for certain needs. In this column, you will write *in concrete terms* what each person or organization could do for you.

Maybe the woman next door who has agoraphobia and never leaves her house is not the person to ask to accompany you to the hospital, but she may be a good candidate to take care of your cat. Maybe your glamorous college roommate doesn't know what to do with your kids but knows tons of doctors and lawyers who would be good sources of information in a crisis.

And after you've completed this, if there are still holes in your support network, at least now you know what those holes are, and you can make it a priority over the next few months to fill them. Make brownies and drop them off at a neighbor's house, or make a lunch date with the head of another department.

After all, if resilience is something that we value and are willing to work toward—like fitness or a savings safety net—then this exercise is like taking stock of our net worth, only what we're looking at here is support equity. If we have left ourselves vulnerable in some way, then the time to fix it is now, before a crisis hits.

What Effect Do You Have on Your Support Network?

One of my patients came in to my office complaining about her friends. "Since the divorce, I need them more than ever. But I just don't feel like anyone is there for me."

It wasn't hard to figure out why Faye's friends were bailing on her. She was wearing them out! First of all, every conversation revolved around her, and every one was a bigger bummer than the last: her ex was vindictive, her lawyer was an idiot, her other friends never failed to let her down, her in-laws had taken his side. The litany of betrayals and disappointments never ended, and there was no room for any good news or joy in the friendship; you certainly couldn't tell Faye what a great weekend you'd had without hearing how lucky you were to have a boyfriend.

I'm sure that her friends felt bad about blowing her off, but after six months of listening sympathetically and commiserating, I can't really blame them for letting her calls go to voice mail. And yet, Faye had no idea that the way she was coping was interfering with her ability to get her needs met.

If you're going to cultivate and use your social network effectively, you must take accountability for your own behavior. What is your emotional effect on others? Do you make others feel empowered by helping you, or do you wear them out with your hopelessness and your need to relate stories of how you were victimized? Do you make others distrust you with all your talk of revenge, lawsuits, and vigilante justice? These are important things to know.

Resilient people pause to reflect on how they affect others.

Trauma is intimidating to people; our friends are often desperately afraid that they're going to say or do the wrong thing. What things can you do to make it easy for others to help you?

Shari's mother passed away and the whole synagogue turned out for the funeral. But the mood was tense, with people lining up to offer self-conscious condolences, until Shari broke the ice with a few funny comments about the irony of everyone's sunglasses on a day so overcast. It reminded everyone that despite the black garb Shari was still herself and it gave others permission to be themselves. Stiff handshakes gave way to warm embraces and familiar dialogue. Humor, it turns out, is one of the tricks of the trade that many resilient survivors use so as not to wear out their supports.

When you are serious and sad, you set the tone. When you are hopeless, others feel it is disrespectful *not* to mirror your emotions. They might feel that telling you about something funny they saw on late-night TV would trivialize your feelings or demean what you've gone through. But sometimes the best thing that could happen would be for someone *not* to allow you to stay in your depressed state. Using humor gives people permission to not be so gloomy around you.

Incidentally, humor also has a normalizing effect on the *person making the joke.* When we allow ourselves to spiral into despair we start thinking like victims, forgetting that we have options. When we begin to feel helpless, we stop being able to problem-solve or to see our way out of the bind we're in. But humor reintroduces us to the noncrisis aspects of our personality and to the coping skills we forget about in times of crisis.

> **When we are being funny, we tap into the resources of an alternate persona within ourselves, a persona that has a perspective that the victim in you does not have.**

Using humor takes you out of victim mode and helps others support you.

Sometimes it doesn't feel like there's anything to laugh at. But when you look at resilient survivors, you will be amazed to find that even when the circumstances are grim they manage to find the irony, crack a joke, or in some other way use humor to lend perspective.

One of my patients in the midst of her cancer treatment joked, "Finally, after years of dieting, I'm a size six!" Another patient of mine, a paramedic who worked at Ground Zero, quipped, "For years I saved lives and no one thought I was a hero. Then 9/11 happened and I saved no one, but suddenly I'm a hero." Victor Frankl, in his book *Man's Search for Meaning,* actually makes a joke *about the showers at Auschwitz.* I feel pretty comfortable stating that there has never been anything less funny in the entire history of the world than the showers at Auschwitz.

Humor makes it easier for people to tolerate being with you when you're going through something heavy. Like Faye, whose bitterness and anger after her divorce alienated her from her support networks, we sometimes (without meaning to) drive people away precisely when we need them most.

On hospital rounds in medical school, I was disturbed to observe how little time was spent in the room of the depressed cancer patient and how much longer we lingered with the woman across the hall who had a whole routine about how easy chemo had made it to style her hair. While the depressed patient likely needed our attention more, it was the woman with the wig jokes who got the support. Her cancer comedy routine served several purposes. It gave her a break from her own tension and intensity, it gave us permission to mirror her light affect, and it also drew people near. Her humor did not negate or make light of her problem, but rather it helped her build a social safety net of support.

When you are in crisis, do you know—emotionally speaking— what you need? Do you need empathy, a sounding board, a dose of reality, a place to safely cry? Do you need someone who will listen without trying to fix things and without giving you the sense that you're being self-indulgent? Do you need someone to jump in and take over?

How do you go about getting those needs met? Is this method usually effective? There are many ways that your behavior can encourage people to give you what you need. Are yours healthy? Does your way of needing help make others feel gratified, or does it make them feel put-upon?

The Power of Others

Resilient survivors know that they need each other. They embrace the concept of community; they embrace the concept of mutuality. These are traits worth emulating. And you can do that only by harvesting evidence that good people are out there and want to help.

My own attitude toward people changed radically when I became a psychiatrist. I had a one-way-mirror perspective on people's lives, one that permitted me to peer deeply into people's lives while remaining unseen myself. And the things my patients shared about themselves defied all my expectations.

I met people filled with kindness, people who were devoted to their family members through the worst of times, people who enjoyed giving and who did so without feeling burdened, people who considered it an honor to be asked to help. I met people who cared deeply about their spouses, their children, their social causes, and the quality and value of their work. I found people impressively articulate and discovered that many of them were capable of truly tremendous acts of empathy and compassion. I met people who were ready to fight for justice, to take on the system, and who expected to win. I saw people struggling through extraordinary difficulties with enormous dignity.

Listening to these people opened my eyes. Certainly it was not possible that it was just my patients who were these loving, courageous, honorable people. Maybe there was a world full of people out there like this that I had been neglecting to notice while wearing my trauma-colored glasses and anticipating the worst. I began to harvest evidence of goodness, of compassion, of generosity of spirit, and of community. And I was richly rewarded for that work. I went from being a person who saw the worst in people to finding that people in general exceeded my expectations. In fact, it's possible that this appreciation for interpersonal connection and the value of community has been the biggest gift of my trauma.

Now, you may find yourself doubting that your outcomes will be as successful as the examples that I give. You may find yourself feeling a lack of self-efficacy, worrying that even if you reach out to others, you won't be effective in gathering the support you need. If these doubts arise, remind yourself that you have been living in permatrauma and that your expectations may be artificially discolored.

If you ask something of someone, or reach out to someone or share with someone, and they don't give you the response you had hoped for, that's their problem, not yours. Remember the trick you employed in the self-efficacy chapter: take credit for what goes well, place blame for what goes badly on external factors. There are bad people out there and selfish people and nasty people. But mostly, there are good, kind, decent, caring people who want to help. Go looking for them, and you will find them.

PART III | Changing How You Feel

| 15 |

Finding Your Stones
How to Replace the Bad with the Good

IN EARLIER CHAPTERS I DESCRIBED a metaphor for getting past your past. I referred to a vase full of liquid into which you drop stones in order to displace the habitual negativity that otherwise fills the vase. For the remainder of the book we will be making this metaphor concrete.

The premise of the vase full of stones is that there is a finite amount of emotion in a day. Because most of us are in the habit of negative thinking, fluid just drips, drips, drips into the vase, filling it to the brim without any effort or awareness on our part. This leaves us feeling lousy without realizing why.

There are two ways to counteract this habitual negativism. You can work at having less bad stuff or you can work at having more good stuff. We are going to pursue both methods.

Some stones will help you catch yourself when you are allowing negativity, pessimism, and victim thinking into your life, so you can slow the flow of liquid into your vase. Other stones will help you "displace" that negativity much as a real stone will overflow its volume's worth of fluid out of a vase.

If you plunk enough good-feeling stones into a container full of bad-feeling liquid, eventually most of that liquid will overflow. Similarly, by taking control of your thoughts and repeatedly wrangling yourself into a more positive way of thinking and feeling, these stones will displace the negativity and bad feelings in your day, replacing them with healthier thoughts and emotions. As you learn new skills and create new habits, your vase will fill with stones representing good-feeling, happy emotions and other essential ones, like healthy entitlement, or appropriate anger, or forgiveness.

Throughout your day you will have many opportunities to cultivate new habits by **working these stones.** But also, when you find yourself feeling badly or when your trauma is triggered, you can reach for them as a coping skill to try to feel better. The concepts from parts I and II of this book will form the theoretical basis for these stones.

> **I encourage you to think of these stones as a kind of holistic pillbox.**

Your selection of stones offers you the opportunity to get yourself a "dose" of the kind of emotions, thoughts, and coping skills that help resilient survivors fight back when their demons rear their ugly heads.

By the end of the book you will have three stones that represent ways to stop the flow of negative thinking and seven stones to use to displace habitual negativity with healthier, more positive, more optimistic thoughts, emotions, and coping skills. Your stones will be tailored to your needs and experiences given who you are and what you went through. They will be designed to be antidotes to the very type of victim thinking that plagues you. The goal will be to eliminate as much of your take-home trauma as possible.

Are they actual stones? Yes! In my practice and in my life, I have collected beautiful polished rocks, smooth river stones, and hefty semiprecious nuggets in a variety of shapes and sizes and colors. Although if you have a particular talisman or amulet, a shell or a button that symbolically crystallizes the exercise you are working on, you may certainly feel free to use that object instead. But there's a reason I personally use stones and encourage my patients to do so as well.

For centuries humans have been using touchstones as a means to relax themselves, remind themselves, and protect themselves. There is something about the heft of a stone in your hand, the way our fingers naturally explore and revisit the shape, the way its ancient and complex molecular structure meets our fingertips, that just feels powerful.

When I am working with a patient on a specific exercise, I offer them a basket of beautifully colored polished stones. I invite them to choose one that will then act as a symbol of that exercise. I love to watch as people rifle through the basket picking up and considering each stone, feeling and examining each one until they find the "right" one for the task at hand.

It is one thing to read about a new way of thinking, feeling, and coping, and another to integrate the resultant actions into a daily practice. The beauty of stones is that you can carry them in your pocket as a reminder. You can use a marker to write a word or symbol on your stone to remind you of the steps you need to take. But also, it is helpful to imagine plunking your stone into a vase filled to the brim with fluid and seeing the volume of liquid displaced. This image drives home the concept of being at the helm of your emotional world. Because to the extent that you are willing to "work your stones" you can fill your head and your heart with a healthy diet of emotions, an empowered way of interacting with the world, and a sense of yourself as the accomplished survivor you are.

If you adopt this practice with discipline, you won't lose your day to permatrauma. Knowing that you have a trail of bread crumbs that you can use to find your way back from feeling trauma-y makes a resilient person better able to take risks—to be vulnerable to a new friend, to push the envelope with a lover, to be emotionally accessible to their kids. It will make you better able to experience a full spectrum of emotions, and that's the way to heal and finally move forward.

How It Works

When you take an ibuprofen, you expect your headache to recede. Similarly, I'd like you to think of your stones as actions designed to deliver you to a "goal feeling."

These feelings are those that trauma victims tend to be low on—and that all survivors need more of. There's a reason we are going to create a slew of stones—some will help you more than others. So use what works, and discard what doesn't. When you feel trauma-y, you can look at your pile of stones and ask yourself: "What's going to work? What do I need right now?"

Once you get the hang of what a stone is and how to work it, you will be free to make many more on your own, with as much complexity as you would like.

My stones represent the things I know I must continually seek to fill my days with in order to have a satisfying and happy life. When I see them together, I know what makes life feel great for me. You will rarely find me without a stone or two in my pocket as a reminder of what I am cultivating in my life, what skills I am working on, what emotions I need more of.

I have, for instance, a pale green stone the color of a tender spring shoot. This is a stone I acquired when I learned I was pregnant with my daughter, because as soon as I found out that I was going to have a baby, Moodith went into overdrive. An occupational hazard of the kind of work that I do is that I hear about a lot of horrible stuff, and to stay with the metaphor, that can increase the flow of liquid into my vase. The idea of bringing a vulnerable new baby into what was feeling like a very harsh world suddenly didn't seem like such a good idea. I was not in an emotional space conducive to raising a child who believed in fairy tales or a young adult who would believe in her own dreams. I didn't want to be a killjoy to this new life I was bringing into the world.

My stone was an anticynicism stone. Every time I reached into my pocket, it was a literal reminder not to stomp on the grass. Working this stone entailed harvesting evidence that the world was not the trauma-riddled painful place I sometimes can feel that it is, and I worked it hard by finding evidence every day and everywhere that there is ample room in the world for tender, innocent things to thrive.

I sought proof—and found it—in people and things and nature. I made playlists that celebrated innocence. I perused Web sites that acknowledged unsolicited acts of kindness. I harvested evidence of all the kids around me living happy, safe lives. In my heart was a balance scale that had temporarily tipped toward evil and I heaped evidence on the opposite side until the cynicism and fear were displaced and the scale tipped back the other way.

The spring-green color of this stone reminded me of what it meant, but most of my stones have a word or symbol on them, often one that would be cryptic or obscure to anyone else looking at them. The more specific the symbol, the more powerful and personalized it is. And while I am happy to share some of my stones with you, the content of them is as close to my soul as anything gets. The symbols I create make me feel like I am speaking my own special language to myself.

I will speak of "working your stones" in a crisis as well as in noncrisis times. It is important to practice using them at times when you are feeling fine so that you can hone your skills and remember how to use them when you need them. I have used them so often that the actions associated with them—and the relief they give me—have become second nature to me. When I backslide or find myself ruminating, I select a powerful one and work it hard, knowing I am off-kilter and need to take this "medicine" to feel well again.

Just as trauma has been a constant character in your life since it occurred, so must your stones now become a constant, talismans that you can carry with you (metaphorically or physically) to have at your disposal whether you're at a crowded party or walking along on a beach.

Together, my vase of stones is a work of art—it is the work of my life, my life's greatest triumphs. They are a daily reminder that someone tried to take away the gift of my life, and for a time I conspired to do the same. But I took life back, pebble by pebble, and so can you.

What Makes a Good Stone?

The best stones are highly ritualized, reliable, symbolic, portable, and associated with a specific action. So, as you go through the process of creating these stones, ask yourself:

Does it tell you what to do (and not just what to think)?

If simply carrying a stone with "hope" written on it could really restore your hope, then you wouldn't need this book. A stone has to have an action associated with it, something easy to remember and execute, even if you are feeling disinclined and trauma-y.

Is it portable?

It has to be convenient. Will you be able to work your stone in traffic, at work, in the middle of the night? In general, trauma-y feelings don't creep up on you under perfect conditions—in your meditation room, for instance. They catch you off guard at the movies, in a meeting, at Thanksgiving dinner. If you can't find a way to work your stone anywhere, then it won't be as useful to you as you need it to be.

Does it resonate with your core values and celebrate the car behind your dent?

Stones are meant to redirect your emotions and help you create and achieve substitute emotions to replace the bad and unproductive ones. But in order to be effective, a stone needs to be more than just a distraction. Distraction is important. But if you're not distracting yourself in a compelling way, it's not going to work; instead, you'll find yourself still feeling terrible while listlessly leafing through a magazine. In order to create a stone that packs a punch, try to tailor it to reflect your signature strengths and core values.

Different Ways to Work Your Stones

As you'll see, stones should be worked in two different ways: as a *maintenance* stone, and *in case of emergency.*

Maintenance stones are like vitamins. Vitamins are not nutrients in and of themselves; technically, they facilitate the chemical reactions necessary to metabolize nutrients. But your body can't function without them, so we need to stockpile them. When we speak of working a stone in a maintenance way, I mean that you are working that stone daily and habitually, not because you are feeling trauma-y, but because it helps you think and live in a less traumatized or victimized way. It helps get you in the habit of positive, optimistic, empowered thinking, which would make anyone feel better.

With this practice, when the day comes that you find yourself feeling lousy—say a crisis challenges your coping skills or something triggers your trauma—you have those skills at your fingertips. Having rehearsed how to work a stone on an ordinary day can prove to be a godsend when you are feeling out of control. When you are feeling depressed, stressed, and miserable, you need stones that can be reliably counted on to splash a substantial volume of negativity out of your vase. These emergency stones are your first-aid toolkit, your bread crumb trail back from feeling awful.

Creating Your Stones

Learning to feel differently means changing some long-standing habits. Doing so will require repetition. Ritualizing your approach to working a stone ensures you get the most juice out of the process and helps you savor your improvement.

When you work a stone, follow these five steps every time:

1. Recognize when you are feeling trauma-y: Your blue list of permatrauma feelings will be useful here. It's essential to recognize your trauma feelings so that when they hit you, you can move swiftly into action.

2. Reach for and work a stone: We will put together ten highly personalized stones for you over the course of this chapter, so that you have a variety of options to reach for. By the end of the book you will have the actions associated with each stone mapped out, actions that will reliably deliver you to a target emotion.

3. Acknowledge the water you've displaced: Some stones work better than others, and some days it's easier to put them into action than others, so every time you work a stone, pause to evaluate its effect. Note the change in your emotional state before and after the exercise. Do you feel better? Relieved? Healthier? More in control? Picture the vase filled with liquid in your mind. Did the stone you plunked in there displace a lot of fluid? Are you getting better at working the stone?

4. Pat yourself on the back for moving from the passive to the active, and note that acquiring this skill increases your resilience for the future: You were willing *not* to get stuck in a negative or unpleasant emotional state, proving that you're not subject to your emotions but are taking charge of them. There is a tremendous amount of pride to be taken in the fact that it occurred to you to reach for a stone instead of just feeling trauma-y—this is a great advancement in itself. It is these small moments that differentiate the version of you that caused you so much pain from the version of you that resembles your heroes. Take the time to pat yourself on the back.

The self-awareness and coping skills you have learned in this book give you resilience, and that means that you can embark courageously on the journey of life knowing that you'll be able to cope, no matter what happens. Take a moment to observe the resilience skills you employed in working your stone. Did you turn to others for support? Did you rosewash? Note that these skills not only work in the present, but will work for you in the future.

5. Savor: Later in the day, make sure to reflect on the fact that you can create pleasure and other good feelings in your current world, and that you are in control now, even if you weren't when your trauma was occurring. Recount the times when you were able to forgo emotional junk food in favor of emotional soul food. Bask in your increased sense of efficacy, power, pleasure, and pride. Share your successes with those in your social network who are likely to appreciate what they mean and who will celebrate how far you've come. (For a printable, wallet-sized reminder of the steps involved with working a stone, please visit aliciasalzer.com.)

The First Three Stones: The Freebies

The first three stones we are going to create are what I call "freebie" stones. These stones require little to no action—except catching yourself in a previously injurious behavior and deciding not to do it. These are the three stones designed to curb the flow of liquid into your vase.

In earlier chapters we discussed some habitual ways of thinking that are injurious to trauma survivors. Chances are, these are things you didn't even know you were doing. And even if you gain nothing else from this book, you'll benefit greatly if you've learned to catch yourself thinking in these negative ways: once you're onto yourself, it becomes very clear how much negativity permeates the course of an ordinary day and how destructive it is.

Freebie Stone #1: Your Spiraling Stone

Every one of us should have a simple stone with a spiral drawn on it to symbolize our tendency to start thinking negative thoughts and get stuck there. When you catch yourself ruminating in the car as you drive, rehashing an argument with someone where you wish you had responded differently, or predicting all day that you'll get fired because of a confrontation with your boss, you can say to yourself, "I'm spiraling," and acknowledge that this type of thinking is a form of emotional junk food. If you think this stone is a lightweight, carry it in your pocket for a day and focus on noticing a habit of negative rumination.

The spiraling stone doesn't require an action to follow up. It's monumental just to catch yourself thinking that bad outcomes are personal, pervasive, and permanent and to call yourself on the fact that your catastrophic "conclusions" are not facts. An important part of feeling well again is hurting yourself less, so when you catch yourself, you get to plunk a spiraling stone into your vase.

But make sure to do all of the five steps: Recognize that it is your own way of thinking that is perpetuating the take-home trauma. Be conscious of how much better you feel. Reward yourself for being willing to try something different. At the end of the day, pause to reflect on how many times you noticed yourself spiraling. And if you choose to work another stone to follow up, replacing those spirally feelings with a healthier snack, observe your own resilience building.

Freebie Stone #2: Your Moodith Stone

This stone can be as simple as a stone with an unhappy face on it, and it doesn't require any action other than to catch Moodith in the act. While your spiraling stone is for when you catch yourself stuck in a cognitive rut, the Moodith stone is for when you notice that buzzkill voice in your ear, talking you out of an impulse that initially felt right.

You get to plunk a Moodith stone whenever you hear your inner voice saying something like:

- Don't bother trying; you'll only fail.
- Don't bother telling; no one will believe you.
- Don't be stupid enough to fall for him; he'll only betray you.
- Don't pursue that fun activity; it's dangerous and you're asking for trouble.

Remind yourself that Moodith is a vestige of your primitive brain, misguidedly trying to protect you from a repeat of your trauma. Just recognizing this—even if you don't yet know how to substitute a kinder, more encouraging voice—is a huge step toward silencing the bad advice.

My Moodith stone has a drawing of a tiny, hideous witch on it; it reminds me of how ugly her advice makes the world. As with the spiraling stone, you may ultimately choose to follow up with one of the seven nonfreebie stones. But for now, all you have to do is note that you are changing a habit and congratulate yourself for taking charge of your thoughts in order to change how you feel.

Freebie Stone #3: Your "Stop Feeding the Monster" Stone

In every given day, there are hundreds of messages from the media, society, and our friends and families that rub salt in our wounds. You get to plunk your "stop feeding your monsters" stone whenever you acknowledge that an external factor is going to have an adverse effect on your mood or your worldview—and you say no. This stone represents the habitual negativity that you avert when you acknowledge that toxic work, toxic media, or toxic people are contributing to the water in your vase and you decide to limit these exposures in the interest of a more balanced emotional diet. In other words, this is another stone that you get simply for *not* doing something that you would have done before reading this book, as when you:

- Opt out of a movie that you know will leave you feeling trauma-y
- Commit to going to the gym each evening instead of watching the evening news, which contributes to your sense of the world being a dangerous place
- Decide not to hang with the family as they watch pay-per-view boxing because you know it will disturb you to hear everyone cheering at the violence
- Constructively limit your interactions with someone who makes you feel more "dent" than "car"

Visualize the volume of water you displaced by blocking the inevitable bad feelings that toxic influence would have resulted in. As with the other freebies, you may want to follow up with an action stone that helps you harvest good feelings. Is there an inspiring documentary about amazing overcomers that you can see instead of that violent movie? Is there a friend or family member you can reach out to who has modeled a nonvictimized way of being? Can you have coffee with someone who makes you feel more like a shiny car than the dent?

My "stop feeding the monster" stone has an octagon on it like a stop sign. Carry yours for a day and see how many opportunities life gives you to say no to influences that put you on red alert or contribute to a victimized worldview.

Now we are going to embark on the task of creating seven action stones. These necessitate that you do something differently from how you did things before.

Stone #4: Your TPA Remedy Stone

By now, you're familiar with some of the unconscious trauma-preserving assumptions that you carry, unhelpful generalizations like "men are all after one thing," or "nighttime is dangerous," or "people can't be trusted." Since the glass is simultaneously half-empty *and* half-full, our goal is not to disprove the validity of your TPA. Rather, since we know that resilient people preferentially attend to the positive, I would like you to spend some time entertaining the possibility that the opposite of your trauma-preserving assumption is *also* true. So choose one of your trauma-preserving assumptions and flip it around to create an alternative.

Here are some examples of remedies for the above TPAs:

- The vast majority of men are decent.
- Lots of great experiences are to be safely had at night.
- The world is full of trustworthy people.

You will work this stone by going out into your life and harvesting evidence to support your TPA remedy.

My pale green anticynicism stone was a TPA remedy stone. By harvesting evidence that innocent vulnerable things could thrive in the world, I was offering myself an alternative to an ugly TPA that made me fear for the safety of my unborn child.

Let's take a detailed look at how to work a TPA remedy stone.

Francesca battles a trauma-preserving assumption that men are dangerous. One afternoon, she got out of her car at a rest area and encountered some teenage boys hanging out in the parking lot being vulgar and lewd. Immediately, a sense of panic set in, and she felt endangered. This is the kind of trigger that might have left her feeling rattled all afternoon. Instead, let's follow Francesca as she works her TPA remedy stone to try to counteract the horrible feelings those teens brought up.

Step One: Recognize That You Are Feeling Trauma-y

Francesca recognized that she was feeling trauma-y—the first step. She felt scared and humiliated that mere boys could make a grown woman feel this way—emotions from her blue list. So she reached for a stone and worked it.

Francesca's TPA remedy stone, which she routinely practiced during peacetime, entailed harvesting evidence that the world is full of kind, good men. So she calmed herself down enough to approach an elderly man for directions. She took careful note of the elaborately detailed instructions he offered, the way he double-checked the directions with his wife and came back to further clarify them. She harvested his soft-spoken manner and warm eye contact—all evidence that the world is full of decent guys, if you are willing to look.

A glance at his bumper sticker told her he was a retired navy man, which added even more fuel to her fire. Here (she imagined) was a man who had subjected himself to danger in order to serve his country. Despite whatever traumas he may himself have endured, he had emerged not bitter or hardened, selfish or angry, but a true gentleman.

When you harvest, you do so with the presumption that you will find what you are looking for.

Francesca knows that the point of working this stone is to cultivate better emotions, so she would have found evidence that men are caring and good pretty much anywhere, even if she had to go on the Internet or call a friend in Spain. In this instance, Francesca was so dedicated to preferentially harvesting the positive that even if the retired navy guy hadn't been so nice, she would still have looked for the best in him and found some evidence in the interaction to prove his decency.

Francesca then took stock of her emotional status, the third step of working her stone. She compared how she felt when she first encountered the teens to how she felt after chatting with the navy man. Vulnerability had been replaced by a more comfortable feeling of being in control. Fear and humiliation had been replaced by a tender affection.

Sometimes it seems as if there are parallel universes. That day Francesca hopped from one universe, in which vulgar boys populate a dangerous world, to another inhabited by chivalrous and decent people, fellow overcomers lending each other a hand.

The fourth step is to pat yourself on the back for your increasing resilience. Francesca had good cause to feel proud of her willingness not to get stuck in a negative emotional state—even if it meant artificially engineering a situation to disprove her trauma-preserving assumption. Had she not, she would have had to get back into her car and drive in that panicky state. She would have had to tend to her children that night feeling distracted and shaken instead of feeling that she could model resilience skills for her kids. Although Francesca cannot change her trauma, she has made real progress in terms of controlling the take-home aspect of it.

And later that afternoon, Francesca might very well have let her mind wander back to those teenagers, imagining what might have happened, rekindling the trauma-y feelings she so successfully squashed earlier in the day. Instead, she did the fifth step and savored her success. She had turned a challenge into a positive experience, turned to someone for social support instead of retreating into a private place to ruminate.

You can see how much more powerful a stone is when you do all five steps. You'll do this not just for this stone, but for all of them.

Stone #5: Your Rx Emotion Stone

After a trauma, our emotional repertoire gets narrowed and we find ourselves missing a whole host of great-feeling emotions. We get careful. We retreat into a shell. Losing these emotions is one of the reasons that trauma is so very painful: these are things that made us uniquely who we are, the very core of our identity.

But, as I have said, it is often these same emotions that we mourn the loss of that wind up being our guideposts back to life. That's why in chapter 7, after we made the lost emotions list, we renamed it the Rx emotion list. Now it's time to make a stone with one of these emotions written on it and figure out how to take it back.

The concept of dosing yourself with an emotion that your soul is craving should not be an alien one. In life, we are constantly going off in search of a particular emotional experience that is not part of our daily routine. We watch the Discovery Channel to appreciate the beauty of nature, we read a great novel to experience the thrill of romance, we go out with friends after work because we know that we need to lighten up and laugh.

Go back to pages 82–83 and look at your Rx emotion list. The Rx emotions that prove to be the most powerful remedies are often the very ones that feel most lost and inaccessible. Try to choose an Rx emotion that feels like it has the power to heal the unique way that what you went through affected you. For example, if you are aware that what you went through left you feeling humiliated or ashamed, consider that your Rx emotion may be pride. Alternatively, if you are aware that what you went through left you with a sense of helplessness, perhaps the Rx emotion that will help you most is power.

So how do you go about reconnecting with a lost emotion? Sometimes a powerful memory of a time or an experience that gave you your Rx feeling is all you need to shake loose a lost emotion. Often, you can rekindle a lost emotion by reintroducing an activity you no longer pursue. But if you are feeling avoidant about the activity or are physically unable, don't be discouraged. As I have often said, my goal is not to get a jogger who was mugged in the woods back to jogging in the woods. But it's worth making it a priority to sit down and brainstorm alternate activities that might give you the same charge.

Sometimes your heart is just unwilling to budge from its stubborn position of feeling lousy, and you need to trick it into letting go and feeling better. I once worked with a group of depressed teens who felt they had good reason to feel bad—and to stay feeling bad. As an exercise in recapturing a lost emotion I had them make collages of magazine cutouts symbolizing the word "triumphant." There was a lot of grousing, but grudgingly, they cut out pictures of hikers atop mountains with their arms raised and sweepstakes winners jumping for joy. As they snipped and pasted and chatted, I could see the emotions getting under their skin. By the time they were done, they were heatedly arguing over whose collage was best, laughing and doing impersonations of the cutouts in their own collages, remembering times they felt that way. In twenty minutes they had found access to a long-buried emotion and the experience did their spirits good.

If collages aren't your thing but you need a boost to get back in touch with your lost emotion, you might try the technique discussed in chapter 11: make a playlist that captures the feeling of your Rx emotion. Consider playlist categories like pride, tenderness, sexuality, gratitude, justice, hope, grief. For any feeling that may be on your Rx emotion list, there are songs that cannot fail to transport you there. Note that not all Rx emotions are "feel-good" ones and that's okay. Some of us are numb and need to cry. Some of us feel helpless and will benefit from getting back in touch with entitled rage. (For a list of the top five Rx emotions, plus suggestions on how to access them, visit aliciasalzer.com, where you can also share how you work your Rx emotion stone.)

Music can change a fragile and jumpy mood to an empowered and brave one. It can help you go from feeling unworthy of love to knowing that you will walk away strong and find something better. Music can help us achieve subtle and complex emotions, even ones we don't quite have words for. I have a playlist of songs that give me a sense that the world is full of abundance and all is well.

But *making* that list of songs may be an even more powerful tool than listening to it. Because as you hunt for songs, you will invariably come across ones that miss the mark, yet you find so compelling that you will want to add them. You must keep asking yourself, "Is this a song that is reinforcing my trauma-preserving assumptions, or is it helping me get in touch with emotions I need more of?"

> **It is your awareness, your lack of passivity about your own mood—the making of that *choice* to pursue a different emotion—that helps.**

I would have missed out on a major teaching opportunity with my collage-making teens if we hadn't paused afterward to acknowledge the amazing feat that they had accomplished on their own behalf. Just as their exercise was not an art project per se, working your stone is much more than making a playlist. That only gets you through step 2: Reach for and work your stone. It is no small thing when you are feeling lousy to take the plunge and try something so alien as making a collage or a playlist. But to do so reflects an empowered willingness to let go of old hurts, to break an old emotional habit, and to try to feel better. So once you make that playlist, you still have steps 3 through 5 to note how much better you feel afterward, appreciate your newfound resilience, and savor it.

Stone #6: Your Distraction Stone

Sometimes when you are feeling lousy, you need to communicate, you need to process, you need to be heard. Other times, as every parent knows, the magic bullet is a distraction. The purpose of a distraction stone is to engage your attention so fully that you cannot stay focused on what was making you feel bad.

But you can't just flip the TV channel to the ball game and say you worked a distraction stone. What makes a distraction stone different from an ordinary distraction is that you are actively training your attention on something, much in the way that people meditate. Working a distraction stone requires stillness and singular focus.

The trickiest part of a distraction stone isn't coming up with something that will work for you—it's convincing yourself to use it in the heat of the moment. When you're feeling trauma-y, it is very hard to convince yourself to let go of those feelings. In fact, if someone popped up midspiral and told you, "Hey, stop ruminating and smell this flower!" you'd probably want to smack them.

I suggest that my patients explore the five senses to find their distraction stones. Not only are sensory experiences always readily at your fingertips, but they can help us make peace with our bodies. A strong sensory experience can really help you pull yourself out of a cognitive, spiraling, ruminative space or a fit of rage. If your trauma-y feelings tend to fall along the painful spectrum of depression, anxiety, grief, or bereavement, then a distraction stone featuring your senses is a great way to introduce a pleasurable counterbalance. Some suggestions follow.

A VISUAL DISTRACTION STONE

Just as video on your computer takes up more space than text files, the data transmitted by sight is some of the most densely packed sensory material you can experience. Looking at something that soothes and inspires you seems like a natural way to distract yourself. But most of us do not know how to look closely and carefully enough to actually deeply engage and distract. Imagine if I were to ask you to memorize your surroundings in preparation for a visual quiz. How many windows are there in that building? How many streetlights line the block? What color skirt is the woman on the bench wearing? This would necessitate much more attentive looking than is typical.

If you are artistic, choose something that is emotionally evocative or invites you to look deeply. Say you look outside and you notice some rippling turquoise water sparkling in the pool. To work that image as a visual distraction stone, let that image of water lead you to associations with your other four senses: the smell of the chlorine in your parents' pool, the squeaky sound of your wet finger on the vinyl raft you floated on in that pool.

Another way to work a visual image as a distraction stone is to attend to colors in your environment the way you would have to if you were mixing the perfect color on a palette and creating a painting. This approach forces a level of detailed observation that can be quite consuming. If your stone simply said "distract yourself," I'm sure you would resent it and resist it. But if you are artistically inclined or love color, an invitation to delve deeply into it may be seductive enough to help you drop your commitment to your bad mood and try something else.

A DISTRACTION STONE USING SMELL

Scent is perhaps the most evocative of all the senses. Your sense of smell is tied to the limbic system, the area of the brain responsible for memories and emotions. Its close connection to this primitive area of the brain is why smell has such a powerful ability to take us back to a place that was safe and happy.

This is not about smelling something "pretty." When you're feeling trauma-y a spritz of perfume is not the answer. Psychologically laden and *emotionally* rich smells will prove to be the most compelling distractors.

Identify a smell memory of a scent that you still have access to. While smelling that smell, make a "photo album" in your mind of all the images it evokes. List as many associations with that smell as you can.

If you don't actually have something evocative to smell, travel the above pathway in reverse: instead of using a smell to launch a memory or feeling, use a memory or an emotion to locate a smell. Recall a wonderful time or a great feeling, and replay the scene trying to recall the smells associated with that memory.

These vague, not-everyday smell memories remind us that there is continuity between where we are now and where we once were. This hardwired reminder of our old identity is a powerful refutation of the trauma-preserving assumption that we have been changed forever by what happened to us.

A TOUCH DISTRACTION STONE

Touch can be a tricky sensation for trauma survivors. If you are uncomfortable with interpersonal touch, you may be able to reintroduce yourself to it in a way that doesn't involve other people, such as through temperature or positional sense.

Focusing on the neurologic aspects of touch is a good place to start. In medical school every student learns about something called the sensory homunculus, a drawing of a weird little guy with a huge head, even huger lips and tongue, and big fingertips. The size of the body parts in the homunculus reflects the proportion of sensory cortex in the brain dedicated to feeling things from that part of the body. Your lips and tongue, then, take up the vast majority of your sensory cortex, while the skin above your navel is pretty numb (although those who have had theirs pierced might disagree).

Exploring your own sensory homunculus can be a fun and safe way to start reexperiencing touch, as well as a way to work a touch distraction stone. Close your eyes and notice how different a Q-tip feels on your knee versus your nose tip, or on your cheekbone versus your forearm. Appreciate how some parts of your body are more gifted at feeling than others.

Notice how you can reach into your pocket and differentiate a penny from a dime simply by the way it feels. How far apart do two pencil points have to be on your skin for you to be able to feel them as two distinct objects? Does this distance differ depending on the part of the body you are touching?

The amazing complexity of our ability to feel touch is a potent reminder of the many things we take for granted, including the many ways our amazing bodies are working for us—and working just fine without us ever noticing or acknowledging what they do. This is why a touch distraction stone may be just the thing if your trauma-preserving assumptions are telling you that your body is your enemy.

A TASTE DISTRACTION STONE

I'm hardly the first to observe that Americans aren't great at slowing down and enjoying and tasting our foods. We are a culture often guilty of eating our food without even focusing on it.

When we work a taste distraction stone, the goal is to focus on taste with the same degree of attention to detail that we observe in the visual realm. To try to achieve this, taste things with your eyes closed. Try eating with your nondominant hand. Use language to describe in detail what you are tasting, as if you are writing a food critique.

Compare your two favorite brands of iced tea, or diet cola, or peanut butter in a blind taste test, and see which you *actually* prefer. Appreciate subtle differences in texture and saltiness, sweetness and aftertaste. Do you like one better while it is in your mouth but the other better after you have swallowed it? You may find that when you open your eyes, you suddenly can't tell whether you liked the Jif or the Skippy better, even though they were so different before.

Once again, the magic of this stone happens because it is engrossing and therefore distracting, but also because of what happens as you go through the remaining four steps. As you savor, notice that this type of taste test carries a powerful message: our inner compass speaks, but sometimes so subtly that we don't hear it unless we are focused.

A SOUND DISTRACTION STONE

The beauty of a sound distraction stone is that it can be worked anywhere, and at any time, simply by focusing keenly on the background noise.

Practice working this stone when you are feeling fine. Go someplace noisy and listen to all the sounds surrounding you. What are the dominant ones? Choose the most obvious sound and follow it for a while, the way you would follow the vocals in a song. Now tune out that dominant noise and listen *between* the sounds. The buzz of the fluorescent lights, the hum of traffic, the elevator music, the other conversations in the room.

This exercise is like listening to music with the melody removed. If you aren't in a noisy place, put on music and follow the different instruments, one by one. What is the drum doing? Can you pick out the bass? Are there backup singers? If so, can you tell how many? Are they male or female?

Of all the senses we have discussed, selective listening is perhaps the most powerful metaphor for the way I am encouraging you to take control over what thoughts you allow to inhabit your mind. Many people cannot tune out the background noise: people with sensory integration problems, schizophrenia, or hearing loss find the clinking of silverware so loud in a restaurant that it overshadows all conversation. Seen from that perspective, our ability to filter is a gift and a relief. All the noises are out there, but just as you can shift your attention to follow different instruments in a song, you can learn to hone your emotional filter and shift your attention to stimuli that make you feel good. This selective listening exercise is a reminder that you can learn to be selective about the emotions you allow in your head—and if you can do that, then you can also take control over the emotions that dominate your day.

Make sure to create a symbol for your distraction stone that reminds you concretely of the action you plan to take when you feel trauma-y. For example, an eye or a musical note.

These five sense distraction stones are very useful, but they aren't the only distractions available to us. As always, the most effective strategy is to follow your signature strengths. The sense distraction stones may be particularly effective for you if your signature strength is an appreciation of beauty and excellence. But if you're someone who is strongly intellectually curious, for instance, perhaps your distraction stone will involve learning something new—like teaching yourself to play chess or watching an online lecture on a topic that interests you.

If your signature strengths lie in the social realm, other people can have a powerfully distracting effect. But if you decide to create a "reach out to someone" distraction stone, then choose wisely! The person on the other end of the phone should be someone who reliably pushes you into a better place, not a worse one. And make sure that you have a handful of people on your list so you don't return to the same well too often. A stone doesn't work if you can't work it, and no one friend is accessible—nor should they be!—all the time.

Stone #7: Your Hero Stone

As you well know by now, there's nothing arbitrary about the heroes we choose. Famous or not, your heroes are often people who embody your signature strengths or who have easy access to your lost emotions. They represent something you want more of—in yourself or in humanity. This is why it's important to know who our heroes are and why we admire and identify with them: they give us insight into our values.

In the very first chapter of this book, we explored your choice of heroes. Armed with that information about yourself, find some version of what your hero does and make it a stone for you. Choose some aspect of their heroism that you seek to emulate, some action that they have taken. Even though we may not have the talents or resources that our heroes do there is always some piece of how they cope, what they do, and what they stand for that we can act on in our daily lives. Doing this connects us with a larger community of people who have triumphed over tragedy, and it enforces our sense of external efficacy. It helps us create a value-driven life and doses us with power.

Many overcomers cope by taking action to help others or by trying to change the world for the better. And while their acts do help others, they need not be *entirely* altruistic—and neither does your hero stone. Engaging in heroic acts gets us a dose of efficacy and power, so we are also helping ourselves. By helping others we are reminded of what we have to offer, which enhances our sense of survivor pride.

Rameck Hunt is one of a trio of men now known as the Three Doctors. He, along with his friends Sampson Davis and George Jenkins, grew up on the streets of Newark, subject to and tempted by all that conspires against the success of young urban men. But the three of them made a vow to support each other in their quest to become doctors, and they succeeded; their memoir of that experience, *The Pact*, is a primer on resilience.

One of Rameck's early heroes was the author of a book about

mentoring fatherless young men. This book spoke so strongly to Rameck that he and his friends started their own grassroots mentoring program for talented inner-city kids, named after a Swahili term in that book. Had Rameck made a hero stone he would have put this word on it, and he would have worked that stone by doing everything necessary to mobilize his organization into existence.

Certainly Rameck wanted to help others. But let's take a look at all the nonaltruistic benefits of a hero stone. Mentoring, even just *setting up* the mentoring program, was an exercise in efficacy, a way for him to see himself as someone accomplished, not just a victim. Rameck needed a concrete exercise to enable him to see himself on the other side of the tracks. In this way, starting a mentoring program was a hero stone that he could reach for as a healthier snack when old junk food emotions got triggered. This accomplishment, Rameck says, was the proudest moment of his life. Not only did it signify a radical change for a guy who, just months earlier, had risked his future by stealing from the campus store and fighting in the dorm, but you can bet that his emotional world felt better when he was acting like his hero, too.

Write the name of your hero on a stone and make yourself a list of things that you can do to emulate whatever aspect of their heroism moves you most. Clearly a hero stone is a great way to introduce value-based actions and positive feelings into your everyday routine, working it as a maintenance stone. But you can also use your hero stone in emergency circumstances. You can't mentor someone in the middle of the night, but you can *make plans*. Research a Big Brothers Big Sisters program where you might volunteer. Or simply imagine that you are a mentor and write a letter to your imaginary mentee sharing what you have to offer. Make a list of the experiences you might want to share with your mentee, outings to empower her and broaden her horizons. Draft an e-mail in support of some new education legislation, or sketch out a plan for a bake sale to raise money to donate to a scholarship.

Remember, the planning of these activities is just as powerful as the doing.

> **Your survivorship is not contingent upon how many of these plans you are able to accomplish.**

What *is* important is that when you feel trauma-y and weak, like you have no voice and no power, when you feel that you are passive and not in control, that you reach for this stone and take an action that alters your reality. Many people say that helping is the best form of healing. You may find that turning your attentions to the needs of others when you are feeling down is a wonderful way to reconnect with a stronger side of yourself.

Stone #8: Your "Car Behind the Dent" Stone

Early on, I talked about how trauma survivors come to see themselves as nothing more than their symptoms or their diagnosis, or the trauma they overcame, while neglecting to appreciate the rest of themselves. I used the analogy of a dent with a car attached.

In that chapter, you compiled a list of things you liked about yourself, as well as activities you enjoyed and were talented at. Another great stone is one that helps you get back to the person you were before the trauma—the person who is undoubtedly still in there, waiting to reemerge.

I recently watched a demonstration of Australian shepherd dogs herding sheep. Watching them—so attentive and alive, so excited and engaged—reminded me of Mihaly Csikszentmihalyi's concept of flow, which we discussed in chapter 1. Activities that give us flow straddle the perfect balance of talent and challenge, resulting in a degree of engagement that is both engrossing and cleansing. Do you recall ever having that feeling? Have you felt that way recently? I believe that each one of us needs to experience flow, just as we need to eat or sleep to refresh ourselves.

If these stones are a holistic pillbox of ways to feel better, then flow is nature's destresser, refresher, and energizer. Whether you experience flow from doing crossword puzzles or long-distance running, these activities are reliable sources of pride, efficacy, pleasure, and general good feelings.

You may find that you can get into a flow activity even when you are feeling lousy, whereas you might not be able to lose yourself in a more commonplace "hobby." This makes a flow stone useful for both maintenance and emergencies. I find that if my patients can identify an activity that does (or used to) give them a dose of flow, then they have a ready-made stone to plunk. The activities and pursuits that put us into flow return us to "the car"—the place we occupied, the people we were, before the trauma happened to us.

Like taking a daily vitamin, maintenance doses of these stones help foster our awareness of a peacetime world, where there is more to us than our damage and our symptoms. Make space for them. We all need engaging diversions and downtime, and reintroducing these stones into your daily life is groundwork for your ability to use them when you really need them. Don't make the mistake of devaluing this stone as a hobby stone. Rediscovering the car behind your dent is often the epiphany moment in a memoir that turns the whole victim story into a survivor story.

Stone #9: Your Rescuer Stone

Bruce was a patient of mine who had spent years as a child living in fear of his raging alcoholic father. As he remembers it, he spent the days and nights of his childhood hiding, hoping to stay out of his dad's path. Whenever there was a shooting star or birthday candle to wish on, Bruce would pray for some kindly and gentle-spirited adult with a confident voice who would extend a hand and lead him out of his frightening world.

When Bruce finally grew up and got out, he became the rescuer he had always dreamed about: he became a firefighter. When I met Bruce, he was already well on his way to healing that childhood trauma, because his job gave him the opportunity every day to refute the ugly trauma-preserving assumption that came out of his childhood trauma—that everyone is alone, that there's no way out, that no one cares. His work gave him daily evidence that the world was a better place than he had been taught it was.

Then 9/11 happened. Bodies fell from the sky. Friends never returned to their sobbing wives. And despite the rescue skills he had acquired there was not much Bruce could do to help. After a few days at Ground Zero, he began to feel lost and disoriented, overwhelmed by hopelessness, trapped and isolated—just as he had as a child.

It's one thing to acknowledge that you aren't feeling well and another thing to recognize that your trauma has been triggered and you are feeling all those blue-list emotions from your permatrauma list. Bruce recognized that while *everybody* at Ground Zero was feeling depressed and rattled, he was experiencing a rekindling of his childhood trauma. "One second I'm working, and then I turn back into a little boy, hiding under the bed in my father's house."

Bruce had already worked his way through step 1 (recognizing when you are feeling trauma-y), but he didn't have a step 2 to turn to. Without any concrete tools to rely on Bruce had no way of regaining control over these emotions. So we embarked immediately on creating a stone for him to firmly grasp when these feelings emerged.

It is fairly common among trauma survivors that they have already done the work of figuring out what they need, but instead of giving it to themselves, they have been busily giving it to others. Bruce had spent years of his early life fantasizing about being rescued, and he had grown up to be a rescuer, generously offering to others the confident, comforting safety he had craved so deeply as a child.

Bruce needed a rescuer stone to help him apply what he knew was needed to himself. To help him make one, I asked him about the rescues he'd performed that gave him the most satisfaction and pride, and the ones he'd heard about that had moved him the most. All the stories had one thing in common: the rescuer was powerful and calm and had things fully under control (or could at least give the illusion of this), so that the person in need of rescue could bask in feeling safe and protected.

Next, we looked at the techniques and skills Bruce had developed to convey that kind of safety to the people he was rescuing. Bruce shared with me a story about his wife at the end of her difficult labor, more vulnerable and afraid than he had ever seen her. He had grasped her hand while looking deeply into her exhausted eyes, and he had told her, "It's okay; I'm here. I've got you." Using touch, eye contact, confidence, and reassurance he was able to create a paternalistic sense of taking over.

What Bruce gave his wife was just what he had needed as a boy and what he didn't get. It told us that Bruce needed to start finding ways to give himself that feeling in his present crisis. This informed his awareness as we began looking for ways for him to work his rescuer stone and get himself a dose of this unique brand of comfort.

First, he realized that rather than wanting to flee from his work, he needed it. Firefighting had helped him see the world as a place populated by people who cared; it had connected him with a community that prioritized rescue and compassion. That worldview was essential to him.

He also had a painfully awkward conversation with his wife, in which he asked her to do for him when he felt panicky what he had done for her in childbirth. His wife had the sense not to make a joke and did just what he asked. She touched him, looked into his eyes, and reassured him she was by his side. So Bruce not only got the type of comfort he needed, he also got further reassurance that his trauma had artificially discolored his worldview. His wife's adaptability gave him evidence to support his TPA remedy—that the world is generously populated with decent people who want to help.

Bruce's rescuer stone has a ladder on it, to remind him both of the ladders he uses as a fire rescuer and also of the rope ladder he used to sneak out his boyhood window and flee when the shouting downstairs got too scary. When he notices himself feeling trauma-y, it reminds him that he has to get a dose of the warm, paternal, "I'm here and I've got you" kind of protective rescue that he dishes out so liberally to others.

He works it in a maintenance way as often as he has the chance, noting all the many people out there offering comfort and rescue to others. This reminds him that the world is not populated by malevolent alcoholics like his father, but with people who are much kinder and better than that. As a result, when trauma-y feelings hit, he is better able to find the specific brand of reassurance that will get him feeling under control.

What are your rescue fantasies for yourself? Do you find that you have pursued work or volunteer opportunities to rescue others? Is this a role you have taken on in your family and among your friends? When you ruminate about what you *wish* had happened in the moment or aftermath of what you went through, what do you learn about what you need? When called upon to rescue someone else going through what you did, what do you offer them?

Acknowledging that this type of rescue is what *you* need to heal, your new healing prescription is to harvest evidence that this type of help is available out in the world. As you start to accumulate evidence, these observations will pave the way to an alternative worldview, one in which you may ultimately be more comfortable finding rescue for yourself.

One of the most powerful moments in my career—and my own personal healing—happened when I was working in a psychiatric ER in New York City. A thirteen-year-old girl came in, covered with bruises after a beating from her father.

I wish I could say that things started getting better for her once she was "safe" in the ER. But Mariposa lay frightened and hurting on a plastic hospital mattress for what seemed like an eternity while the staff went about executing social and legal interventions on her behalf. Arrangements were made that would be suboptimal at best. And it only got worse: the policemen who came to photograph her bruises were businesslike and insensitive. Facing the wall afterward, she cried, refusing to speak or eat. My heart ached for her, but I did as I had been trained and carried on the long-standing tradition that we don't touch, we don't hug, we don't share; we remain in control and keep our boundaries intact.

I left the hospital when my shift ended, but on my way home, I thought of her spending the night in the hospital and I threw up. Mariposa's plight would have left anyone feeling ill, but in her age, her helplessness, and her aloneness, I recognized many things about my own trauma at age thirteen, at the hands of a sadistic pedophilic physician. I knew all too well what it felt like to be thirteen, in a hospital, feeling alone, wishing my ordeal was over but knowing it likely was not.

I had made a career out of helping, and I had mostly found it gratifying and healing to do so. But that day, I felt like a complete failure: what on earth could I possibly offer a girl like Mariposa, with my white lab coat and clipboard? That night, as I thought about what I had—and had not—done for Mariposa, I decided to bust down some of the walls that psychiatric training builds between you and your patients.

At the start of my shift the next morning, I sat down next to Mariposa with a box of tissues in my hand, and with tearful indignation, I proceeded to list for her all the injustices she was facing. I apologized for the plastic mattress and the crappy, see-through, open-in-the-back hospital gown, for the lousy ER rule that you can't have your own belongings (a rule made for psychotic and violent patients that didn't pertain to her), for the lack of cozy sheets and fuzzy PJs, for the fact that we had no pillows, only folded-up towels. I apologized for the cold room, the cold cops, and the deeply, deeply broken system. I told her that I thought she had gotten a raw deal in life, with her abusive dad and a mom who had left her kids behind. And while I didn't share my own story, I did let her know that something horrible had happened to me, too, when I was her age. I told her that at age thirteen, I didn't think that my circumstances would ever change, or that I would ever stop feeling the way I felt, but that I had, and I believed she would, too.

Somewhere along the way, she looked up and started making eye contact. She even laughed when I ranted about the pajamas. We both went through a lot of tissues. I would like to believe that I made a difference in Mariposa's life as she moved out of the ER and on to the next phase of her life; I know for sure she made a big difference in mine. I was able to learn a few important things about the practice of trauma psychiatry and about myself.

I couldn't rescue Mariposa, but I could offer to walk by her side on this scary journey, listening, validating, and helping her contain the emotions that threatened to overwhelm her. I could allow myself to cry and I could share her tissues, to offer a reality check that what she found in her world was neither normal nor acceptable, and to let her know that there was a world of people out there who found her circumstances horrifying and heartbreaking and her father despicable. I could model appropriate indignation and rage on her behalf. I could plant a seed that she might just have the strength to overcome and that she wouldn't have to do it alone.

My rescue stone has her name on it (her real one, which is not Mariposa), and it reminds me that I need all the same things. When I am feeling trauma-y, I need to feel heard and believed, to know that I am not crazy—as I felt I was at thirteen—and that I make sense. It reminds me that if I choose to seek out companionship in these moments, it needs to be with someone who can tolerate my sadness without devaluing my feelings or discrediting my story. It reminds me that while I couldn't do anything differently when I was thirteen,

I am in a blessedly different place now, in which I control the take-home aspect of my trauma.

As I watched Mariposa struggle to find her words it was clear to me that her difficulties were no fault of her own. Many things defy description in the limited vocabulary and life experience of a thirteen-year-old. So my rescuer stone reminds me to feel compassionate toward the people in my life who I felt failed me at the time, because they didn't miraculously see what I could not say, and because they didn't seem to believe me when I tried.

I work this stone by channeling my inner Bull. I am armed with plenty of songs and quotes (like the one at the start of this book) that can give me a kick-start if I don't know how to get there. My imaginary rescuer is fierce and angry, an agent of change, an instrument of justice, a compassionate protector. But the way I learned to work this stone for myself, all these healing, soothing tricks, is the gift that Mariposa gave me: the insight that often, what we feel so powerfully and poignantly for others is what we need to be feeling toward ourselves.

Stone #10: Your Gratitude Stone

There is a little soothing chant that we used to sing to my daughter when she was distressed. It starts: "You've got your mommy, you've got your lambie . . ." We'd name all her friends, every relative, every fuzzy toy in her bed—everything in her life that she loved and that loved her back.

It was very distracting and comforting—for all of us—to remember what was good in her world. As my daughter grew older, she became able to list these things for herself, filling in the blanks as I sang, and it delighted her to search her world and to think of things to add to the list.

Our little song is an exercise in gratitude. Exercises like writing a gratitude letter and reading it to its intended recipient are reliably effective in giving a feel-good boost. But when positive psychology exercises such as this are ritualized so as to make them a part of your daily life they can have a major and lasting impact. Like all stones designed to cultivate a nontraumatized worldview, a gratitude stone needs to be worked as a maintenance stone, so that you know it's there when you need it most.

I suggest categorizing the things you are grateful for. One week, for instance, pause routinely to reflect and list all the people and relationships you are grateful for. The next week, create a daily habit of listing your gratitude for the ways in which the universe is abundant. Seeds, sun, clear water, and brown dirt combine somehow to make sweet, jewel-toned, nutritious fruits—what's the difference between that and magic? The next week, pause daily for a few moments to meditate on the ways you are grateful for your body and how well it functions.

One patient of mine worked a gratitude stone to combat fearful and vulnerable feelings that he was left with after a natural disaster. When he was triggered and found himself feeling thin-skinned and fragile he worked a stone on which he had written the words "gentle rain." This stone was a reminder for him to pause and focus with gratitude on the environment, the weather, noticing how well-suited and well-adapted he was to withstand the elements. How rain might fall from such a great height yet not injure him. The stone didn't require the presence of rain to be effective—although it was during a rainstorm that he first had the idea to create his particular gratitude stone. At any moment he could pause to gratefully reflect on the fact that, with the exception of those rare days when natural disaster strikes, our bodies prove hearty and strong and up to the task of facing the elements.

Listing all the things in your life that you are grateful for, that you like about yourself or that define who you are, is a great way to work a gratitude stone. List all the people you love. List all the lessons you've learned. Acknowledge all the roofs you've had over your head. One family I work with made this a mealtime ritual: each individual in turn tells each of his family members something about them for which he is grateful.

But the best part of this stone is sitting back and savoring as you acknowledge how radical the change in your outlook has been. You have moved from a place of pained rumination to a place of awe, wonder, and thankfulness. It is more possible than ever that the day will come when your vase habitually fills with good.

YOUR CHART

I am a survivor of _____.

The car behind my dent is _____, _____, _____.

My trauma-preserving assumptions are _____, _____,

_____.

I am a Bull/Bee/Mouse/Wolf (circle the ones that apply).

My signature strengths are _____, _____, _____.

My #1 hero is _____, because he/she demonstrates _____ as a coping style and as a value in action.

The following are resilience traits I am cultivating in myself: flexibility, accountability, rosewashing, community, internal efficacy, external efficacy (circle all that apply).

When I feel trauma-y, I feel _____, _____, _____.

My Rx emotions are _____, _____, _____.

My stones are:

1. Spiraling

2. Moodith

3. Stop feeding the monster

4. TPA remedy (write in your own symbol on the line): _____; how I work it: _____

5. Rx emotion: _____; how I work it: _____

6. Distraction: visual, auditory, taste, olfactory, touch (circle which work best for you); how I work it: _____

7. Hero: _____; how I work it: _____

8. Car behind my dent: _____; how I work it: _____

9. Rescuer: _____; how I work it: _____

10. Gratitude: _____; how I work it _____

| CONCLUSION |

AFTER HER MASTECTOMY, Geralyn Lucas was asked to pose topless for *Self* magazine. She was told that the portrait would be done by a famous photographer known for huge-format, eight-foot-tall Polaroids. Hoping to show others that a woman with one breast can be beautiful, Geralyn agreed. But on the day of the shoot, faced with a room full of stylists and assistants, she panicked.

Her breast reconstruction was asymmetric and still lacked a nipple, so she had assumed she would be draped or covered in some manner. But there was to be no artful pose. Instead, the photographer positioned her with hands on hips, facing the camera. Geralyn felt vulnerable and exposed, and just as she considered backing out of her promise to pose, the photographer clicked the picture. She said of that moment, there she stood, with "one breast that nursed a baby and one breast that nearly killed me. It is this contradiction that has vexed me: life and death are so close to my heart now."

In our lives as survivors, we have all stood with darkness on our left side and life to our right. There have been times when we have faced left and have had to kick and scratch to keep that darkness at bay. At other times, we have faced to the right, living greedily, as if our good fortune and happiness might end at any moment. Both states are illusory; our feet were always in the same place.

We all live in that space between life and death, between courage and bravery, between shame and pride. Survivors just know all too well what's on either side, and that knowledge informs the way we live. This knowledge is a universal aspect of survivorship; it is both trauma's biggest gift as well as our biggest obstacle to healing.

When the enormous Polaroid was hung on the wall to develop, Geralyn watched with fear, afraid to look. But as the image emerged, she fell in love with a new and different version of herself. "I don't recognize myself. I see my eyes and a depth I have never seen before. I see a journey. . . . This famous photographer has worked her magic. She has captured the courage that was mingled with my fear and turned out a beauty so honest and raw it is unfamiliar." Geralyn sees herself as a survivor. And that beauty is enhanced, not diminished, by the scar of a survivor's knowledge that life lives so close to death, shame so close to pride, fear so close to courage.

It is an amazing grace that washes over you when you realize you can stop fighting and just *be*. It's that moment in "The Star-Spangled Banner" when the smoke clears and you see that the flag is still there. That what's done is done. That life has been waiting for you to get back to it. That although death hovers alongside life, you can stop fighting death on the left and gobbling life on the right, and just stand strong between them—a survivor. That what remains is a scar—but also, all the rest of you.

Nothing can erase what happened to you; you can't go back. And, even if you could, there are gifts you have gained that you would likely not want to trade. What we survivors know makes us uniquely equipped to live full, vibrant, courageous lives. Our experiences have given us an exquisite, and sometimes painful, sensitivity. We are stronger, wiser, more compassionate, more appreciative, and more real because of what we have endured. We have acquired the ability to see things more clearly and more beautifully, to live more fully and more meaningfully. We are a proud tribe.

I hope that this book has been a mirror for you, one that has helped you see the beauty in your own eyes, the gift in your own journey. And I hope that, armed with a handful of stones, you find yourself ready to embark on the rich, full life that awaits you.

| ACKNOWLEDGMENTS |

NO FLOWER HAS EVER GROWN without roots and water and sunshine. For me, my spouse, Leslie, has been all three. At every fork in the road you have said to me, "Yes." Because of your faith I have had the chance to explore the far reaches of my talents and interests, knowing that no matter the outcome, you would be there, like the ground beneath my feet.

I am also profoundly grateful to my parents, Rita and Jerry, who have always been prepared to move mountains for their kids. You raised us to think outside the box, and I know there were times you wished I'd not jumped quite so far out of it. But I have watched you reach and grow to follow me, and I love you both for it.

I also acknowledge my older brother, Steve. You have gone places and done things I would not have thought possible if I hadn't watched you with my own eyes. My bar is higher because of your lead.

Equally important as my family are my friends. Christina, best friend and minister rolled into one. How can I thank you enough for reintroducing me to all the faith and grace, the fun and play, the life and love that got packed away during medical school? Tony and

Gary, you are my brothers from another mother. You have taught me so much about the magic that happens when we approach life with an open heart and an outstretched hand. Julie and Joy, you are my soul sisters and my safety net. Thank you also to Evie and Michael, owners of Doma, the café that thought it was a writers' colony. I feel lucky to have had so fertile a place to create, where if I got stuck there was likely to be some variety of writer at the table next to me with whom to share ideas.

At several junctures of my professional life the following people have shown faith in me or taken me under their wing in a way that deserves special thanks. To Ira Lesser, M.D., for allowing me to host a radio show during psychiatric residency. Because of you I have made a career of taking psychiatry to the streets. To Garrett Simmons, whenever I am at a crossroads, there you are. Some kind of magic. So much good in my life dates back to you. To Diane Rappoport and Nancy Walzog, you knew I had so much to say and decided I should say it on TV. To Montel Williams, you taught me that myelin, both literal and emotional, are a nerve's best friend, but sometimes you have to function without it. Fierce fighter of other people's battles, thank you so much for helping me find my loud voice.

When this book was just an egg, I brought it to my friend Alexis Hurley at Inkwell Management, who polished it with her gentle advice and sent it back to incubate and grow. In your hands, Alexis, it hatched into a bird, and before I knew what had hit me, you had jettisoned it out of the nest and into flight. Sometimes life comes full circle in amazing ways.

It takes a village, and this book has been blessed with a brilliant and loving bevy of editors at HarperCollins. To Caroline Sutton, who originally acquired this project, you were the first "stranger" to read this book. Until that moment, one never knows for sure if the passion one pours onto the page makes any sense. Learning that it did is a moment of light I will never forget. Mary Ellen O'Neill came to the project with unbridled enthusiasm at a time when forces bigger than both of us might have swept it out to sea. When I told you this book was a bible of sorts, you not only didn't laugh, you took it and me to heart. Your strength and spirit inspire me. Laurie Chittenden, your faith in me as a first-time author and in this new approach to healing is such a gift. Thank you for believing in this material and helping me spread the word.

I would also like to acknowledge the following people at Harper-Collins: Through it all, the patient and organized Mac Mackie kept the machine moving smoothly and taught me the publishing lingo. Thanks, Mac, for keeping me supplied with great novels and for keeping a smile on my face. Mumtaz Mustafa designed the book's cover. I hear authors never like the first pass of a cover, but when I saw your design it was love at first sight. Aja Pollock filled the margins with notes and when she was done everything was silky smooth.

Enormous thanks go to my cowriter, Laura Tucker. There was not a note, anecdote, or page of research that you did not pull deeply into your heart, examine with your own soul, and offer back to me for the page. You have helped me understand myself, find my voice, and figure out how to get it all into chapter form.

Finally, there is this. Way before I was an author or a doctor or even a woman, I was a girl in need of someone who saw past the anger. I was fortunate in that dark period of my life to have the quiet companionship of my grandmother Gussie. One night shortly before she died, she sat me down and listed all the good she saw in me, all the promise of a bright future, which at that time was unimaginable to me. This was Gussie's great, great gift to me. It is my hope that if this book helped you, you will remember what a difference one conversation can make in a life and that you will find opportunities to offer a seed of hope to someone who might seem, on the outside, to be pushing you away. Gussie, I have been thanking you ever since.

| NOTES |

INTRODUCTION

xix   *half of all patients fail to respond*   R. A. Bryant, K. Felmingham, A. Kemp, P. Das, G. Hughes, A. Peduto, and L. Williams. 2008. "Amygdala and ventral anterior cingulate activation predicts treatment response to cognitive behaviour therapy for post-traumatic stress disorder." *Psychological Medicine* 38: 555–61.

xx   *Another study looked at*   S. C. Rose, J. Bisson, R. Churchill, and S. Wessely. 2008. "Psychological debriefing for preventing post traumatic stress disorder (PTSD)." *Cochrane Database of Systematic Reviews* 2: art. no. CD000560. DOI: 10.1002/14651858.CD000560.

xx   *debriefing doesn't prevent PTSD*   J. W. Pennebaker and K. D. Harber. 1993. "A social stage model of collective coping: The Loma Prieta earthquake and the Persian Gulf War." *Journal of Social Issues* 49: 125–45.

CHAPTER 1

7   *The list in this chapter comes from*   C. Peterson and M. E. P. Seligman. 2004. *Character Strengths and Virtues: A Handbook and Classification.* New York: Oxford University Press; Washington, D.C.: American Psychological Association.

13   *he called this state* flow   Mihaly Csikszentmihalyi. 1991. *Flow: The Psychology of Optimal Experience.* New York: HarperCollins.

CHAPTER 2

25   *When Charlize Theron was fifteen*   Lisa Sewards. 2009. "Charlize Theron: I Stole Bread to Get My Big Break." *Daily Express,* March 12.

30   *Psychologist Christopher Peterson*   C. Peterson, N. Park, and M. E. P. Seligman. 2006. "Strengths of character and recovery." *Journal of Positive Psychology* 1: 17–26.

32   *quotes the work of Jeff Moore*   Ben Sherwood. 2009. *The Survivor's Club: The Secrets and Science That Could Save Your Life.* New York: Grand Central Publishing.

40   *at risk of something called* stress contagion   Stevan E. Hobfoll. 1986. *Stress, Social Support, and Women: Series in Clinical and Community Psychology.* Philadelphia: Taylor & Francis.

CHAPTER 3

43   *personalize, generalize, and catastrophize*   A. T. Beck, A. J. Rush, B. E. Shaw, and G. Emery. 1979. *Cognitive Therapy of Depression.* New York: Guilford.

44   *"optimistic explanatory style"*   Edward C. Chang, ed. 2001. *Optimism & Pessimism: Implications for Theory, Research, and Practice.* Washington, D.C.: American Psychological Association, xxi, 53–75, 395.

CHAPTER 4

50   *In her book* I Can't Get Over It   Aphrodite Matsakis. 1992. *I Can't Get Over It: A Handbook for Trauma Survivors.* California: New Harbinger Publications.

CHAPTER 5

70   *A researcher named Barbara Fredrickson*   B. L. Fredrickson. 2001. "The role of positive emotions in positive psychology: The broaden-and-build theory of positive emotions." *American Psychologist* 56: 218–26.

CHAPTER 13

175 *how we both "construct and construe"* S. Gonca and I. Savasir. 2001. "The relationship between interpersonal schemas and depressive symptomatology." *Journal of Counseling Psychology* 48: 359–64.

178 *positive emotions like contentment* B. L. Fredrickson. 2003. "The value of positive emotions." *American Scientist* 91: 330–35.

CHAPTER 14

189 *So what traits really are associated* W. Fleeson, A. B. Malanos, and N. M. Achille. 2002. "An intraindividual process approach to the relationship between extraversion and positive affect: Is acting extraverted as 'good' as being extraverted?" *Journal of Personality and Social Psychology* 83: 1409–22.

| RECOMMENDED READING |

On Optimism, Positive Psychology, and Happiness

Happy for No Reason: 7 Steps to Being Happy from the Inside Out by Marci Shimoff with Carol Kline (Free Press, 2008).

Authentic Happiness: Using the New Positive Psychology to Realize Your Potential for Lasting Fulfillment by Martin Seligman (Free Press, 2002).

What Happy Women Know: How New Findings in Positive Psychology Can Change Women's Lives for the Better by Dan Baker, Ph.D., Cathy Greenberg, Ph.D., and Ina Yalof (Rodale, 2007).

www.authentichappiness.sas.upenn.edu
Learn more about Martin Seligman, the father of positive psychology, and his team at the University of Pennsylvania. On this Web site you can take self-tests to assess your own optimism, gratitude, perseverance, and other traits related to life satisfaction and happiness.

To Learn More About What Gives Your Life Meaning

www.viastrengths.org
The Web site of the Values in Action Institute, where you can take an online test to learn your signature strengths and learn more about the impact of living a value-driven life.

Character Strengths and Virtues: A Handbook and Classification by Christopher Peterson and Martin E. P. Seligman (Oxford University Press, Values in Action Institute, American Psychological Association, 2004).

To Learn More About Coping in a Crisis and Finding Positive Ways to Move Forward
Welcome to Your Crisis: How to Use the Power of Crisis to Create the Life You Want by Laura Day (Little, Brown and Company, 2006).

How Did I Get Here? Finding Your Way to Renewed Hope and Happiness When Life and Love Take Unexpected Turns by Barbara De Angelis (St. Martin's Griffin, 2006).

Get Out of Your Own Way: Overcoming Self-Defeating Behavior by Mark Goulston, M.D., and Philip Goldberg (Perigree, 2006).

To Learn More About Being Present and Focused as a Means to Contain Strong Emotions
Mindfulness for Beginners by Jon Kabat-Zinn, audiobook (Sounds True, 2006).

To Learn More About the Emotional State Called "Flow"
Flow: The Psychology of Optimal Experience by Mihaly Csikszentmihalyi (Harper & Row, 1990).

To Learn Effective Communication Skills When You Need to Set Limits with Others
The Complete Idiot's Guide to Assertiveness by Jeff Davidson (Alpha Books, 1997).

To Learn More About the Traits That Enable Children to Be Resilient in the Face of Obstacles and Thrive Despite Them
Raising Our Children to Be Resilient: A Guide to Helping Children Cope with Trauma in Today's World by Linda Goldman (Routledge, 2006).

The Freedom Writers Diary: How a Teacher and 150 Teens Used Writing to Change Themselves and the World Around Them by the Freedom Writers with Erin Gruwell (Broadway Books, 1999).

To Learn More About "Secondary Wounding"

I Can't Get Over It: A Handbook for Trauma Survivors by Aphrodite
  Matsakis, Ph.D. (New Harbinger Publications Inc., 1992).

On Learning from Our Heroes

*Great Failures of the Extremely Successful: Mistakes, Adversity, Failure
  and Other Steppingstones to Success* by Steve Young (Tallfellow Press,
  2002).

The Hero Book: Learning Lessons from the People You Admire by Ellen
  Sabin (The Watering Can Press, 2004). A book for children ages 6–12.

The Survivors Club: The Secrets and Science That Could Save Your Life
  by Ben Sherwood (Grand Central Publishing, 2009).

For Veterans Facing the Challenge of Returning to Civilian Life

*Courage After Fire: Coping Strategies for Troops Returning Home from Iraq
  and Afghanistan and their Families* by Keith Armstrong, Suzanne Best,
  and Paula Domenici (Ulysses Press, 2006).

**News Sources for Soul-Nourishing Good News That Won't Feed Your
Monsters**

www.goodnewsnetwork.org
www.only-positive-news.com
www.gimundo.com

Memorable and Positive Memoirs by Overcomers We Can Learn From

A Three Dog Life: A Memoir by Abigail Thomas (Harcourt Books, 2006).
  This memoir offers a portrait of a woman who throws guilt and
  self-pity out the window. When her husband suffers a brain injury,
  the author's life is changed forever. This is a fascinating peek into the
  mind of a person who, rather than mourn the past, learns what there
  is to love about her new life and the very changed man to whom she is
  married.

Happens Every Day: An All-Too-True Story by Isabel Gillies (Scribner, 2009).
  When her perfect life is shattered by the betrayal of her husband, this
  author has to figure out how to re-create her identity and her life.
  If you are a person who copes by leaning on others for support and

finding the humor in a tough situation, you will resonate with this author's path as she discovers that no one can take away the things you truly like best about yourself.

Celebrity Detox: The Fame Game by Rosie O'Donnell (Grand Central Publishing, 2007).
A survivor of both childhood abuse and the death of her mother, the author is a master in recognizing when her trauma is rearing its head and shares the specifics of how she uses art, music, and time with her children as stones to soothe, comfort, and inspire herself in the face of these challenges.

Why I Wore Lipstick to My Mastectomy by Geralyn Lucas (St. Martin's Press, 2004).
Refusing to lose sight of the car behind her dent, the author of this funny and insightful memoir refused to surrender her precancer identity and assume the role of a sick person. This is a great opportunity to peek into the thought process of someone who believes in internal efficacy and has the discipline to wrestle her thoughts to a more positive place. It is also a portrait of a girl-next-door hero with wisdom to share about how to refuse to allow your trauma to derail the life you had planned for yourself.

Golden Bones: An Extraordinary Journey from Hell in Cambodia to a New Life in America by Sichan Siv (HarperCollins, 2008).
If you are a person who copes using mental discipline and perseverance, this memoir will appeal to you. Whether fleeing a terrorist regime in his homeland, keeping his hope intact in a refugee camp, or making his way in a new country filled with challenges, the author's powerful and productive work ethic, patience, and persistence allow him to triumph and rise to serve as a UN ambassador.

The Pact: Three Young Men Make a Promise and Fulfill a Dream by Sampson Davis, George Jenkins, and Rameck Hunt with Lisa Frazier Page (Riverhead Books, 2002).
This memoir is a primer of resilience and a tribute to the power of mentorship. Three young men from the inner city resolve to help one another achieve their dream of becoming doctors. They offer insight

into the many obstacles that almost defeated them and tools they used to help rewrite a fate they refused to accept.

Resilience: Reflections on the Burdens and Gifts of Facing Life's Adversities by Elizabeth Edwards (Broadway Books, 2009).
Whether coping with her son's death, her husband's infidelity, or her own cancer, the author is candid about her self-defeating behaviors and offers insights into the changes she made to persist in living a value-driven life. This memoir demonstrates the way that mastering the art of coping in one challenge bolsters you in subsequent ones.

Always Looking Up: The Adventures of an Incurable Optimist by Michael J. Fox (Hyperion, 2009).
Many of us cope by taking charge and taking action, and this memoir is a portrait of such a man. Determined to assert his own sense of efficacy in the face of Parkinson's disease, the author's trauma fuels his activism. This is a portrait of a man who copes with humor, uses his social supports to effect change, and continually challenges feelings of hopelessness by paving a way for progress.

Tuesdays with Morrie: An Old Man, a Young Man, and Life's Greatest Lesson by Mitch Albom (Broadway Books, 1997).
The silver lining in many a trauma is that it shows us what is truly important in life. This memoir shares the wisdom of a man with a fatal illness: how to retain dignity, seize life, love well, and bask in gratitude for what the day brings.

Man's Search for Meaning by Viktor E. Frankl (Beacon Press, 2006).
For some, having overcome their life's traumas is a great and proud achievement. The author reflects on how he and others coped while in a Nazi concentration camp. With an emphasis on retaining one's dignity and finding a sense of personal meaning in what we have endured, Frankl believes that the way we cope with life's inevitable challenges forges our character and becomes a testament to the life we have lived.

Rosa Parks by Douglas Brinkley (Viking Penguin, 2000).
There is much to learn about coping from civil rights leaders who have faced ongoing oppression such as racism. Racism is in itself a trauma that attempts to devalue and disempower. A portrait of a

woman whose life and life's work were shaped by an awareness of her values, this biography offers a peek into the mind and the coping techniques of a woman who sustained her esteem and her sense of efficacy over a lifetime of setbacks and slow progress.

Long Walk to Freedom: An Autobiography of Nelson Mandela by Nelson Mandela (Back Bay Books/Little, Brown and Company, 1995). We don't often think of the author of this memoir as a trauma survivor. Here is a portrait of a man who emerged from twenty-seven years in prison neither bitter nor defeated. From his story we see how an optimistic survivor and heroic overcomer envisions a better world and creates a life path out of pursuing it. This book will speak to anyone whose signature strengths lie in the areas of justice, leadership, and kinship with others.

For Those Who Prefer Their Inspiration in Fictional Form
The Secret Life of Bees by Sue Monk Kidd (Penguin Books, 2003). A girl finds healing as she rediscovers emotions that disappeared from her emotional repertoire after her trauma. If spirituality, kindness, and love are your signature strengths, this story will offer many coping techniques that will speak to your love of beauty, your desire for emotional comfort, and your need for human connection.

Web Sites
www.suicidepreventionlifeline.org
1 (800) 273-TALK
National Suicide Prevention Lifeline. A free confidential 24/7 hotline for people in crisis. Also offers a hotline and online chat for veterans.

www.militaryonesource.com
Provided by the Department of Defense for active-duty guard and reserve service members and their families, this site offers information and resources about combat stress as well as a host of other topics. With few exceptions, the service is completely private and confidential.

www.actsofkindness.org
The Random Acts of Kindness Foundation was started in 1995 as a resource for those dedicated to spreading kindness. Their site

offers educational materials, articles on the benefits of kindness, and inspiring ways to "pass it on."

www.ndvh.org
> The National Domestic Violence Hotline, 1 (800) 799-SAFE
> Offering support and information as well as a twenty-four-hour confidential hotline.

www.rainn.org
> The Rape, Abuse and Incest National Network
> Offering support and information as well as a twenty-four-hour confidential hotline.

www.compassionatefriends.org
> Compassionate Friends supports families after a child dies. Six hundred chapters across the United States put you in touch with others who understand the unique pain of losing a child.

www.afsp.org
> The American Foundation for Suicide Prevention offers support for those who have lost someone to suicide, including an e-network and ways to get involved in legislation and suicide prevention and awareness.

www.ptsdsupport.net
> A source of information and support for combat veterans suffering from PTSD.

www.livestrong.org
> Information and support for those with cancer and their caregivers, financial resources, and survivor stories.

| INDEX |